CHILDSTRESS!

Books by Mary Susan Miller

STRAIGHT TALK TO PARENTS, with Samm Sinclair Baker
A TEACHER'S ROUNDTABLE ON SEX EDUCATION
SAS EXERCISES IN THE CHAIR, with Dr. Folke Mossfeldt
BRINGING LEARNING HOME
CHILDSTRESS!

CHILDSTRESS!

Understanding and Answering Stress Signals of Infants, Children and Teenagers

Mary Susan Miller

Doubleday & Company, Inc., Garden City, New York   1982

Excerpt from the poem "The Fortress" from *All By Pretty Ones* by Anne
Sexton. Copyright © 1961, 1962 by Anne Sexton. Reprinted by permission of Houghton Mifflin Company.

ISBN: 0-385-15906-4
Library of Congress Catalog Card Number 81–43327
Copyright © 1982 by Mary Susan Miller
All Rights Reserved
Printed in the United States of America
First Edition

To Darcy, Noah, Abby and Alexa . . .
with love and hope

Foreword

❖

There are many books on stress written for adults, but to my knowledge none has wholly devoted itself to the subject of informing adults about the stress experienced by children. Yet it is extremely important to begin teaching the stress concept to children at a very early age, because all codes of behavior sink in best if they are established over a long period.

Ms. Miller's *Childstress!* provides what has proved to be a missing link in the vast area of stress-related studies—an examination of stress in children and an inquiry into methods by which adults can help them manage stress. I have often equated stress with life, and yet children have been consistently omitted from stress research as if life did not apply to them.

Both pleasant and unpleasant experiences cause stress in children. The student caught cheating who learns he will be expelled from school, and the student who did excellently on an exam and learns he will receive a desired medal both experience a rapid heartbeat, rising blood pressure and other physical symptoms caused by stress. Though distress is much more likely than eustress [the stress response to positive stimuli] to cause alarm, there is evidence that, in excess, both can be harmful. However, eustress is less likely to be harmful—probably because it rarely equals the intensity and duration of suffering.

There are a number of everyday manifestations of unhealthy response to stress. We would be well advised to be aware of these, so that if they appear in our children or students we can make an effort to divert them from stress-causing activity.

Without being aware of it, for example, parents sometimes expose their children to tremendous stresses whose results may be carried into adulthood. Children are often pressured to conform to their parents' aspirations and ambitions. If these are very different from the children's desires, or beyond their capacities, deep feelings of guilt, unworthiness and suppressed anger may develop in the children. Such anger may surface years later in the form of drug taking, dropping out of school, running away and other destructive acts. Even before that, such tension in children can silently reverberate across the family circle, disrupting harmonious relationships.

Childstress! is an invaluable guide, for both parents and educators, to understanding children and their plight in today's society. Ms. Miller strips childhood of its idyllic myth and exposes the hardship of youth. The warmth and understanding with which she examines the problem never turns to condescension, for she has rightfully granted children equal status with their elders in the ongoing study of stress.

Hans Selye, C.C., M.D., Ph.D., D.Sc.
President, International Institute of Stress

Contents

❖

Introduction

◈

"Parents will greatly minimize stress when they realize that not all of their children are racehorses; some are turtles." Hans Selye said that to me the first time I met him.

I had flown to Montreal to see him after a year of corresponding by mail and twenty years of reading his books. Now as I sat opposite him in his office at the University of Montreal, I felt what a young man told me he felt upon meeting the Maharishi—"guru-ed out." I was clenching and unclenching my hands, breathing hard and listening in embarrassment to my heart's pounding. What I really was feeling was stress.

Surely there was no more appropriate place to feel stress than two feet away from Hans Selye, the doctor who pioneered studies leading to the creation of the International Institute of Stress, of which he is President. Nor was there a more appropriate person to inspire awe than the tiny, strikingly handsome, almost fleshless man who was speaking to me; for in his three quarters of a century he has uncloseted an illness from which over half the population suffers. With three earned doctorates, nineteen degrees from universities all over the world and a room filled with medals and awards of highest recognition, he not only has communicated the first word on stress, but *is* currently the last word.

What is stress? And what has it to do with racehorses and turtles? An answer may be found if we begin with what stress is *not*. It is not *tension*, such as you have from job pressures or marital discord, nor *anxiety*—over a hospitalized child, for instance. Tension and anxiety are *symptoms of stress*. Neither is it the job itself, the nagging wife or the sick child; those are *causes of stress—stressors*, in Hans Selye's language.

Stress is the way our mind and body responds to a stressor. For instance, if we grow up unable to accept ourselves as we are—our weaknesses along with our strengths—we develop feelings of inadequacy; these are *stressors*. When we become tense, we show *symptoms of stress*. Our mind and our body begins to wear and tear; that is *stress*. If, as a result, we punch someone in the nose, that is *adaptive behavior* as a response to stress. In the metaphor of racehorses and turtles, Hans Selye attributed to stress a great deal of the unhappiness and ensuing "bad" behavior I have seen in young people.

As I sat in his office that day almost two years ago, I suddenly felt the way the ugly duckling must have felt when he joined his genus of swans. For seventeen years as a teacher and principal, I had observed destructive behavior in children from nursery school up to college. While my colleagues referred to these children in names ranging from "animals" to the unprintable, I could see them only as troubled kids who needed help.

No child starts life with the ambition of becoming an outcast. It is far more fun to remain inside, nibbling the sweets of accomplishment which society passes to its respected sons and daughters. Outside, it is cold with little more for nourishment than self-hate. Yet, every year I saw hundreds of children behaving in ways that relegated them to the latter course.

Why? I wondered. Why *are so many so miserable?* Then Hans Selye introduced me to racehorses and turtles, and I knew that like the ugly duckling, I had come home. The so-called problem children over whom I had wept and worried were not "bad," despite the labels pinned on them; they were children in stress, whose antisocial behavior was their way of responding to that stress. It was a cry for help which I heard but could not interpret, a cry which many adults did not even hear.

Since leaving Dr. Selye's office, I have thought back over the thousands of children whose cries have pierced my heart, wondering who finally heard, who finally answered and what happened if nobody did. I have remembered my own children—Chris, Eric and Amy, referred to in the book—in their times of pain and in the pain they inflicted on me. I have looked around me at my grandchildren—Darcy, Noah, Abby and Alexa—as their parents now reach out to them in their stress. And I have pored over many hundreds of stress studies of children and adolescents collected in Hans Selye's world renowned stress library in Montreal. What I have seen, what I have heard, what I have read and what I have come to understand are the body of this book about your child's signals of stress.

Until recently only a few adults have taken children's stress seriously. Perhaps we have been hoodwinked by the myth that childhood is a carefree time of life—"the apple tree, the singing and the gold." Or it may ease our own stress to cling to the make-believe child of nostalgia, even though that child is a figment of imagination. Have we so long concealed in the dark corners of our mind the child we actually were that we have lost her? If we listen, we may hear our own childhood cries for help misunderstood, ignored, like those of our children today. We may discover the real child we used to be.

Where is the three-year-old who held back tears as a new baby gurgled and got everyone's attention?

Where the five-year-old who, abandoned at the kindergarten door, faced a foreign land alone and alien?

Have we forgotten the ten-year-old praying to be picked for a team before the teacher assigned the stragglers that neither captain chose?

And the twelve-year-old who sneaked a nickel from his mother's purse to "buy" a best friend?

Remember the teenager whom no one invited to the dance?

Or the one whose father was too busy to attend Fathers' Day?

Or the one who let his parents down by not getting into Colgate?

Where is the fat one? . . . The one with a funny dress? . . . Where is the one who can't read? . . . who wears eyeglasses? . . . whose skin is black?

Can't we find the child crying alone in her room? . . . and the child afraid of the dark? . . . and the child whose parents are fighting? . . . the child of divorce?

These are the real children we were before our memory lost them.

More to the point, they are also our children—living with us, attending our schools, hiding their pain as we hid ours a generation ago. They are the children we overlook when we are busy . . . and scold for their failures (or for ours); the children for whom we set unattainable goals . . . whom we over-plan for and under-listen to. They are the children we love—and forget to let them know. They are our turtles and racehorses running at the wrong speed. In thirty years will they, too, create myths?

Probably. But what about today?

A study conducted some years ago in four disparate cities revealed some startling facts about childhood. In a big city school, seventy-five percent of the children showed evidence of serious stress—not surprising, perhaps, in the light of overcrowding and racial tension. However, in a small school in a town described as "at peace with itself," fifty percent of the children showed stress symptoms. Children in two other cities fell in between with sixty-one and sixty-five percent under heavy stress.

Yet adults are unaware. Even with their children's tensions straining relationships and the atmosphere within their homes and schools, they are oblivious. A group of parents and students questioned separately surprised each other. The parents, asked to rate their children's "happiness," answered in overwhelming majority, "Very happy." Their children, on the other hand, rated themselves from "Miserable" to "Unhappy." Only a small percentage considered themselves "Happy." In a group discussion later, the children pointed out fears and pressures which their parents considered only minimally important. Almost half the children expressed a feeling of isolation that their parents had totally overlooked.

Why this disparity? The mythology parents create is only part of the answer. The other part lies in young people themselves. They do not articulate their stress. "There is nothing I can say," wrote a young boy before putting a bullet through his head, "that would make you see what is happening to me." "I wish I could tell Mother how torn I am—like two people pulling me apart," wrote a girl in her diary before slashing her wrists.

They were aware of their anguish. Other young people are not. When asked why he knifes and kills people he robs, a young prison inmate answered, "I dunno. It just makes me feel better." What he was unable to answer was, "I get all tight from hostility when my father beats me; so I get rid of it on other people." It is difficult for society to hear what is not articulated.

Many young people deliberately immure themselves against hurt. The fortress they build walls in their deeper feelings, the vulnerabilities they dare not share. They unhesitatingly bemoan the obvious: "I hate my teacher" or "My mother makes me mad" or "I'm scared of this exam." But the deep-lying stressors stay taut within: sexual wonderings, pressure to succeed, fear of failure, face-saving, hurt of rejection, hopelessness, injustice, loneliness. Above all, the impersonal quality of the life they live.

While young people are adept at demanding surface needs, they are paralyzed in demanding help for their deeper needs. They cannot cry, "I am hurting. Help me." The sound of their voice merely intensifies the pain, and so they remain silent.

They cry out in other ways, however. When they are afraid, they clown or act the bully; they join cults or run away. When they feel rejected, they attack—rebel and steal and vandalize. When they fail, they cop out—cut class, drop out of school, withdraw from their friends.

Adults do not hear the fear trembling inside a child. They have not learned the language of their children's behavior, and so they punish.

Adults do not know the hurt of rejection throbbing inside. They know only rebellion, thieving and destruction. And they clamp on restraints.

Adults do not understand the sense of failure weeping within a child. They understand only antisocial behavior and disobedience. And they moralize.

The child's hurt grows deeper, his loneliness more intense. He cries louder for help. He no longer clowns; he burns an old man on the Bowery. He no longer fights; he kills a store owner. He no longer cuts class; he gets drunk and pops pills and shoots dope.

Still adults do not get the message. They spank the "naughty" child; they expel the "incorrigible" teenager; they imprison the "hardened criminal" of fourteen. And they shake their heads woefully over the state of youth today.

"Drug taking," says Dr. Norman Levy of the New York State Substance Abuse Control Commission, "is an attempt to escape the experiencing of anxiety through narcotizing it." So are running away and murdering and playing with sex and suicide. Young people find the drug that "makes them feel better."

Stress has always been with young people. Why suddenly have they gone wild, spewing terrifying statistics on us?

First of all, young people are more alone than they have ever been before . . . and stress increases without the touch of a calming hand. The family that used to be their mainstay has crumbled: aunts and uncles live in distant cities; cousins pass briefly at weddings and funerals; and for every two marriages in the United States, there is one divorce. It is hardly a joke that the nursery school story of Goldilocks today deals with Baby Bear, Mama Bear and Stepfather Bear.

More married women are working today than are staying home. More husbands are battering their wives; more parents are abusing their children. More husbands and wives have extramarital sex. A suburban housewife said the other day, "My child came home from school crying—he was the only one in his class living with both parents."

With the family shifting, where does the young person go for support? Not to church—he has not been raised as an attender. Not to school—the old teacher who cared has retired. Not to the community—the family has been transplanted so often in father's upward mobility that the child has no community.

No, today's youth finds support in his peer group. And these young people, like him, are scared and stress-burdened and themselves unsupported. They lean against one another like a house of cards.

Secondly, today's young people are pushed into greater competition than ever before. There are more of them in sheer numbers struggling for first place: to get the best mark, the most money, the highest football score, the most dates. They are rated by judges who set up the criteria for success, often arbitrarily. They are intelligent or slow according to Stanford-Binet's definition of IQ. They are popular according to the head cheerleader's or football captain's model. They get into college if their talents match those that Educational

Testing Service holds up as important. So the struggle becomes one, not only for success, but also for conformity. The loner is doomed to the stress of failure. The group is doomed to the stress of competition.

Society, which is merely a conglomerate of parents, teachers and community members, teaches young people to measure self-worth against success. So they dare not be less than best. Some are lucky and learn to accept second-best.

Finally, never before have children been so indulged, so prized, so placated as today. The cause may be parental guilt or that old chestnut, "I want her to have more than I had." No matter—the result is the same: a generation of young people who cannot cope with the negatives the rest of us had to grow accustomed to. They get what they want—at no little expense to their parents—from birth through adolescence. They get what they see on television. They get what their friends have. Parents seem afraid to say "No."

The easy life leaves children with little sense of accountability. Parents team up to help them switch the blame. A child does poorly in school—Mother says the teacher is no good. A sixteen-year-old wants liquor at his party—Dad winks at the law. One mother boasted, "I will never let Rachel be upset if I can possibly prevent it." She prevented it, and Rachel is now at a psychiatrist's. She is six years old.

Way back in the 1700s, that famous spokeswoman for children, Mother Goose, defined children:

> *What are little boys made of?*
> *Snips and snails*
> *And puppy-dogs' tails,*
> *That's what little boys are made of.*

> *What are little girls made of?*
> *Sugar and spice*
> *And all that's nice,*
> *That's what little girls are made of.*

Apparently children were living a myth even then. With mythology and memory peeled away, however, perhaps children will be able to grow in the light of truth. Perhaps in the glare, adults will be able at last to understand them.

Behind the myth—in life and in Mother Goose—lie the hurts and stresses that make up a child's everyday life: spiders, empty cupboards, tattletales, barking dogs, spankings, dead birds and scary old men and women. One wonders why it has taken us so long to learn.

Now we find ourselves in the 1980s, in a world where the myth of childhood is being torn to bits . . . where children are beset with stress they are ill-equipped to handle . . . in a world where, unable to *scream* out, they *act* out their hurt . . . in a world where we adults, unable to interpret their screams, react only to their behavior. For we are deaf to our own cries of fear.

This book is an attempt to translate children's cries for help while there is still time to answer them. It is divided into 3 parts.

PART ONE presents stress and stressors as they exist in the lives of children today—from birth through the teenage years.

PART TWO probes into different ways in which children respond to stress—the adaptive behavior that adults label as "bad."

PART THREE offers concrete suggestions to parents and to teachers—ways they can help children handle stress and ways they can avoid creating it.

As a whole, the book endeavors to do more than enable adults merely to help their children. It endeavors to enable them to equip children to help themselves.

It is hoped that this book will put Mother Goose's children—and our children—into the real world. For it is with the real world that they must cope.

PART ONE

◆

How Happy Is Childhood?

Monday's child is fair of face,
Tuesday's child is full of grace,
Wednesday's child is full of woe,
Thursday's child has far to go,
Friday's child is loving and giving,
Saturday's child works hard for his living,
And the child that is born on the Sabbath day
Is bonny and blithe, and good and gay.

CHAPTER I

◆

Stress Is Always There

This is the farmer sowing the corn,
That kept the cock that crowed in the morn,
That waked the priest all shaven and shorn,
That married the man all tattered and torn,
That kissed the maiden all forlorn,
That milked the cow with the crumpled horn,
That tossed the dog
That worried the cat
That killed the rat
That ate the malt
That lay in the house that Jack built.

WHO EXPERIENCES STRESS?

A fifteen-year-old girl in her first long dress struggles with an unruly curl as she stares at herself in the mirror. Her hand trembles. Her date, stiff in his rented tuxedo, adjusts his bow tie as, gardenia under his arm, he rings her doorbell. Rivulets of perspiration trickle down his face. The boy and the girl are experiencing stress. They experienced it long before this anxiety-filled evening, however: long before tests in school, over which they sweated; long before jealousy over siblings; long before the first slap on the hand told them Mother meant business. They knew stress in the womb as, floating warm in protective fluid, they kicked against the uterine wall. They knew it again as their head pushed against an ever-widening cervix. They were old hands at stress as, thrust amidst blood into a bright, cold world, they felt a sharp slap on the behind and began to breathe.

The two young people above have never been without stress, not since a chance sperm united with one month's ejected ovum and began to create the individual they became. Stress was a part of their conception and a part of the long nine months' wait and a part of their daily survival, as it had been for their parents . . . and their parents . . . and their parents. As it was for the first caveman and *Homo erectus* before him and the mastodon and the dinosaur and the reptile and the fish and the paramecium and the amoeba. We might say the amoeba, that minuscule one-celled animal for whom life became so complex that he had to figure out a way to survive, *discovered* stress. The amoeba's answer was to develop a second cell to handle more specialized mechanisms. And so evolution began.

If we are to credit the amoeba with the discovery of stress, we must admit that it has a good P.R. man on board in the person of Hans Selye to spread the word. As an eighteen-year-old medical student in Prague fifty-eight years ago, Selye came upon what he called "the syndrome of being sick." No one before him—neither researchers nor medical doctors—had noticed that all sick people developed the same three symptoms no matter what their specific sickness was. Dr. Selye called this the triad: the adrenal glands swelled, producing unusually high levels of cortisone and the pituitary hormone ACTH; lymphatic tissues—the thymus gland, the spleen and the lymph nodes—shrank; and bleeding ulcers formed in the lining of the stomach.

These three body changes Hans Selye called the stress response to sickness—or, simply, *stress*. Since that time, more and more professionals and lay people alike have discarded the old definitions of stress and accepted his definition: "Stress is a nonspecific response of the body to any demand." The involuntary way our body's physical and mental components react to whatever it is forced to do: that is stress.

While the initial biochemical response is always the same, no matter what the stressor may be—always a change in adrenals, lymph nodes and stomach lining—secondary reactions take on their own identity as stressors differ. For instance, if we cut our finger and develop an infection, inflammation arises. Pus forms and the finger swells. This is the body's answer to the infection's call to duty. It is stress.

Similarly, if we walk in the winter's cold without gloves, our hands turn red because our circulatory system sends an added supply of blood in an effort to lend additional warmth. If we stay outside too long, however, the blood sent to warm our hands can no longer do the job. It is withdrawn and used instead to fill the more vital need of protecting internal organs. Our hands turn white and may become frostbitten. This too is stress. Stress makes blisters form when our shoes rub, makes us sweat when we square-dance in August and shiver when we face February winds, makes us cough when a crumb lodges in our pharynx. Stress makes us swallow when our mouth is full and vomit when our stomach is too full.

But stress is not always a response to unpleasantness. It tightens our throat when we have won an award. It shoots extra adrenalin into our system when we compete in sports. It makes our heart pound if we win a lottery. And it pulls out all the stops of orgasm when we have sex.

Neither is stress only physical; it is psychological as well. It makes us faint at the sight of blood, sob in grief. It raises our blood pressure when we grow angry and paralyzes us with fear. Stress makes us "go crazy" or lose touch with reality when problems seem insurmountable, and it even lets us die when we no longer have the will to live. On the pleasanter side, it makes us protect our babies. It makes us gregarious. It makes us fall in love.

As a matter of fact, stress unifies our physical and psychological beings: one affects the other. For instance, if someone hits us, we get angry: there we go from physical to psychological. Contrarily, if we are frightened, we often have difficulty breathing. Here we go in the other direction, from psychological to physical. The two are inextricably tied together.

While the body responds involuntarily to stressors, the same stressor may have different effects, depending on the circumstances. Let's take a noise on the stair. You are alone at night in bed in the dark, and you hear a creak. Though hardly audible, it awakens you like thunder. Who can be there? Your breath comes fast and hard. Your heart pounds. You tremble and may break out in a cold sweat. On the other hand, if you are expecting someone—a lover perhaps, or a child who has been away—you hear a footfall. You think you hear it a hundred times before it actually comes. And then it does come. Again you breathe hard and tremble and sweat. Stress caused by terror or by excitement evidences itself the same way: through involuntary body responses. That is what stress is.

Stress can stimulate and spur us on to work and support a family, to fight in defense of our home and country, to learn and invent, to give the world art, to mature and grow wise. Or stress can drain and debilitate, fill us with fear that takes control of our lives, block our thinking with hatred, create pressures that drive us to madness and death. Whatever it does to us, however, it remains for as long as we live. We are always in stress. As a house of cards stands only so long as the stress of one card against the other holds up, so we live only so long as we have stress. When there is no more, we are dead. We strive no more. No longer does the system struggle to retain its temperature at 98.6 degrees. No longer does the heart pump blood upward from the extremities. In the non-stress of death, the body quickly takes on the temperature of its environment: a snowflake does not melt on the cheek.

The person we are does not change in death. Our body decomposes and wears away like rock dust, but this is nature at work, not ourselves. We give up at death. Change creates stress, and only living brings change. Constant change. A mature adult has responded in a lifetime to the changes of television and automation, air travel and atomic energy. In one year we respond to the changes of government and taxes and work habits and aging. Even in a day we respond to innumerable changes of temperature and clothing and food, of people around us and of our own thoughts and feelings. Each minute leaves us different from the minute that went before and the one that will come after. And each change foretells stress.

Yet the paradox is that it is stress which brings about change. Not only does the body change in stress, but the world changes as well. Hunger may produce effective methods of farming. Disease may produce cures. Alexander Graham Bell's deafness led him to invent the telephone, and Louis Braille's blindness motivated him to devise a system of reading with the fingertips. Physical longings unite to produce offspring, and physical hurt sometimes produces murder. Greed and ego needs produce war. A soul in pain may produce poetry.

"Stress develops in people whenever survival is at stake," Hans Selye and Jean Tache wrote in their paper "On Stress and Coping Mechanisms." In short, stress makes people change. Change, therefore, is the survival technique—remember the amoeba. We call it adaptation.

WHAT IS ADAPTATION?

Early in his studies Hans Selye concluded that the body reacts to stress in what he calls the General Adaptation Syndrome, the G.A.S. First, when you encounter a stressor, you react with *alarm*. If the stressor does not immediately kill you, as a bullet or a bolt of lightning or the shock of bad news might, you gather your forces and prepare for Reaction Two. This is the stage of *resistance* (or coping). Your mobilized defense system wards off the stressor for as long as it can. If successful in its resistance, your body drives off the stressor and returns to normal. If not successful, it continues to resist until it reaches the stage of Reaction Three. This is *exhaustion*. At this point your body is no longer able to resist and must resign itself to inevitable defeat.

On the simplest level we see the General Adaptation Syndrome at work when we have an infection. A cut may be the stressor, to which your body reacts in alarm. You bleed in order to carry away infectious bacteria. If bacteria remain, however, your body prepares itself to resist them by setting up a wall of inflammation around the cut, which is intended to confine the infection. In addition, your body sends armies of white blood cells to overcome the germ warfare. If your body wins, the infection is contained and finally wears itself out and disappears. If, on the other hand, your body loses, the infection spreads beyond the wall of inflammation, poisoning other parts of the body. Other inflammatory walls of defense are set up there, and new battles ensue. This resistance effort continues until one side wins. Either your body wins and the infection disappears or the bacteria win, taking over your body until it surrenders and dies.

Fortunately, in most cases of infection the body wins, but even a small cut infested with a lethal germ such as staphylococcus can result in death.

The General Adaptation Syndrome works similarly at a psychological or emotional level. The stressor may be a bad marriage. The first stage or shock may come, as they say, when the honeymoon is over. The second stage, resistance, may endure through years of unhappiness. You may be lucky and win by turning a poor relationship into a fulfilling one. If, however, you are not so lucky, you end up in the third stage, exhaustion, either resigning yourself to the inevitable or packing up for Reno and a divorce.

You can resist during stage two in one of three ways: you can *fight* the stressor; you can *run away* from it; or you can *ignore* it. Your body selects one of the three involuntarily when resisting physical stress, whereas you may make a more conscious choice in coping with emotional stress. For instance, in dealing with the bad marriage outlined above, you might opt for any one of the three resistance methods. If you choose to fight, you may do just that—physically and verbally fight in order to change the factors causing marital discord. Or you may choose more subtle means of fighting: you may humiliate your spouse, nag, lash out with sarcasm, taunt, withhold favors. However, you may go the second route—not fight, but flight, in which case you resist through different means. You may move into separate bedrooms, take separate vacations; you may develop your own interests and friends, maybe even take a lover in order to escape the source of stress. Some people escape so successfully that they actually delude themselves into believing their marriage is what they want or by living in daydreams and fantasy. If you eschew both fight and flight, you resist the third way, by ignoring the problem. In this case, you immerse yourself in activities that keep your mind off your marriage, allowing yourself no time for worry or unhappiness. In addition, you minimize the problem areas by dwelling on your spouse's positive qualities which support rather than break down the relationship.

Whichever of these three methods you select, or whatever combination of methods, you are operating at the second stage in the General Adaptation Syndrome. You are resisting the stressor. When you resist it successfully, you do not pass on to the third stage, exhaustion.

According to Hans Selye, "Adaptation is probably the most distinctive characteristic of life." Even without labeling it, we adapt all the time. And we get better and better as we practice. An infant, relatively new at adaptation, as he is at life itself, is little able to cope with hunger. The instant he feels the first pang, he cries and continues crying until breast or bottle is brought forth to satisfy him. As he gets older and more experienced, his body handles hunger with greater sophistication: no longer does he instantly cry, but waits until mealtime.

If you have ever gone swimming in cold water, you have seen your own adaptation skills improve with practice. When you first plunge in, your body responds in shivers, breathlessness and goose pimples. Shortly, however, the water feels less cold as you grow used to it. Similarly, when you learn to drive a car, you are overwhelmed by the pressure of remembering what to do when: push clutch, shift gear, turn wheel, release brake, push gas pedal, clutch again, gear shift, gas wheel—so many motions to coordinate. But as you get used to driving, you adapt to the confusion: each single motion blends with the overall motion of driving a car, and you perform it instinctively. The same happens when you jog or play an active sport. At the start your body is limited in its performance: it can't take more than one block of running or one set of tennis. But as you continue pushing yourself a step more, a game more, every day, your body adapts, and you find yourself running two miles or playing three sets without trouble.

According to Hans Selye, adaptation energy, however, is not infinite. We are born with a limited amount that is not replenished throughout our life. Rest replenishes our physical and emotional energy, but it does no good for our adaptation energy. The limit of that is predetermined—no one knows exactly how—at birth. The only control we have over its depletion is the rate at which we use it.

In addition, our bodies and emotions can take only so much wear and tear without falling apart. No matter how efficaciously our adaptation energy works, we cannot continually resist stress without debilitation. There is an end to what we can take. There is a point at which we say, "No more," and give up.

As we combine these two realities—limited ability to adapt to stress and limited ability to withstand stress—a loud word of warning emerges. USE YOUR ADAPTATION ENERGY WISELY. Like a child with a lollypop who takes an occasional lick sparingly, we must make it last as long as possible. To help us do this, scientists like Hans Selye and others continue to study stress attentively. As they reveal major causes of stress, they enable us to gain insight into the stressors in our individual lives. With greater insight, we are more adequately equipped both to avoid unnecessary stress areas and to successfully handle those we are forced to contend with.

Stress is identified in a variety of ways. In some studies respondents are interviewed in depth and followed for periods of their life, at home and at work, during crises and everyday routines. In others they are asked to fill in questionnaires on a regular basis or to become part of a panel scrutinized by a stress center. On the other hand, modern technology may be applied to stress identification—electrocardiograms and electromyograms can chart the course of reaction to imposed stressors. One of the newer methods is the galvanic skin resistance test, which monitors sweat in the palm of the hand in response to a weak electrical current. No single test is significant, however, according to the experts: only a battery of tests can give anywhere near a reliable measurement.

The National Institute of Occupational Safety and Health has identified a major area of stress in the lives of many Americans. They have found that the stress of routine, repeated work such as that of an assembly line or of punching computer cards can actually produce physical illness. In a Midwestern plant, women assembling lawn furniture developed headaches, dizziness, weakness and bad tastes in their mouths. The symptoms were attributed to their stressful work. In other places around the country rapid breathing and spasms have also developed. This syndrome has been labeled "assembly-line hysteria" and, once again, is attributed to boredom and monotony as stressors.

Dr. George Engel of Rochester identifies from his studies eight stressors that may lead to psychological stress and even resultant death:

1. Death of a person close to you
2. Acute grief

3. Threat of loss
4. Mourning
5. Loss of status or self-cstccm
6. Personal danger
7. The time after the danger is over
8. Reunion, triumph and happy ending

One of the most interesting, and surely one of the most applicable, stress tests is the Life Event Scale developed by Dr. Thomas Holmes and Dr. Richard Rahe. They have developed a list of forty-three major events which may occur in an adult's life to cause varying degrees of stress. A rating number is given to each event in descending order of the stress intensity.

You can give yourself this test. Read down the list of life events listed below, circling those which apply to you. Total the value of the life events you have circled, and you will have the score of your current stress potential.

LIFE EVENT	VALUE
1. Death of spouse	100
2. Divorce	73
3. Marital separation	65
4. Jail term	63
5. Death of close family member	63
6. Personal injury or illness	53
7. Marriage	50
8. Fired from job	47
9. Marital reconciliation	45
10. Retirement	45
11. Change in health of family member	44
12. Pregnancy	40
13. Sex difficulties	39
14. Gain of new family member	39
15. Business readjustment	39
16. Change in financial state	38
17. Death of close friend	37
18. Change to different line of work	36
19. Change in number of arguments with spouse	35

LIFE EVENT	VALUE
20. Mortgage over $10,000 [this might be higher now]	31
21. Foreclosure of mortgage or loan	30
22. Change in responsibilities at work	29
23. Son or daughter leaving home	29
24. Trouble with in-laws	29
25. Outstanding personal achievement	28
26. Wife begins or stops work	26
27. Begin or end school	26
28. Change in living conditions	25
29. Revision of personal habits	24
30. Trouble with boss	23
31. Change in work hours or conditions	20
32. Change in residence	20
33. Change in schools	20
34. Change in recreation	19
35. Change in church activities	19
36. Change in social activities	18
37. Mortgage or loan less than $10,000	17
38. Change in sleeping habits	16
39. Change in number of family get-togethers	15
40. Change in eating habits	15
41. Vacation	13
42. Christmas	12
43. Minor violations of the law	11

You may interpret your score as follows:

SCORE	STRESS POTENTIAL	
150–199	Moderate	37%
200–299	Medium	51%
300 or more	Severe	79%

Hundreds of studies are being made in the areas of stress. Scientists and social scientists are investigating stress in the handicapped, in minorities, in housewives; they are studying executive stress, stress of the liberated woman and of her toppling chauvinist husband; they are uncovering facts about the stress of depression, disease and death. There remains, it seems, only one group whose stress until recently has been all but ignored, one group whose stress is still only hesitatingly being acknowledged, one group whose stress has rarely been viewed with compassion. That is our children.

WHAT STRESS CAN A CHILD HAVE?

Since most adults view a child's world from their own frame of reference, it is difficult for them to imagine any life but their own as stressful. There are several possible explanations. First of all, adults brim over with nostalgia in remembrance of childhood. It is the carefree time, the days of innocence, from which they have been thrust and to which they *think* they long to return. "Backward, turn backward, O Time, in your flight,/Make me a child again just for to-night!" So pines Elizabeth Akers Allen. How can stress be permitted a place in such a fantasy?

Secondly, adults tend to treat children's pains and problems patronizingly. They consider them insignificant in comparison to their own: what is a lost "best friend" compared to the divorce over which they may be agonizing? How serious can a failed test be alongside losing one's job? Wearing the wrong dress to a party can't possibly create the anxiety of spying the first gray hair and wrinkle. Yet the tragedy of a best friend lost to a ten-year-old may produce the same sense of isolation and abandonment as a divorce to her parents. Her self-esteem drops as low over an F on a midterm as her father's does over losing his job. Her feeling of being lost to the mainstream in the wrong dress is as keen as her mother's in the face of age signs. Adults should not judge troubles by their size, but by the size of the pain they produce.

Thirdly, adults rarely put themselves inside young people. Don't judge a person, the old Indian proverb warned, until you have walked a mile in his moccasins. Most adults take no more than a few steps in their children's moccasins and cannot, therefore, know what their world is like, cannot feel what they feel. They can only superimpose their own opinions and feelings, attributing them to their children. It is safer this way, for they can avoid confrontations with realities that may differ from their own. Children sense this; that is why they rarely communicate honestly with adults. Adults, however, are less wise; they *think* they communicate.

However, adult recognition or nonrecognition of the stress under which children live changes nothing. The stress is there. Anyone doubting it need only look at the results of adult stress studies and apply them to the lives of children. The Holmes and Rahe Life Event Scale serves as a clear example.

You will find below the same forty-three life events, adjusted to fit situations in the life of a child—that is, "spouse" is changed to "parent," "work" to "school," etc. The value of each life event remains the same.

LIFE EVENT	VALUE
1. Death of a parent	100
2. Divorce of parents	73
3. Separation of parents	65
4. Parent's jail term	63
5. Death of a close family member (i.e., grandparent)	63
6. Personal injury or illness	53
7. Parent's remarriage	50
8. Suspension or expulsion from school	47
9. Parents' reconciliation	45
10. Long vacation (Christmas, summer, etc.)	45
11. Parent or sibling sickness	44
12. Mother's pregnancy	40
13. Anxiety over sex	39
14. Birth of new baby (or adoption)	39
15. New school or new classroom or new teacher	39
16. Money problems at home	38
17. Death (or moving away) of close friend	37
18. Change in studies	36
19. More quarrels with parents (or parents quarreling more)	35
20. Not applicable to a child	
21. Not applicable to a child	
22. Change in school responsibilities	29
23. Sibling going away to school	29

LIFE EVENT   VALUE

24. Family arguments with grandparents   29
25. Winning school or community awards   28
26. Mother going to work or stopping work   26
27. School beginning or ending   26
28. Family's living standard changing   25
29. Change in personal habits—i.e., bedtime, homework, etc. 24
30. Trouble with parents—lack of communication,
    hostility, etc.   23
31. Change in school hours, schedule or courses   20
32. Family's moving   20
33. A new school   20
34. New sports, hobbies, family recreation activities   19
35. Change in church activities—more involvement or less   19
36. Change in social activities—new friends, loss
    of old ones, peer pressures   18
37. Not applicable to a child
38. Change in sleeping habits—staying up later,
    giving up nap, etc.   16
39. Change in number of family get-togethers   15
40. Change in eating habits—going on or off diet,
    new way of family cooking   15
41. Vacation   13
42. Christmas   12
43. Breaking home, school or community rules   11

Totaling the score, you may be surprised to find how quickly an average child can reach the 300 level of severe stress potential. Changes occur rapidly in his life, far more rapidly than in the life of his parents. Six hours of school alone subjects him to Life Events 8, 10, 15, 18, 22, 25, 27, 31, 33, 41 and 43 on almost a routine basis. In addition, the ups and downs of his social life add the stress of Life Events 13, 17, 32, 35, 36, 39, 41. He is far more susceptible to personal injury because of the high percentage of his time spent in physical activities such as bike riding or skating. In addition, he may fall victim to every contagious disease that strikes the school.

Other measurements of adult stress are equally applicable to children. Hans Selye in his book *The Stress of Life* lists eleven areas as major causes of stress in the lives of adults: job, human relations, climate, crowding, boredom, loneliness, captivity, relocation, urbanization, catastrophe and anxiety. Applied to children, they become the fiber of their everyday life:

Job (*in the case of children, school*) — The typical six-hour school day is fraught with problems and pressures creating stress—in academics, sports, in peer relationships and in interchanges with teachers. Survival of the self-image is on the line every minute.

Human relations — A child has many relationships to juggle in the normal course of a day, at home, in school and in his afterschool activities. Furthermore, he takes his relationships intensely, running the gamut of love, hate, anger and envy. Indifference in relationships is alien to most children.

Climate — A child, of course, lives with this as much as an adult does. Some teachers feel, moreover, that children react to weather changes more forcefully than adults do. Schools are louder on rainy days; children are more uncontrollable on gray days; more work is accomplished when the sun shines.

Crowding — Since studies prove that even rats grow hostile in overcrowded conditions, it is foolish to ignore the pressures of overcrowding on children. Schools across the country are notoriously too full: there is too little space per pupil and there are too many pupils per teacher. Many teachers relate the degree of aggressive behavior in their classrooms to both size and space, particularly in the early grades.

Boredom — One of the current American tragedies is the plague of boredom blighting the lives of young people. "What can I do?" is a familiar cry at home. Too often the answer is television—up to forty hours a week of it. Most schools do equally little to relieve the tedium of routine studies; children expect to be bored. Except in those few schools with individualization and creative programs, students "get through another day," rather than get stimulated.

Loneliness — Psychologists point out that adolescence tends to be a lonely time. A time of mourning, they call it, when young people grieve for the security of childhood while also longing for adult independence. Even younger children, as young as three or four, have a sense of not belonging. While preadolescents and teenagers cling to the peer group to ward off loneliness, younger children may cling to parents and to a single friend, to what is familiar and secure.

Captivity—The stress of captivity vibrates in any institution where juveniles are confined. Yet all children live in a kind of captivity, similarly stress-producing. They have little say about the rules and regulations set up at home, less to say about those set up at school, both of which together confine them twenty-four hours a day. They are subject to even larger laws over which they have no control, such as how long they must attend school, with whom they have to live, at what age they can work. It is little wonder that they rebel with the battle cry of freedom.

Relocation—School can be regarded as a continual relocation for children. Each day they switch from class to class and subject to subject. Each year they switch teachers and classrooms. Periodically they switch buildings since, except for a relatively few remaining central schools, different school levels are housed separately. In addition, the usual family relocations affect them as well: they are forced to leave friends and familiar routines for a reward no more personal than Dad's new job, Mother's divorce and remarriage or the family's upward mobility.

Urbanization—Although the increasing urbanization of life is comparable for children and adults, it probably affects children more destructively. Where do they ride their bikes? Where do they pull together a ball game? Where do they contact nature, or even themselves, alone in the quiet? Since parents rarely do those things, city life is less of a hindrance to them. To their children, however, it can be stifling, alienating.

Catastrophe—Children do not require earthquakes and floods: a failed test is their catastrophe, or a disloyal friend, a dog run over by a car, ridicule by a teacher. These they meet and are forced to live with routinely.

Anxiety—Anxiety is almost a normal state for children, for their lives are uncertain: Will they succeed in school? Will they please their parents? Will their peers accept them? Will they get thin . . . or fat . . . or pretty . . . or strong? Will they make the team? Will they get the part in the play? A character in a soap opera lives under no more anxiety than the average child, and, according to investigators Cecil Reynolds and Bert Raymond in their study of children's anxiety, the younger the child, the greater his anxiety.

Management consultant Gerard Fisher, greatly concerned with stress in business executives, identifies sources of stress through what he calls the "Life Diamond": job, family, society and sense of self. In various combinations these, he says, account for the stress that executives relieve in assorted ways, from a three-martini lunch to a screaming fit at their secretary. While to young people both of these outlets are off limits, the stressors in their Life Diamond are probably as intense, or even more so, than those of their executive parents.

We cannot avoid the fact that children are in constant stress. Yet few parents and teachers, who in most cases are the stressors themselves, acknowledge the scope, the intensity or the damaging effects of this stress. Since they want to think of their children as happy, they have to consider overstressed children as aberrations rather than the norm. Their inability to face the reality of a child's life not only prevents them from helping their child; it actually creates and reinforces the problem.

Erik Erikson associates a large part of childhood stress with fear. He has isolated eleven separate fears, not remote, but woven into the everyday fiber of their lives. Like soldiers in battle, children face fear daily; and like soldiers, when not actually facing it, they frequently anticipate it. These eleven basic fears have been prevalent in the life of your child, adding to her stress even if you have been loving and thoughtful.

1. FEAR OF WITHDRAWAL OF SUPPORT

Even the newest infant has a fear of falling. The older baby will cling to any neck for support. Many a toddler shies away from swings and seesaws, despite parental urgings; she is more comfortable on terra firma. Support is more than physical, however, and while few parents and teachers would let a child physically fall, they are apt to withdraw *emotional* support heedlessly. A new mother and father I know are proud of themselves for letting their infant son cry himself to sleep for several nights in a row. "It hurt us more than it did him," they boast. I doubt it. The older child neglected by parents too busy to become involved is also left hanging in midair, but unlike a trapeze artist, with no reassurance of support below: the parental mainstay is gone. The teenager reprimanded for "letting his parents down" is in even worse shape; he suffers not only the fear of loss of support, but the guilt of having pushed it away himself.

Fear of support withdrawal is a major pressure for children in school. With any failed paper, they lose teacher support—or with an incorrect answer in class or with even trivial misdemeanors. An English teacher in a school where I once taught withdrew support to the point of refusing to correct a student's papers anymore. A fourth-grade teacher played such favorites with a select few that two thirds of the class complained, "She doesn't care if I learn."

More important, children fear the loss of support from their classmates for what to us seem like trivialities—wearing the wrong clothes or being different or challenging peer values. Being too smart or not smart enough can turn peers away. And sometimes there is no reason at all.

2. FEAR OF SUDDENNESS

Parents move in slow, easy patterns around an infant for they know that sudden motion frightens them. Yet they respond to their growing children with terrifying leaps and starts. Many are inconsistent in everything but their inconsistency. A parent scolds one minute and cajoles the next; she agrees to TV on Monday and demands it be turned off on Tuesday. Hospital regulations usually forbid visits by children under twelve, yet parents bring newborn infants from the maternity ward into the home with a suddenness that all nine months of preparation cannot ease. As a three-year-old complained about her attention-getting five-day-old brother, "Maybe he'll go 'way tomorrow. He wasn't here last time."

Even the most careful of parents subject their children to suddenness and its ensuing fear. They move into a new house, new neighborhood, new locale; they change jobs; they get divorced; they go back to school. Whereas for them the action may have been deliberated and planned for months before the actual step was taken, for the child it happened all of a sudden. Even when it has been discussed with him, it does not become a reality until the words become the act.

The very essence of school is sudden change. Bells ring, and children jump to switch subjects, classes, rooms and sometimes even buildings. Teachers are in school one day and gone the next: they get sick or married or frustrated enough to quit. Studies of high teacher turnover show seriously deleterious effects on students. In addition, during the course of normal school routine, fire drills break into quiet and study; the principal's voice interrupts over the loudspeaker, and teacher and student outbursts resound with a startling shock.

3. FEAR OF NOISE

Infants start at noise and begin to cry, so we learn to talk softly to them, to coo like doves with gentle sounds. Yet children are forced to live amidst almost intolerable noise every day. Parents scream at them, and at each other in their presence. How frightening is that noise at night as a child lies awake in bed, chilled by the hostile sounds of his parents! Siblings yell; radios blare; telephones ring, and brothers shout upstairs, "It's for you!" Doors bang, pots and pans rattle. All this, before nature intrudes with a clap of thunder or a dog's barking and before civilization intrudes with buses, cabs, police sirens, construction drills, blastings and jets taking off and landing. One of my favorite two-year-olds has learned about noise: every time she does something "naughty," she runs to her somewhat volatile mother, holding both hands over her ears.

Noise at school emanates from all directions—band practice in the auditorium, recess on the playground, lunch lines in the cafeteria and cheers for the basketball team from the gym. Children talk at once, teachers shouting above them to be heard. Bells ring, feet tramp down the hall, sibilant commands of quiet hiss like snakes about to strike. Even the clocks tick audibly, clicking each time the hand moves a minute. One of the best teachers I know conducts her classes in a whisper in order to tone down the whole decibel level.

4. FEAR OF BEING MANIPULATED

Because babies hate having their arms and legs shoved into sleeves and pants, they often are at their worst while being dressed. Diapering can become a tourney between mother and baby with large pins as weapons. Those operations are necessary, yet parents continue to manipulate a child in ways far less necessary and far more fearful. They often set up rules for their own convenience, passing them off to the child as aids for him—for instance, "You don't like living in a messy room." The truth is, Mom can't stand it. Or they impose their values on the child under the guise that they are his own values—like, "We know you wouldn't cheat." Of course he would, if cheating gets him the mark his parents demand. They create an image of him in their own minds, establishing it for him and the rest of the world to accept as reality. "Jimmy is the smart one of the family," they may say. "Janie is our personality girl." And they ensure the success of their manipulative efforts by rewarding both for playing the part.

School too manipulates. It persuades young people to perform by awarding them gold stars and A's and by reading their names on the honor roll. The successful student, therefore, is one manipulated into writing not what he may think, but what he is told he should think. One of the most horrifying examples of manipulation is the ubiquitous teacher who will not let a child back in class until he says, "I'm sorry." What latent aggression that innocent two-word phrase contains!

5. FEAR OF INTERRUPTION OF A VITAL ACTIVITY

A child's concentration on an activity is forever being interrupted by his parents because they do not consider that activity as vital as he does. A talk with a friend, a book being read, a block house being built or just plain sitting and doing nothing seem far less important than time for dinner, time for school, time for our visit, time to mow the lawn, time for bed. A confused five-year-old asked his highly organized mother, "When is it time for me?" I suspect adults would be far less amiable in the face of continual interruptions than their children are.

The clockwork of school precludes long periods of involvement in anything. Just as a student gets absorbed in one subject, it is time for another. Teachers, after all, must follow their lesson plans, and the principal demands that certain curriculum be covered. In fact, the almighty schedule is one of the most self-defeating aspects of any school, determining what courses a student may or may not take, at what time and with what teachers. A student I know, unable to fit advanced courses in both biology and creative writing into his schedule, opted for the former. I cannot help wondering whether the computer's limitations deprived the world of a poet!

In order to combat the choppiness of education as it exists in most schools, the Gill School in New Jersey and a few scattered others attempted intensive study in which students concentrate their efforts on only one subject for several weeks at a time. Unfortunately, the plan has not caught on widely, and children are still forced to conform to the school schedule, despite differences in their interests or powers of concentration.

6. FEAR OF BEING DEPRIVED OF A VALUABLE POSSESSION

Anyone who has ever raised a child is aware of his possessiveness. He hates to part with anything, from the B.M. he howls to see flushed down the toilet and the hair he hates having cut, to the toy you wish he would share with your friend's baby. As children mature, they attach themselves to other valuable possessions, of which just as often parents heedlessly deprive them. As a little girl, I had to give my dog away because his fur shed. I wept and called my mother "a rat" and ran away from home. Over forty years later I can still relive the shock and feeling of helplessness, the depth of which my parents never realized.

I know a mother who threw out her son's drooping plant because it was dead. He was devastated. Many a rock collection or bag of string or cache of matchboxes, unappreciated by parents, has thoughtlessly gone out with the garbage—and been wept over. What a sacrifice the tiny cherub makes in "The Littlest Angel" as he hands over his box of "treasures" to the baby Jesus on Christmas Eve. Can parents value their own cherub's treasures less highly?

In this day of increased crime and intense coverage by the media, there is a new fear of loss which children encounter: stealing. Stealing in schools is rampant. I have encountered a fourth-grader who memorized locker combinations in order to help himself with ease to his classmates' possessions. I know a second-grader who stole a camera from his classmate's schoolbag. Children's drawings demonstrate the intensity of this fear: when asked to illustrate their dreams or night thoughts, they draw guns, men entering their houses, their favorite toys being thrown from windows. And, of course, children are always vulnerable to other, less tangible possessions being taken away—a best friend, a position on a team, their standing in class.

7. FEAR OF RESTRAINT

Babies hate to be held down, which is another reason for tears at dressing time. Yet children's lives involve a series of continual restraints. They must obey, not as their logic or needs dictate, but as arbitrary rules demand. At home they dress pretty much as they are told, eat what is served and follow parental rules. They are required to attend school, which they often hate, and forbidden activities which they enjoy. They are awakened by alarms in the morning, shoved out the door, ordered to be home at a certain time and sent to bed "when Mother says so." Parents are probably correct when they warn that young people are ignorant of the responsibility that accompanies the freedom they struggle for; however, reality, or their blindness to it, does not minimize the stress that stems from the absence of freedom with which they are forced to live.

In school as well as at home, restraints are tight. To begin with, children have to sit still for long hours, constraining bodies that are made for action. In addition, few schools involve students in decision-making, so they are psychologically held down by rules and regulations that may seem remote and irrelevant. Should they stray, disciplinary measures add further restraints: recess—one of the few periods of free play—is taken away; or athletics are restricted, with extra hours in study hall or the library as an alternative. Whether kept *in* after school, sent *out* during class, or just living through a normal day, most children feel tied down by school. A group of junior high students were asked to check off from a list of fifty words those they thought best described their school. The winning word was "prison."

8. FEAR OF HAVING NO IMPOSED CONTROLS

Too much freedom is as fearsome to a child as too little: it places on his shoulders more independence than he can handle. Haven't we all seen the three-year-old, unable to decide what to choose for lunch, throw a temper tantrum and eat nothing? Similarly, haven't we seen the preadolescent filled with self-loathing over an act he committed? Excessive freedom creates guilt and self-doubt, and although growing up is synonymous with fighting to obtain that freedom, being granted it too soon is synonymous with unhappiness. That is the paradox of childhood: simultaneous striving for and turning away from independence. There is no winning.

Permissive schools, like permissive parents, are self-defeating. While they intend to help a child grow in self-confidence, they do the opposite: they weaken his ability to cope. By "permissive schools" I do not mean open schools with carefully planned and executed programs. On the contrary, these are far from permissive, holding children strictly accountable for their work. By "permissive" I mean schools in which children are turned loose to do their own things, with no one guiding them to follow a plan of learning. Like water bugs, they scoot from activity to activity, receiving little fulfillment or sense of accomplishment. In such situations the children's discomfort manifests itself frequently in excessively aggressive behavior, a sure sign of stress.

9. FEAR OF INSPECTION OR OF BEING EXPOSED

Children instinctively dread the doctor or dentist, not so much because he hurts them as because he inspects them. While parents may be sympathetic to this kind of fear—and certainly doctors are, if the proffered lollypops are an indication—still they subject their children to hundreds of similar inspections. They give them a nightly bath, probing cavities, often for far too many years. I know a mother who is still bathing her eleven-year-old boy "because he would never get himself clean." Parents peer into closets and bureau drawers, regardless of privacy. Some open letters, listen in on phone calls and open diaries which, in their innocence, children trust to cheap little locks. One even sniffs her daughter's socks to ascertain that they are clean before she puts them on each morning. Children are vulnerable: inspection and exposure deprive them of dignity.

Teachers inspect children to a lesser degree, although they too check lockers, cubbyholes and desks for orderliness. In some urban schools where lice are prevalent, children line up each morning before the teacher or nurse for hair inspection. It is exposure rather than inspection to which schools mercilessly subject children. They are exposed by the return of papers as classmates look and whisper, "What did you get?" They are exposed when marks are posted and honor rolls read aloud, when athletic awards are given (and not given!) and journals kept to be read weekly by the teacher. They are exposed when they have to speak before the class and when their papers are read aloud and criticized. They are exposed on visiting days when their parents show up—or fail to show up—in school. Let them injudiciously break a rule, be it ever so slight, and through a cruel grapevine they are exposed to the entire community.

10. FEAR OF BEING OR REMAINING SMALL

Bigness is a status symbol in America: we brag about the size of our houses, our automobiles (before the gas shortage) and our babies at birth. Athletes are tall; models are tall; movie stars who are not tall survive on elevator shoes. Children are little in a world of giants, always confronting knees or navels or straining to look up, like the audience in the front row at the ballet, awkward and sore-necked. Parents tend to reinforce their children's feelings of littleness. "You are acting like a baby," they say; or, "She's our littlest." A father I know takes pride in the fact that his daughter, shortest in her class, always leads the line as they march to assembly. His daughter dreams of being even second in line someday. My 6'2" son Chris is so sensitive to the disparity in size between his two daughters and himself that he has gotten into the habit of kneeling whenever he speaks to them. "I like meeting them eyeball to eyeball," he says.

Shortness is intensified in school because the older students loom so much larger. Have any of us not experienced the shock of observing a group of eighth-graders and remembering how huge they looked when we were in elementary school? Size is important to a child's self-image. Boys hide in the lavatory to compare penis length; girls vie to be the first to wear a bra. Tall boys have always been school heroes; the advent of girls' competitive sports has made tall girls heroes as well. The nickname "Shorty" is second only to "Fatso" in causing pain.

11. FEAR OF BEING LEFT ALONE

Children, particularly girls, are afraid of being left alone. This accounts in part for the strong and often ruthless cliques associated with preteen girls. One of the greatest causes of stress in young children is separation from their mother—often if she merely leaves the room, later on when she leaves them at the kindergarten door. Actually, recent tests reveal that children can stand separation from their mother when the door through which she passed remains open. Children harbor a subconscious fear that their parents will die, and, of course, many children while still young have to face the death of grandparents. Parental routines tend to reinforce this fear without parents' awareness: they leave children alone in bed each night in the isolating dark. Sometimes parents are ill and go to the hospital, leaving children; or they have babies and leave them temporarily. Sometimes they separate and get divorced. In America's cities, tens of thousands of "latchkey children" come home from school every day to an empty house. There they wait alone until parents return from work, or they join the gang on the street for company.

Recent teacher turnover has proved unsettling to children. Since young children attach themselves to their teacher as a substitute mother, her leaving becomes almost as traumatic. Even steadier schools with little turnover magnify a child's fear of being alone: teachers punish by excluding a child from the group, sending him alone into the hall or keeping him alone in the room while the class plays in the yard. I ran into a teacher who actually kept a large box in the hall; she closed in any unruly child, taking a cue, I guess, from a prison's use of solitary confinement. One of the saddest sights in my memory is a little blond second-grader who sat alone at school every afternoon waiting for his father to pick him up at five o'clock. When his father was late, he would tell me, "He's going to come." I always felt he was reassuring himself rather than me.

In examining the application of these eleven basic fears of children to situations at home and at school, parents will not, I hope, exclaim as one parent did, "My God, I'm doing everything wrong!"

Parents are *not* doing everything wrong, nor are teachers. No judgment is intended. They are doing in most cases what they have to do by temperament and circumstances. My object in outlining these fears is to alert adults to what goes on inside their children. My object in pointing out the hundreds of fears that children face every day is to alert adults to what goes on inside their homes and their schools. *The very nature of home and school creates stress in children.* The best parents and teachers in the world could not eliminate all of this stress if they tried.

Actually, they should not eliminate all stress even if they could. It is essential to their child's growth. There are some things they should do, however:

— They should realize that their children live under constant stress.
— They should recognize the stressful factors that they and their environment create.
— They should eliminate unnecessary stressors.
— They should help children cope with the stressors that remain around them.

Chapter I of this book has tried to make readers aware of the first two points, that children live under constant stress in both the home and the school environment. The rest of the book will deal with these two points in fuller detail and will offer guidelines for Points 3 and 4.

> *"Put off, or put on,*
> *Youth hurts. And then*
> *It's gone."*

Those are the concluding lines of James Emanuel's poem, "The Young Ones, Flip Side." They tell the story of childhood. What they do not tell, however, is an answer to the eternal question: why do some children react positively to the stressors in their lives and others, subjected to the same stressors, react negatively? Why does Winston Churchill, a failure at his studies, become a world hero? And a thousand other school dropouts die from an overdose of drugs?

No one really knows. However, the question is currently being explored. Many knowledgeable people claim that children are born either with or without the ability to cope. Surely infants react differently to the stressors in their environment. It has even been proved through chemically produced uterine contractions that unborn babies react differently to stress. Yet, as child psychiatrist Dr. Lee Salk explains, "It is hard to isolate the genetic factor, although we think maybe some kids are programmed to be stronger than others."

More people accept the explanation that children develop coping techniques at home. They become what Dr. James Anthony of Washington University calls either "vulnerable or invulnerable," the latter able to find ways of living through even the worst of conditions, the former falling apart under the least strain. The anonymous author of "Mother Goose" seems to have known this all along. Wednesday's child is the vulnerable one—ill-equipped to cope, "full of woe." The Sabbath day child is the invulnerable one—the coping child, "bonny and blithe and good and gay."

In my search for an answer to this unanswerable question, I put the question directly to acknowledged experts.

I asked Lee Salk, "What accounts for a child's ability to handle stress successfully?"

"The family is the key social unit from which children learn how to deal with life," he replied.

I asked Hans Selye, "What is the simplest way you could explain the difference between a child able to handle stress and a child unable to handle it?"

He made it simple, all right—he gave me a two-word answer: "His mother."

Paul Zindel's play The Effects of Gamma Rays on Man-in-the-Moon Marigolds might challenge them both. Two daughters, Ruth and Mathilda, respond to their emotionally paralyzed, fantasy-living mother in opposite ways. Ruth succumbs; Mathilda escapes into the world of intellect and scientific discovery. We are left with the same old question: why?

"Mishaps are like knives," the poet James Russell Lowell said, "that either serve us or cut us, as we grasp them by the blade or the handle."

Maybe that is where the answer lies. The Sabbath day child grasps knives by the handle and uses them; Wednesday's child grasps knives by the blade and cuts himself. In between are the millions of children who grasp them both ways.

CHAPTER II

◆

The Child That's Born on the Sabbath Day

Little Jack Horner sat in the corner
Eating a Christmas pie.
He put in his thumb,
And pulled out a plum,
And said, "What a good boy am I!"

Little Jack Horner is a Sabbath day child: he can cope. Even from children's short, four-line acquaintance with him, they know that. They meet him sitting in the corner for some unexplained reason. If by choice, they can't help realizing that he enjoys his own company —a sure sign of coping. If he is there as punishment, they must admit he holds no grudge—another sign of coping. Either way, his appetite holds up.

Jack is daring as he faces the unknown: unaware of what lies beneath the piecrust, he fearlessly plunges in his thumb. He shows no signs of revulsion over the gooey plum filling, nor does he show signs of fear over possible maternal disapproval.

Upon extracting a plum, he feels neither guilt nor shame, nor does he attempt to hide his deed. He is proud of what he has done. In full, free expression, he shouts his feelings to the world and to future generations of readers. Since critics probe all literature for meanings and morals, we must unearth one in the opus of Jack Horner. "What can you lose by trying?" it seems to dare us.

Jack is obviously a happy child, one that parents—all but Craig's wife and those others obsessed with neatness—would willingly claim as their own, because happiness is what parents truly want for their children. They may nag ceaselessly over minutiae: "Put your clothes away . . . clear the table . . . hang up the towels . . . do your homework . . . turn off the television . . . be quiet . . . eat your vegetables . . . stop teasing your sister." And their efforts may seem to focus on subjects far removed from happiness, like marks, manners and morality. That is because the everyday business of living diverts their attention from what really matters. Sometimes at night when the house is quiet, when it has been a good day and thoughts of children are mellow, parents reveal the concerns that lie underneath the day's trivia. That is when they talk of happiness. If they see it only in terms of their own happiness or in their own definition, they cannot be faulted. That is what they know.

Several years ago at a school where I was speaking, I asked the sixty parents attending to complete an open-ended statement. "I hope my child . . ." the sentence began. They were to fill in whatever came to mind. A third of the parents used the word "happy" or "happiness" in answering. Another third used words like "fulfilled," "contented," "well-adjusted." In other words, a large majority—two thirds—held the equivalent of happiness as the major goal for their children. Only two mentioned "success" as their hope.

Happy children, like happy adults, are not those without problems. Very often they may be those with the most severe problems. In thinking back over the happiest children I have known in my twenty-three years of educating and thirty-three years of parenting, I have to include a little girl with only one leg, an overweight teenager with two slim, beautiful sisters, a child too indigent to have anything but secondhand clothes, and a wizened little boy laughed at by his classmates because he played the violin. These were not looked on as fortunate children; they had serious problems. They were, however, happy children—far happier than many of the healthy, wealthy and beautiful children I have known—for they had learned to handle their problems. They were in control.

That is what coping is—being in control: recognizing the problem, accepting it for what it is; considering alternative solutions; making a decision and following through. When children are master of the situation, the problem does not overcome them; they overcome it. Only when they cannot handle a situation is it insurmountable, for then the problem is in control, not they themselves.

I saw both of these situations the other day with three-year-old Darcy. She wanted to put together a jigsaw puzzle, but instead of selecting one, she took out three. The first two, though difficult, she struggled with excitedly and put together. When she could not find a piece, she ran her fingers through the remaining pieces, studying the shape and color of each. When one did not fit, she turned it around until it slid in. Though frustrated, she kept at her job, chatting away with comments such as, "That's a dumb piece," or "Good for you." By the time she reached the third puzzle, however, she was worn out and could no longer cope. Whereas she had been master of the first two puzzles, the third puzzle took possession of her, and she was overwhelmed. She cried and kicked and finally threw the pieces on the floor. Her wise mother prevented a sense of total failure by suggesting, "Let's leave the puzzle and finish it later this afternoon." By then she would once again be in control.

In 1939 a man named William T. Grant endowed a study, later called the Grant Study, which was to determine "the kinds of people who are well and do well." A group of college men who were coping successfully in the areas of family life, health and academics were selected for the study and were followed for thirty years, their health, attitudes and personal and professional life charted. Reporting on the study, George Vaillant in his book *Adaptation to Life* found that as their fiftieth birthdays rolled around, most of these men were healthy, ninety percent had stable marriages and families and all had successful careers. They considered themselves happy, both by their standards and by the world's. "Yet," writes the author, "there is not one of the men who has had clear sailing." Their happiness, like yours, your children's and everybody else's, stemmed not from the absence of problems, but from their ability to cope.

HOW CHILDREN COPE

Children, like the men of the Grant Study, are happy when they can cope. Edward Whymper, who, after six brutal failures, became the first man to scale the dreaded Matterhorn, wrote, "The thing to be wished for is not that the mountains should become easier, but that men should become wiser and stronger." The child who is born on the Sabbath day is wise enough and strong enough to scale his own Matterhorns as they loom before him.

According to Hans Selye, when faced with stress, people have four main ways of coping:

— They can remove the stressor.
— They can refuse to allow neutral situations to become stressors.
— They can deal directly with the stressor.
— They can find ways of relaxing to ease the tension of stress.

When we apply each of these four coping techniques to a single stressor, we may better understand the way the Sabbath child works. Let us use Edward Whymper's mountain as an example.

Here is the child, confronted with a mountain in her pathway to a goal. At the first level, she will remove the stressor: in this case, she will detour and walk around it. At the second level, she will not let the mountain become a cause of stress: "It is only a mountain," she will say. "I will either climb it or not climb it. It doesn't really matter." At the third level she will deal with the mountain: she will map out the best route for ascending it and take lessons in mountain climbing. At the fourth level she will relax: "The hell with it," she will say and sit down under a tree to read Louisa May Alcott. No matter which of the four methods she selects, she will have mastered the stress created by an obstruction in the way of her goal. She will have conquered the mountain.

Children use these four coping techniques every day in the face of stressors—the mountains put in their way by parents, siblings, teachers and by fate itself.

1. HOW CHILDREN REMOVE STRESSORS

It is not easy, sometimes downright impossible, for a child to remove some of the major stressors in his life because, locked into them, he has little power. For instance, if he has a learning disability, he may be stuck with it. However, he can work around it, cultivating skills in other areas, such as athletics, the arts or working with people.

Sabbath children learn to remove stressors in a variety of creative ways. Matthew, aged thirteen, puts on his radio earphones when his parents begin to fight. Marcie takes her sister to the Y on Saturdays to escape the weekly bargain-hunting trips her mother insists on. Even two-year-old Jeff has learned to cope by removing a stressor: when the five-year-old neighborhood bully knocks on the door, he runs and hides in his playhouse.

Fortunately, of the stressors in a child's life, there are many that he can remove. The Sabbath child seems to identify these stressors readily, inventing means of getting them out of the way. A junior high friend of mine saw herself being pulled into the drug scene by her group of friends. Torn by the conflicting pressures of either belonging to her peer group or of doing what she felt was right, she suffered for months before making a decision. At that point she coped with the stressor by removing it: she cut herself off from the group. Another child, somewhat younger, uses a similar technique: when her little brother screams when she is on the telephone, she excuses herself with, "I've got to put *him* in another room," then goes on with her conversation. When five-year-old Mark's dog started eating the play dough with which he was making cakes, he quietly dragged the dog into the closet. Even Anna, just two, removes her stressors adeptly: a farm girl, unused to strangers, she is timid of her grandmother's doorman when she visits in New York— so she covers her eyes and makes him vanish. Similarly, when the witch on *The Wizard of Oz* record frightened her, she held her ears until she felt brave enough to listen.

2. HOW CHILDREN PREVENT NEUTRAL SITUATIONS FROM BECOMING STRESSORS

Many neutral situations in a child's life are turned into stressors by adults. Exams, for instance, should be regarded as mere checkpoints for the teacher to determine how much material she has successfully covered; instead they become one of the greatest causes of anxiety and stress in school age children. Acceptance or rejection, not only by teachers but, more importantly, by parents as well, hinges on them. Similarly, many of the rules established at home become major stressors in the hands of parents. "Clean your room," rather than remaining a somewhat dull chore, turns into a war cry in a battle which is waged, more often than not, for dominance rather than for cleanliness. Even pleasant events can be magnified into sources of extreme stress. A trip to the circus, too long anticipated and built up, may result not in the expected fun and excitement, but in temper tantrums. A birthday party may end in tears. I know a teenager who is so stressed before going on a date that she locks herself in the bathroom and has to be coaxed or threatened out.

Despite all the hoopla, however, coping children find ways to keep events that should be neutral, neutral. Selma, whose mother was close to hysteria over her forthcoming Sweet Sixteen party, kept it in perspective with a laugh. "How come I didn't have a Fat Fifteen party?" she asked, "and will you spring for a Sexy Seventeen next year?" The Sabbath child tends to keep cool at term's end, while other children boil over in the face of exams. "Why shouldn't I do O.K.?" she asks. "I've done O.K. so far." She is in fact statistically correct: a study of elementary school children conducted by Jerome and Joan Dusek of Syracuse University revealed that children with low test anxiety do far better on tests than those with high test anxiety.

Perhaps the ultimate indication of a child's ability to keep life events in their proper place is the story (apocryphal or not) of Joan, whose aunt died. While her mother explained the inevitability and finality of death, Joan listened attentively. Relieved, her mother finished by asking whether the little girl had any questions. She had just one: "When you die, who's going to get the piano?"

My son Chris's four-year-old Abigail also put death in perspective. When it was explained that in dying, her aunt had gone to another world, Abigail's pragmatism took over. "Did she," she asked, "take her lunch?"

3. HOW CHILDREN FACE AND DEAL WITH STRESSORS

Dealing with a stressor entails confronting it and figuring out a way around it. It is more difficult, however, than it sounds—even for adults. The man who continually gets fired and blames the boss, the job or his co-workers, is not dealing with the cause of his failure: he is not even admitting it. The stressor may be his inadequacy or bad temper or laziness or a dozen more problems of his own making that he avoids facing up to. Similarly, a child who is disciplined by a teacher or who gets into a fight with a sibling may avoid the issue by putting the blame on them, rather than by looking objectively at the situation.

The Sabbath child is, more often than not, able to stand off, size up a situation and then plan a course of action that leads to a solution. For instance, if exams are the stressor, he will not simply worry and complain; he will study. If a classmate's misbehavior presents more temptation than he can resist, he will not continue getting into trouble with him; he will move his seat. My older brother used to plead with my mother when, as youngsters, we ran into conflicts, "Can I hit her just once, Mom, please?" Because the answer was always, "No," he invented another solution. "I'll let you call me the worst name you want," he would offer, "if you'll only be quiet during the ball game" . . . or "if you'll tell me where you hid my book," etc. In great delight I would shout, "Dumbbell!" and scoot off to my room. "Dumbbell"!—that shows how long ago I was a child.

Lorrie is a Sabbath child: she went on a diet and lost fifteen pounds when she got tired of being teased for being overweight. Greg is a Sabbath child: he studied art one summer, becoming a proficient watercolorist, rather than compete with an older brother who was an academic whiz. Then there was little Freddie, who grew frustrated when he had trouble sticking his father's stamps onto the dining room table; so he smeared them with glue and beamed with pride. Beth, aged three, solved her boredom while mother was entertaining friends by learning how to turn on the kitchen faucets and "wash" her hair. It is easy to see why parents sometimes have to discourage the Sabbath child's stress-solving techniques!

An infant is particularly adept at finding ways of dealing with his stressors. He solves the monotony of lying in a crib by discovering his feet and playing with those curious attachments called toes. He needs to suck, and, unable to communicate the message to his mother, sticks his thumb in his mouth. Speaking of communicating, a baby solves the isolation of being unable to join in adult conversations by learning to talk!

4. HOW CHILDREN RELAX IN THE FACE OF STRESS

The last level of coping with stress, which is through relaxation, is probably the least used by children. Adults, on the other hand, use it constantly. The executive plays golf or tennis; the housewife meets her friends for coffee or joins an exercise class at the Y. Joggers fill early morning streets in cities, while hikers take to the hills and bicyclists pedal their way into calm. In the past decade hundreds of thousands of adults in all parts of the country have taken up Transcendental Meditation as a way to ease tensions and restore energy drained by stress.

Unfortunately, the relaxation activities of children are for the most part either frowned upon or so highly organized as to be no longer relaxing. For instance, gym is required in school and often becomes competition rather than relaxation—thereby increasing, not lessening, stress. Even the casual after-school or weekend sports that children indulge in tend to become competitive—Little League, ski meets, competitive ice skating, team bowling and such. They need not be, but somehow the "Got to win" attitude slides in and with it, the stressor of proving oneself.

Relaxation that is frowned upon may not be considered damaging in itself, but is discouraged because it replaces chores and homework. All too often parents seem unable to resist nagging when they see their children watching television, knitting, reading a non-school book, making a model airplane and particularly just sitting and doing nothing. They call it "wasting time," and urge its replacement by more profitable activities. Children feel they are always being told to "get going."

Sabbath children find ways to relax, however, dealing with their stress constructively. They can be seen skiing alone down a mountain, doing untimed laps in a pool, climbing trees. They enjoy hobbies as passive as collecting stamps and postmarks or as active as gardening and barbells. Many children use some form of art for relaxation—they play a musical instrument, paint, or dance. Liz, who at twelve was a fine pianist, found an escape from stress by playing the easy pieces she had mastered years before. Small children can relax at a moment's notice, falling asleep in the middle of a story or game: I found my two-year-old son Eric out cold on top of a dresser one day. Others, too keyed up to sleep, will simply lie down and talk quietly to themselves. Ellie likes to sit alone and sing. Jamie at one and a half turns the pages of a book and "reads."

My daughter Amy reminded me the other day of a little poem my mother used to recite to her. She said she loved it because it expressed exactly what she felt so often amidst the stress and strain of life:

> *I wish I was a rock a-settin' on a hill;*
> *I wan't doing nothin' but just a-settin' still.*
> *I wouldn't eat, I wouldn't sleep,*
> *I wouldn't even wash.*
> *Just set there a thousand years or so*
> *And rest myself, by gosh!*

That rock *has* to be a Sabbath child!

WHO IS THE COPING CHILD?

Dr. Paul Gabriel, Child Psychiatrist at New York University Medical Center and Associate Professor of Psychiatry, claims that children who can cope display three abilities strongly.

First, *they can concentrate.* We have all seen children who jump from one activity to another. They pass notes in class, talk in the library over books they should be reading, find a dozen excuses to interrupt homework. Even pleasurable activities cannot hold them: they start books which they never finish; knit half a sweater, keep urging friends, "Let's play a different game." Younger children, whose powers of concentration are naturally more limited, often dart from one activity to the next with the erratic speed of a hummingbird. I remember timing two-year-old Chris as he was playing with his Christmas toys—one minute; forty seconds; thirty seconds, and so on. I am happy to report—let parents take note—that Chris has since grown up and has learned to concentrate long enough to become a microbiology professor!

This "scooter bug" kind of child is not born on the Sabbath day. Sabbath children tend to have longer attention spans. When of school age, they listen and get assignments done and participate in class. They are interested in what they do. When preschoolers, they sit still for a story all the way through, stick to block building even when the tower tumbles and they have to start over again. At home they play repeated sessions of house or school or hospital or other make-believes, and they have to be torn away from their games at the bathtub. I have seen a toddler spend half an hour building a house of grass while I was attempting to walk down the road to the mailbox with her. Just as I thought she was through and had some hope of mailing my letters, she began collecting stones, arranging them around her grass house. Looking at me with the same intensity I have seen on my husband's face as he struggles over his income tax, she said, "See, the stones have to look at me build my house."

Secondly, *coping children can tolerate frustration.* I have seen teenagers so frustrated by exams that they stormed out of the room . . . so frustrated by trying to match pieces of a model airplane that they threw it down, smashing it with their feet . . . so frustrated by their own clumsiness that they kicked chairs over which they stumbled, breaking a toe. We have all lived through temper tantrums in small children. We have seen babies cry when they can't reach a rattle they want. We have panicked when, holding their breath in response to our "No," they have begun to turn blue. I recall my daughter Amy at two and a half having screaming hysterics because she could not communicate to me that she wanted a musical toy called Melody Bells. It kept coming out "Ma-ya-dee Buzz," which sounded like an obscure foreign language until her brother Eric translated.

Sabbath children learn to handle frustration. They struggle with a job until successfully accomplishing it—like Joshua in shop class, trying to make the corners of his kitchen shelf meet squarely. Or they accept the inevitable—like Mary, who wants to go to the movies, but has to stay home and baby-sit. Or they seek alternatives that bring satisfaction—like year-old Alexa, who falls down five times in her efforts to reach the table where her sister is playing and finally settles for crawling there. Monica handles frustration well: although at two and a half she insists on dressing herself and struggles into shirt and trousers, when it comes to shoes, she gives a hopeful try anew each morning, then holds them out to her mother saying, "You help."

Finally, Dr. Gabriel points out that *coping children are able to postpone gratification*. The decade of the 1970s has despairingly been labeled the Age of Instant Gratification. We have forgotten how to wait for things, sociologists tell us. If we want homemade cake, we defrost; mashed potatoes, we add water; entertainment, we turn on television. We pop pills for instant joy, drink alcohol for instant forgetfulness and smoke pot for instant "experience." We live together for instant sex, marry for as instant as babies can be and divorce for instant problem-solving.

Young people have been pulled into this syndrome. Statistics on drug abuse, drinking, sexual activity and crime need not be laid out as proof: newspaper headlines reinforce them every day. Teenagers have learned to get what they want and get it right away. Younger children have learned too. Drug abuse begins in elementary school now, as low as third and fourth grades. Drinking as well. Cheating is rife: children who want a good mark can find easier and quicker ways than studying. Stealing is rampant: kids want money. Shoplifting causes millions of dollars of loss to retail stores: young people want toys and clothes and gadgets. Even very young children, remote from criminal thoughts or activity, find ways to satisfy their needs: they nag for a toy like Billy's; they whine for a new dress. Making themselves all but impossible to live with, they force their parents to give in, and they get what they want. A mother of two young children complained to me that she did not know what to get them for Christmas. "They already have everything," she sighed.

Children who cope with stress are far less demanding of instant gratification. They can save their allowance for the treasure they spy in a store window, even though Billy already has it. They can stand the effort of schoolwork if getting a good mark matters to them. They are willing to live without momentary thrills or to enjoy through anticipation those that may come at a later date; they do not have to devise new pathways to new thrills with each leisure moment. Even young children can accept Mother's promise of, "We'll do that next week," without demanding "Now." Little Winnie's parents informed her in March that they would be going to Cape

Cod for a week in June without her. Nana and Willy, her grandparents, they explained, would come and take care of her; they
would even take her to McDonald's for a well-advertised "Happy
Lunch." Every morning for the more than two months Winnie had
to wait, her first words on awakening were, "Nana, Willy, go
Happy?" Patiently she accepted her parents' answer, "Not today."
She was willing to wait.

So was little Katie, with whom I was wandering around a store
one day in December, letting her play with various toys. "Would
you like me to buy you one?" I asked.

"No," she replied, "we get some for Christmas."

Reinhold Niebuhr expressed himself in a prayer that has become
famous: "God, give us grace to accept with serenity the things that
cannot be changed, courage to change the things which should be
changed, and the wisdom to distinguish the one from the other."

This might well be the Sabbath child speaking—the child whose
qualities enable her to focus attention, to persist in her efforts and
to wait for what she wants. The child who can cope with stress.

What kind of children are Sabbath children? Are they smart?
Good students? Are they popular? Pretty? Handsome? Not necessarily. There are, however, certain qualities that distinguish them.

They are primarily self-accepting.

Acknowledging their shortcomings, they do not need to punish
themselves by self-flagellation. They may be a few pounds overweight but do not strive to emulate the starved look of a model;
they may be too thin but will not resent having to try for the track
rather than the football team. They may not rank first in their class,
but will work adequately to maintain a B average; they will develop
other abilities, taking pride in their accomplishments. If they are not
the most popular, they find fulfillment in a few close friends. In
short, they know their limitations and *accept* them as part of themselves.

On the other hand, acknowledging their strengths, they have no
need to boost their egos by feeling superior. They take their abilities
more as gifts than as personal achievements. "I'm lucky," a high
school Merit Scholar replied when asked how she achieved top rank-
ing in the national scholarships awards. That is how coping children
tend to feel—lucky that they are intelligent or good-looking or tal-

ented. There is no ulterior motive in their abilities; they do not turn them into commodities for buying ego satisfaction. Born with gifts, they derive pleasure from using, not from flaunting them.

Coping children know who they are. They are willing to be that person because, as Saul Bellow says of Herzog, "There is no one else to do the job."

Secondly, coping children are individualistic.

While they are intimate with friends and enjoy get-togethers with classmates, they manage to retain their own identity. They do not give themselves over to peer groups to the extent that other children do. Professor Lawrence Fuchs, author of *Family Matters*, believes that "peer-oriented children are less sure of themselves . . . and think less of themselves" than individualistic children. Sabbath children prove him true—they do not have to run with the crowd.

Under peer pressure, they yield to themselves, finding strength to say "No" when the peer decision differs from theirs. They are the sixth-grade boy who would not look at the test answers a classmate had slipped from the teacher's desk drawer. They are the seventh-grade girl who accepted being ostracized when she refused to shoplift with her crowd of friends. They are the third-grader who cried when his neighborhood playmates threw stones at a stray dog. They are even the preschooler who stared in horror as her little friends defied parental orders by crossing the street alone.

Oftentimes coping children find ways to influence the group, bringing it around to their own way of thinking. This was evident with the eighth-grade girl who, instead of joining the others in excluding a new classmate from the clique, persuaded them to bring her in. It was evident as well when the sixth-grade boys decided to boycott the chorus that the music teacher wanted to organize: two boys agreed to join, finally involving the others. It is frequently evident when a group of preschoolers playing together differ over an activity: the coping child can make his choice attractive enough to win. Darcy did this at two when her four-year-old cousin Abigail, wanting to be "Mommy" as they played house, relegated Darcy to be "the baby." So vociferously did she enact her assigned part that the highly impressed Abigail stared at her and said, "O.K. Now I'll be the baby."

Third, coping children are feeling.

Not all children allow themselves to feel. Some are too out of touch with themselves; others are too fearful; still others lack examples to teach them. Some children feel only the most basic emotions, such as anger and fear. Sabbath children, however, feel intensely and fully, running the whole gamut of emotions. They *love*—parents and a special teacher, a best friend, a grandparent, the new baby, their dog, an old doll. And they *hate*—often the same person, in moments of frustration and hurt. They *pity*—the stray kitten, a sick mommy, a disabled friend, the little boy with no daddy. They feel *fear*—perhaps of thunder or big dogs, of being spanked or of hearing their parents fight; and they grow *angry*—when parents say "No," when siblings tease, when friends reject them, when teachers are unfair. Even very young, they can *grieve*—over a lost parent or grandparent or close friend; over a pet—be it a dog, a canary or even a guppie.

As with most children, the emotions of Sabbath children may not be long-lasting: the person hated today may be loved tomorrow; grief for a lost pet may be displaced by joy over a new one. Yet, while their emotions last, they are intense and real. Turning themselves over to their feelings, children become vulnerable, their defenses down. Since feelings often hurt, they are safer without them; since feelings churn up and tear apart, they lose some control; since feelings raise questions about oneself, they create disquietude. Yet despite all this, coping children continue allowing themselves to feel.

Furthermore, coping children are able to express feelings.

Not concerned with the effect that expressing feelings will have on others, Sabbath children make no effort to repress what they feel. They are unashamed to show love through kissing and touching, through acts of giving, and unafraid to show hate, probably through hitting or running away as a small child and when older, through words. They do not repress anger as something "bad," but allow themselves to communicate it—perhaps in a temper tantrum at two, in a fight at seven and in a verbal confrontation at twelve. At three, Cindy combined the last two when she told her best friend, "I love you and I'm going to marry you."

"I'm not going to marry you," he answered.

At this point Cindy threw a handful of sand at him, insisting, "Yes, you will."

Sabbath children are not embarrassed to offer help to a suffering animal, be it even so small as a lady bug that they release from a windowsill, or to cry over a pet that dies. They will admit their fears, even those of fantasy objects that appear at night in the dark, or those that may make their classmates call them "sissy." They may often be hurt as a result of their honest expression: they may be rejected and laughed at, even punched in the nose on occasion. They will, however, survive, for though *hurt*, they will not be *damaged*. There is a difference.

Coping children have a great deal of self-motivation.

They have what educator Jerome Bruner calls "intrinsic motives for learning"—curiosity, the desire to achieve competence and the joy of working with others. Even in their first year, eighty percent of coping infants' learning is self-initiated, according to a study conducted by Harvard's Burton White. These are the children who grow up working not for marks and parental approval, but for the fun of discovery. These are the children who do not wait to be told what to do, but who are continually in the midst of their own adventures—whether decorating their room, undertaking a scientific experiment or building a tree house. Linda at seventeen months was found one morning toddling out to the barn with her little yellow pail, to learn how to milk the cow.

Self-motivated children do not contribute to the statistic we read about in media reports: forty hours of televiewing for the average child; they have other things to do. They do not hang on Mother's skirt, whining, "What can I do?" They know—and are probably already in the process of doing it. They do, in Dr. Lee Salk's words, "the right thing for the right reason"—because they want to.

Coping children have the courage to try and fail.

Piet Hein in his little book *Grooks* writes the following:

> *The road to wisdom—*
> *well, it's plain and*
> *simple to express:*
> *Err*
> *And err*
> *And err again*
> *But less*
> *And less*
> *And less.*

Sabbath children accept this philosophy far more than others. I know a little boy who won't even attempt to build blocks with me. He says he can't. His parents explain that he is afraid to try, but this is not accurate. The truth of the matter is that he is afraid to fail. Children are unafraid to try anything in which they are assured a chance of success. It is when the fear of failure overrides the desire for success that they are stymied.

Sabbath children take failure in stride; it holds less stigma for them. Where failure denotes personal inadequacy to my non-block-building friend, to coping children it means, "It didn't work." Their personal success or failure does not ride on the outcome. Even in school, where failure is marked with a scarlet letter "F" almost as painful as Hester Prynne's "A," Sabbath children dare to stick their necks out. They answer questions in class, try out for plays, tackle independent projects, ask girls for dates. When their endeavors do not succeed, they feel awful for a few minutes, then put themselves in perspective and try something else. Mark Twain felt that "all you need in this life is ignorance and confidence and then Success is sure." If he was right, coping children are halfway there.

Finally, coping children have a general liking for people.

They trust new people they meet, both adults and peers. They neither anticipate malevolence nor fear it. To them, as to America's system of justice, everyone is innocent until proved guilty. Sabbath children do not whisper behind their classmates' backs; they do not spread rumors—they do not have to put anyone down in order to build themselves up. They do not automatically hate their teachers, nor are they against the system, whatever system it is, merely because it is run by grownups. They may come to disapprove of people or even to rebel against systems through contact with them—like the toddler I know who used to rush to hug every child he saw, leaving his toys behind. Slowly he learned that other children escaped his embrace to make a dash for his toys, carting them away. Now he still runs smiling into embraces, but he takes his toys with him.

When we compound all these qualities, coping children have one outstanding characteristic, which comes packaged in a phrase so overworked in recent times that I hesitate to use it—self-image. *Coping children have a positive self-image.* They trust themselves.

They possess what Arthur Jersild in *The Psychology of Adolescence* defines as "a kind of inner freedom to make it possible to venture, to dare and to do."

Circumstances tend not to alter self-image, for we find it in diverse environments—from Grosse Point to the ghetto, in outstanding students and in mediocre ones, in the beautiful and in the plain. Dr. Gabriel, mentioned earlier, who works with children with fatal diseases, finds it even among the dying. It is a feeling that says, "Whatever I am, I am unique. For every moment in time, from the first human being until the last, from every corner of the universe and even beyond, into undiscovered galaxies, there is only one me." Recognition of that fact leads to the positive self-image we would like to see in all children:

"I'm a wonder!" a fifth-grader told me in awe.

"I'm pretty good," a sophomore admitted.

"I guess I'm sort of special," a junior high-schooler discovered.

Muhammad Ali said it best of all: "I'm the greatest!"

WHERE DOES THE POSITIVE SELF-IMAGE COME FROM?

A child's positive self-image begins long before birth. It begins with the kind of marriage parents have, a relationship of love, with two mature people willing to grow both as individuals and as partners. It begins with pregnancy, a wanted baby, a baby to be brought into the world for its own sake, not to satisfy the unmet needs of parents. It begins in the womb, where a mother nurtures the fetus with proper food and care and protection.

The positive self-image may well be under way at birth, an easy rather than a long labor, a relaxed rather than a tense mother. Otto Rank traced a great deal of emotional illness to the birth trauma, relieving later neuroses through psychoanalysis. The Primal Scream approach of Dr. Arthur Janov attempts to regress patients so that they may relive the birth trauma, thus purging themselves of its negative effects. Recently, tried and true methods of delivering babies are being questioned, with speculation emerging that they intensify the birth trauma through the use of drugs, anesthesia, harsh lights, impersonal contact with the baby and an umbilical cord cut too soon.

In response, other methods are being tried. More and more women are having their babies at home in gentle, intimate environments. Others, though giving birth in the hospital, are taking their babies home in a matter of hours. Millions of men and women together are undergoing Lamaze training in natural childbirth and working through labor and delivery to assure a less stressful birth. Probably the most radical deviation from traditional birth methods is that of Dr. Frederick Leboyer, whose babies and those of his followers are brought into the world in dimly lit rooms, placed immediately on the mother's abdomen and gently massaged until the cord ceases to pulsate, at which time it is cut and the baby placed in a warm bath. Although the value of the Leboyer method is a moot point, a recent test by Alice Slater, a Massachusetts nurse, indicates that Leboyer babies are more alert and cry less.

Whether the actual method of birth affects babies' personalities we do not know for certain. However, we do know that the treatment they receive during the early years, and even days, has a powerful effect. Professor Burton White goes so far as to say that it's all over by the age of three, which any teacher will refute. Studies are showing, though, that babies held and cooed over the first day of their birth develop more positively than those cuddled a few days later. It is further shown that toddlers whose mothers talk to them, play with them, and fondle them become more responsive to people and to the world around them. We can surely conclude that the early days and years greatly influence the development of children.

Although we read cases of infant neglect and maltreatment, it is difficult not to be a good mother to an infant: its helplessness calls forth our most basic maternal instincts. As a child grows up, however, it becomes less easy: older children demand more, get in the way more, irritate more and call more upon parents' own coping skills to do a good job. Often, their own adaptation energy depleted, they respond to the stress of their children with their own stress, compounding the problem. Angry at their children's anger or frustrated by their frustration, they may turn away, unable to cope. Or, frightened by dangers besetting their children and guilty over their own inadequacy as parents, they may cling, sheltering them beyond need.

What does one do in order to be a good parent? Dr. Lee Salk gives only two warnings: "Don't overprotect your children and don't ignore them." The parents of Sabbath children seem to heed him instinctively, turning his warning against destructive parenting into its constructive corollary.

First, they give their children room to grow. Although it is easier to do everything for children, ease is not the name of the game. "I will never let Rachel be upset if I can possibly prevent it," that proud young mother told me. She was foolish. What is more, she was selfish: she would not expose herself to the pain of seeing her child struggle. Eliminating her daughter's pain eliminated her own. What she failed to foresee, however, was that it also eliminated the little girl's growth. She is growing up insecure, afraid to try and fail, filled with self-doubt. Her loving mother has made her that way.

The parents of coping children let them learn to cope, and there is only one way: by letting them face stressors and overcome them, if not the first time, the second or third or fourth. Children learn to crawl when they want to get somewhere; parents see them struggle, encouraging their efforts when they may cry to be carried. Children learn to accept responsibility in order to earn independence; parents have to help them be accountable when they shirk it. Children learn to be honest and to work hard and to play fair only when their parents are strong enough not to remove painful roadblocks on the way. The mother who told me, "I never even let my son get his own glass of water when he was growing up," is a destroyer. No wonder her son is a helpless, selfish husband and father today.

We shall be discussing this a great deal more fully in Chapter X. Let it suffice to say at this point that children will not learn to walk unless their parents let them try. Trying means repeated falls, bumped heads, scraped knees, tears and momentary heartbreak for children; it means twice the pain for parents. Coping children's parents have let them fall; they have winced and probably shed tears of their own, but they have steadfastly endured. For they know that is the only way to *help* their child walk, become a person, cope with life.

Secondly, parents of the Sabbath children love them. They don't just talk of love; they show it. That entails giving time, being interested, sacrificing some adult pleasures and intimacies they were able to share before they became parents. They don't love their children's *accomplishments*; they love *them*, supporting them in their failures. They do not feel that because their children have made mistakes, they are any less worthy as people. Nor do they feel that exposure of their children's weaknesses reflects on them, that their children have let them down. Parents of coping children do not push them to be the best and the biggest; they find other ways of gaining status. Glad and thankful, they take their children as they come.

These, then, are the children born on the Sabbath day. How wise Mother Goose was! How far ahead of her time! Children who can cope with life's stresses are surely "bonny and blithe, and good and gay." Why shouldn't they be? As Thoreau said, "Public opinion is a weak tyrant compared with our own private opinion. What a man thinks of himself, that is which determines . . . his fate."

CHAPTER III

◈

Wednesday's Child

There was a crooked man,
And he walked a crooked mile.
He found a crooked sixpence
Against a crooked stile;
He bought a crooked cat,
Which caught a crooked mouse,
And they all lived together in a little crooked house.

On a hot July night, sixteen-year-old Andrew Zimmer, it was charged, set fire to the jail cell in which he was being held as a runaway. Forty-two people died. Andy lived . . . but, now severely burned, he lived on in the pain which had been with him his entire life.

As a baby Andy was quiet, the kind of baby easily ignored. As a preschooler, he was quickly angered, always on the verge of screaming. During his school years he grew too quickly, becoming bigger and heavier than his classmates. "Fatty," they called him to torment. A slow learner, a poor athlete, lonely and unhappy, he cried in frustration and humiliation instead of fighting back. Almost to the point of torture he baited neighborhood dogs and bullied smaller children. Soon he was accused of setting fires, and although his mother covered up for him, he was referred by the court for help.

Unfortunately, he received little, for he ran away from a home for disturbed boys (one of the few good ones, which claims seventy percent success). Five weeks later he allegedly started the fire that killed forty-two people.

Andrew Zimmer is Wednesday's child, filled with woe, incapable of handling the stress in his life. Like the crooked man in the familiar Mother Goose rhyme, he was out of shape, and everything in his life was out of shape. He was unable to straighten it out.

Andy's inability to cope was dramatic, making headlines in newspapers across the country. We read about thousands of Andys. We do not read, however, about Margaret, and there are *millions* of Margarets—as miserable and as non-coping as Andy.

Margaret was the third child, born twelve years after her brother, eight years after her sister. She felt she was a mistake. Her parents were too old for another child, too tired, too preoccupied. In her own words she was "a bland child"—not pretty enough to be admired nor smart enough nor good enough. She was not even homely enough or bad enough to get attention.

In order to gain a place, she threw temper tantrums until her exhausted parents sent her to boarding school, where her fondest wish was to have a best friend. She had no friends and ate away her loneliness, gaining thirty-five pounds. In college she slept more than she attended class and was expelled. As a final try, she entered art school, where she became a secret drinker. Not until she was thirty-four years old did she admit she was trying to cope through alcohol and was failing. She sought help through Alcoholics Anonymous, where she was able to leave Wednesday's child and begin to function.

Like Andy, Margaret shaped the course of her life by reinforcing her inability to cope. "Everything always goes wrong," she used to whine in self-pity. Now she knows better. "I made everything go wrong," she says, having gained confidence that she can similarly make everything go right. With help, after a childhood and young adulthood of distress, she is becoming a child of the Sabbath day.

WHO IS WEDNESDAY'S CHILD?

Why one child handles stress and another is warped by it is a complex syndrome: there is no simple cause and effect. Eleanor

Roosevelt felt as unwanted and bland as Margaret; yet she pushed herself to world leadership. Stress strengthened her, enabling her to face problems. This happens to many children, as a Chicago study recently pointed out. It was evidenced that some children went to pieces when their first-grade teacher left in the middle of the year, while others took the loss in stride. What accounted for the difference? Were some children more attached to the teacher than others? Were some children more mature than others? Were some less feeling? No, all these factors were ruled out. What was found is that those children who coped with the teacher's leaving had been in kindergartens where a teacher also left midway through the year. Having suffered through the experience once, they had the confidence to cope with it a second time.

We are reminded of the football coach who whipped his team into such nervous tension before the league competition that they rushed onto the field in a frenzy.

"You forgot the ball," the coach shouted.

The captain shouted back, "Who needs one!"

Stress was their spur.

Whatever the causes of non-coping may be, examples of it abound from early infancy. For instance, a group of foreign women who moved to Germany in order to obtain work some years ago found their new surroundings highly stressful. Later on, their babies, which were conceived, carried and born while they were in Germany, displayed a rate of abnormality far above the expected norm. Were the babies' fetal bodies unable to cope with their mothers' stress? It appears so.

Examples of Wednesday's children are evident through the school years. Alicia is three. She finds the stress of a new brother too much to bear. She has begun wetting her pants again, throws tantrums and wakes up with nightmares. Yesterday she pushed her baby brother down the stairs.

Kurt is five. He won't go to kindergarten because he is afraid his mother will not pick him up on her way home from work. He screams and kicks the teacher as she attempts to coax him into the classroom.

Charlie is nine. His parents fight a lot, and he has gotten used to retreating to the basement, where he won't hear them. He has no friends, and spends more and more time sitting in the basement with a toy panda he had as a baby.

Barbara is thirteen. Her parents are unaware that she smokes a joint on her way to school every day. Everyone in her crowd does it. They think it is "cool."

Joe is sixteen. He got caught stealing a record at Caldor's a month ago. He put on such a scene of shame and apology that the manager let him go without even telling his parents. He did not know that Joe has been shoplifting for a year. He has taken two records since then. How else, he feels, can he get what the other kids have? He has no money.

These are all Wednesday's children. Unable to handle the stressors that beset them, they find ways to handle at least the bad feelings the stressors create. They do the best they can; unfortunately, the best is often the worst—for them and for society.

In the preceding chapter we examined the Sabbath child. Let us here take a look at Wednesday's child. Who is she? Who is he? How do these non-coping children differ from their peers?

WEDNESDAY'S CHILDREN HATE THEMSELVES

Primarily, Wednesday's children do not accept what they are. While Sabbath children believe in themselves and, therefore, take life as it comes, Wednesday's children falter.

"So what," coping children say, "I can handle it." And handle it they do, withstanding the blood, sweat and tears with which the problem may burden them.

Non-coping children, on the other hand, collapse. "I'm not good enough to cope," is their attitude. Deep inside they feel, "Actually, I deserve this," adding guilt to the pain of feeling worthless.

The market has been flooded during the last decade with books and articles interpreting what is called "identity crisis" for the American public. This is a catchall term most frequently used to describe young people's turbulence as they grow through dependence on their parents into independence, as they become their own person. In order to undergo an identity crisis, which healthfully happens at adolescence, young people need to feel capable of a separate existence. A fungus ripped from a tree trunk cannot live independent of the sustenance derived from the tree. Coping children are not fungi.

If we seek a comparison in nature, we could say they are young koala bears, clinging to their mother for protection, learning the tricks of life's trade as they watch her seek food and ward off danger. Soon they will let go, eager to test their own mettle. Koala parents, instinctively wise, urge their cubs to go it alone when the time comes; they even pry them loose if necessary.

Human parents, however, perhaps less sure of their role than koalas, support clinging children far longer—through school and college and graduate studies, often into marriage, family, divorce, remarriage and their own grave. They display a lack of confidence in their children of which the animal world would never be guilty. In an interview, Samuel Pisar, author of *Of Blood and Hope*, capsulized this human trait when he said, "The last time my mother saw me before she died, she would have been amazed at what I would be able to do!"

Wednesday's children see themselves as poor specimens of human beings. "I used to be someone else, but I traded myself in," is their slogan, as it was in an ad for Antonioni's movie *The Passenger* several years ago. Wednesday's children must have responded in droves at the box office, for it expresses their fondest fantasy. If they could be someone else, they would no longer hate themselves. So they tailor-make their heroes and heroines. Girls would be any glamorous TV star—Brooke Shields, Cheryl Ladd and company—beautiful and thin and sexy with thick wavy hair cascading down their back. Boys would be Burt Reynolds, Clint Eastwood, Robert Redford— tough sex symbols, rugged, fearless.

Caroline is a sad example. She was the best-looking girl in a well-to-do community, but she never felt pretty enough. She wanted to look like Marilyn Monroe. She wore heavy makeup, but that did not help. She bleached her hair, wore provocative see-through blouses, but they didn't help either. She was the first to go steady and have sex. By the time she graduated, she had good looks and promiscuity all mixed up in her mind. She is twenty-two now and has made four X-rated movies. People say she is beautiful, but she doesn't believe them. She is still trying.

The newspaper gave us a tragic example several years ago in a young man who went berserk and killed with abandon. Described by neighbors as quiet and withdrawn, he shocked everyone with his outburst of violence. Yet during the investigation, police found in his apartment a closet with a secret cache of pictures, stories and memorabilia of the hero he idolized—Adolf Hitler. Like Caroline, this young man traded himself in for a hero embodying the qualities he lacked and longed for. Absorbing what he romanticized as Hitler's strength and daring, he could admire himself in the closet. One day he and Hitler emerged.

Many non-coping children, though not so extreme as the two above, turn to cults as a panacea for the hurt that self-hate brings. The cult leader is strong, offering Wednesday's children a hero to whom they can attach themselves and from whom they can suck the nourishment they lack within themselves. Whether they follow a flesh-and-blood hero like Charles Manson or the Reverend Moon, or a spiritual hero as the Hare Krishnas do, these non-coping young people are drawn by charisma. A friend of mine whose daughter has been a "Moonie" for ten years was stunned when, finally allowed to visit her, she found her room plastered with pictures of her idol.

"He is so homely," she told me later, recalling the glamorous movie stars that had adorned her daughter's walls in high school. Homely, perhaps. But powerful, pervasive, magnetic.

Cult life is designed for Wednesday's children. They feel they cannot cope: the cult agrees. It goes even further: it eliminates their need to cope. It eliminates the possibility. The organization provides for their needs—food, shelter, friendship. Any questions they may ask it answers with pat phrases easily committed to memory. It eases the pain of self-loathing, for it gives them a group to which they can belong. It makes them feel beautiful, needed and loved. What more could any young person want?

Under such conditions stress cannot exist; there are no stressors. But as Hans Selye says, "Stress is the spice of life." For the cultist there is no more stress than for the person drugged, lobotomized, dead. Life is stress. It means problems to solve, hurdles to climb over, pain to endure so that one can see himself grow in strength and capability and self-confidence . . . so that one can face life proudly with a shout of, "I can!" Cult life reinforces a whimper of,

"I can't." Even more debilitating, it echoes a sigh of, "I don't have to." That sound is music to the ears of Wednesday's child.

Non-coping children view life as a contest in which they have lost. A look at our society proves them not far wrong, for in most areas of life we *do* set up competitions. Rarely do we enable children simply to relax and *be*. Rarely do we accept them for themselves. In school, we do not let them merely learn; we force them to compete with their classmates. What is worse, we publicize the results of the competition by giving them marks and class rank, by posting honor rolls and mailing home report cards.

At home as well we compel them to fight for rank. Many parents demand that their children be "best"—sometimes through subtle praise, other times through outright orders. Children read well the signs of parental disappointment, no matter how softly they are couched.

"You will do better next time" translates clearly, "You failed."

"I suppose you did your best" comes across as, "You dummy."

Siblings maneuver and play power games of which parents are not even aware, struggling as they feel they must for favor. Parents need not actually speak the dreaded words "Why can't you be good like your brother?"—although they often do. They need only act the thought out like a game of charades, with smiles and favors and pats of pride—which they *always* do.

The peer group forces competition too. Children must be popular, racking up an evening's phone calls like notches on a gun. Class cliques can write the labels of success or failure. If children are "in," they struggle to stay; if they are out, they struggle to get "in." Either way they struggle by acquiescing to peer standards. They strive to look like their peers, act like them, be like them. The peer group replaces the television idol Wednesday's children struggle to become. The closer they get, the more they win. I know a fourteen-year-old who purposely dropped his standing in academics so he would not appear smarter than the classmates he wanted to be friends with.

Since the world seems to be designed for competition, it should come as little surprise that the non-copers come out losers. Lacking self-confidence to fight the fight, they fail. Failing, they continue to fail. Continuing to fail, they expect to fail, and soon they no longer try. According to the ground rules, they assume the role of failures in society. Actually, they knew it before anyone else did: that's why they hated themselves and failed in the first place. Oh what a vicious cycle!

Is it any wonder then that Wednesday's children do poorly in school? A recent test at Australia's University of Melbourne indicates that students with continual failures have both lower self-esteem and higher anxiety than students who regularly succeed. We need no test for proof, though: any teacher knows that children who expect to do poorly fulfill their expectations, and vice versa.

Unwittingly even parents send out signals that say, "We don't love you . . . not really." Many are too busy to listen to children, too self-involved to play with them, too insecure themselves to guide them, too forgetful of their own childhood to take their problems seriously, and too unfulfilled to stop forcing their children into extensions of themselves.

"Ma always liked you best," says Tommy Smothers, working for a laugh. Wednesday's children know what he means, and it is not funny.

"I wanted a little girl that I could dress up," a young mother told me the other day. Her two-year-old son watched her as she spoke, and I can only project his feelings as he grows up: "I let my mother down." How can he ever accept himself?

Wednesday's children are lonely. If they are shy, they are considered automatic outcasts, for the "Pepsi generation" compels everyone to be the life of the party. If they have only one friend, they are labeled as "queers." If they try to become one of a group, they are rejected. If they are different, they are either teased and mocked or simply ignored. Dr. Theodore Rubin in a *Ladies' Home Journal* article entitled "How Teenagers Can Survive" points out that "the need for group acceptance, coupled with feelings of inadequacy, often leads to a compulsive need to be liked." Wednesday's child finds it impossible to fill that need.

Competition per se is not destructive. Often, in fact, it has a positive effect—when a child wants to compete, for instance, and feels adequate to meet competition. On the other hand, "Competition is unhealthy," Arthur Jersild writes in *Child Psychology*, "if a child's own estimate of his worth is tied to it." That is the case with Wednesday's children.

When they receive low marks in school, they do not settle for an evaluation of themselves as poor students—they feel like poor human beings. When they look in the mirror, they do not see merely the stringy hair they may have—they see an unbeautiful person. When they fail to catch a ball, they do not limit their weakness to a bad catch—they become bad people. When their sibling excels, they do not accept her success on its own terms, but interpret it as "I'm not so good as she." Any failure they have, no matter how limited, makes them in their minds a *total* failure.

As avowed failures, therefore, non-coping children find themselves less and less able to deal with stressors that beset them. Many of them curl up and die inside. Others lash out and hurt or kill—like the thirteen-year-old Texan who, receiving a failing grade, shot and killed his teacher. However they express it, their sense of failure leaves them lonely, unloving and loveless. John F. Kennedy summed it up after the disaster of the Bay of Pigs. "Success has a hundred fathers," he said. "Failure is an orphan."

The behavior through which Wednesday's children express their feelings of worthlessness are as varied as the children themselves.

Donna is ten. "What can I do?" she whines after her mother whenever she is out of school. Bored and listless, she has no inner resources on which to draw.

Marti is easily frustrated. At eight, she flies into rages. The other day, unable to untie a knot in her shoe, she threw the shoe across the room and broke a porcelain vase.

Peter, thirteen, wants whatever his friends have. Last week it was a BB gun; this week it is a Brooks Brothers suit. Even when his parents concede, he is dissatisfied after a few minutes, nagging for something else.

"I can't," is the most repeated phrase in five-year-old Seth's vocabulary. He says it before he even tries—to dress himself, read a picture book, play a game. His mother has to sit outside the kindergarten class or he "can't" go to school.

Susie wears a scowl. "A ten-year-old business executive," her father calls her. She does not laugh. She does not answer him. Susie keeps her thoughts and feelings to herself—and keeps on scowling.

Joe is the butt of his classmates' jokes because, although in the eighth grade, he reads at fourth-grade level and cannot put together a coherent paragraph. He gets even, though: he takes their things—money and books. He took a sneaker yesterday and an autograph album. He trips younger kids in the hall as they go to class.

Paulette is a high school junior. She would be a fairly good student except for the fact that she is absent several days a week. She has stomachaches.

Warren can't seem to get his papers in to the teacher on time. He always has an excuse. When he is accorded an extension, he misses that deadline too.

Bob has no friends. Aaron fights with everyone. Tina watches television all day. Marge cuts classes. Cathy eats in secret. Ronald boasts he can make it with any girl in the back seat of his car. Alice bites her fingernails. Matthew stammers.

These are Wednesday's children. Not bad or rebellious or surly or disobedient or dishonest or babyish or lazy or hostile or aggressive or all the other names by which the adults in their lives label them. They are children filled with woe. Their low self-image is showing. Unable to cope with the life Fate has meted out to them, they attempt to relieve themselves of its pain in any way they can. They are shouting out for help, yet their parents and their teachers often fail to hear. Deafened by their disappointment in the children, parents and teachers intensify their pain. "Why don't you try?" they nag. In fact, these children try with their last ounce of energy. They try to cope. They try to ease the pain. They try to make life work out right. The problem is that the adults in their lives do not hear. They do not see. They are too busy criticizing.

The irony is that Wednesday's children are products of adults who in turn damn them for being what they are. Caught in a vicious cycle, they cannot even grope for a way out. Caught like hamsters on a wheel, there is no way to jump off and begin anew. They are fixed in a pattern of defeat.

FROM WHERE DOES LOW SELF-IMAGE SPRING?

What smothers the self-assurance with which an infant demands his mother's breast? The same infant may become a toddler fearful to throw a ball; a preschooler tearful to leave his mother; a ten-year-old or teenager afraid to make friends or do his homework. Where does the change take place? From what does it stem?

1. FROM PHYSICAL PROBLEMS

At the most obvious level, a child's physical being can be the source of his self-hate. Americans feel they have to meet prescribed standards of appearance. Magazine ads, television and movies are eternal reminders. Books published by the hundreds and thousands hold out promises to make readers thin, tall, handsome, pretty, young, lithe . . . to make them what everyone else is striving to become.

Yet nearly eight million school-age children in this country have no chance of meeting those standards. They are blind, deaf, handicapped, retarded or beset with learning disabilities. That figure automatically removes one in ten American children from the world of the accepted, the beautiful, the successful. Without special education, care and understanding and love, these children will be doomed to be full of woe, Wednesday's children.

A look back in time shows the young Helen Keller—frustrated by her multiple handicap, unable to cope—raging like a caged animal. Had not Anne Sullivan fallen, like Mary Poppins, into her life, Helen Keller's contributions would have been stifled by resentment and frustration; she would have grown up unfulfilled, empty of the love and giving her life exemplified.

Lucinda Hebbeler, New York State's 1980 Teacher of the Year, was born deaf and would have grown up non-speaking had her parents not determined that she would learn to communicate in a speaking world. Now, teaching other deaf children, she confronts their greatest problem. "Not lack of hearing, but their low self-image," she explains. "They regard themselves as losers."

Physical problems that make a child feel different and inadequate can be as seemingly insignificant as myopia. A child fitted with glasses is able to see as well as one with 20-20 vision; yet his classmates perpetuate the difference. He is "four eyes"; he drops his glasses when he runs; he has to tie them on during gym; he cries when they hide his glasses; he gets in trouble when he breaks them. Myopia is mountainous to him.

Or the problem may be as truly insurmountable as cerebral palsy. The child is stared at, whispered about, pitied by older children, feared by younger. Even many adults are loath to accept the shaking, misshapen cerebral palsy child as a fit playmate for their own children.

In between these two extremes are millions of other children whose bodies are in some way not quite normal. They may be overweight and be nagged by parents, teased by peers, singled out to spend summers in "fat camps." Or they may be hyperkinetic children whose behavior is uncontrolled and uncontrollable either by themselves or by the adults that surround them—victims of circumstances as beyond their control as their own metabolism's inability to handle diet as other children do. They become known as the bad kids. The handicapped may be asthmatic children—pale, with circles under their eyes, wheezing, easily fatigued, unable to keep up with the others. Or they may be knock-kneed, limping children, or those born with stubs for arms, vulnerable in their visibility.

Or they may be neurologically misconnected or psychologically unsound, with hidden distortions that grow in isolation. Maybe they are simply unlovely—coarse-featured, freckled, plain. Our world worships good looks; those who fall short of the criteria can only find displeasure in themselves. Even teachers, studies reveal, bestow more favors on attractive students—more personal attention and higher grades.

Dr. Charlotte Buhler presents findings of R. I. Sandwich in her book *From Birth to Maturity*. They spotlight the relationship between physical problems and self-image in high school students, at the same time referring to similar tests in primary and elementary schools. In a large class studied, the most physically perfect students ranked as the top forty in point average; the least physically perfect ranked as the bottom forty. It is evident that a child's body can be a major factor in determining stress and, if not handled correctly, a major contributor to his feeling of worthlessness.

2. FROM SOCIAL HANDICAPS

We cannot help rising to the injustice that places so heavy a physical burden upon one child, while freeing another to beauty and happiness. Yet worse is still to come. Many children, helpless thralls of their families and society, are crushed into self-hatred not by physical handicaps, but by social circumstances farther beyond their control than even their own bodies.

According to the last census, about twelve percent of the nation's families live in poverty: their children feel alone and different. So do the half million out-of-wedlock children, the numberless children beaten and sexually abused by their parents. Children who shudder nightly, feeling somehow responsible, as their parents fight, wither under the shadow of guilt. Fifteen percent of children have behavior problems when siblings are born. With almost one in two marriages ending in divorce these days, children are confounded, caught in the middle of a struggle they do not understand. Did they drive Daddy away? Do they make Mommy cry? I know of one suburban community where a fourth-grade class of thirty-six children has only four children living with both natural parents—a mere eleven percent.

3. FROM LIFE EVENTS

Other events present equally heavy stressors that lie beyond a child's control. Death of a parent is the greatest—especially a parent of the same sex who dies during the child's third or fourth year. When Joannie's mother died, the little girl turned against her father, refusing to talk to him. She grew belligerent toward her grandparents and refused to return to nursery school. The sitter was unable to control her. Deeply stressed by her mother's death, she sought protection from further hurts by breaking off all adult relationships. She was only three years old, yet she employed the same coping device seen frequently in widows and divorcees.

Moving is stressful for children, causing active problems in twenty percent of the cases. Leaving their security behind, children are forced to enter a new neighborhood and a new school as well, where friendships are already formed and they, the outsiders, have to find a place. Some are too withdrawn to try. Others attempt to prove themselves through outrageous behavior. A little boy I know who had never been violent became a virtual prizefighter in training during the first week in a new school.

"I can beat you up," he threatened me as we talked.

"I know, but it would hurt," I answered. He burst into tears.

Where parents live, what jobs they have, how they look—all these directly affect the self-image of children. Alma was embarrassed by a white-haired older mother; Ann avoided school activities because her mother drank; Bob kept his paunchy father away from Scouts; Will never had friends over because he shared a room with a cousin and two brothers. Gloria lied because her father was a garbage collector; George lied because his father was an undertaker; Eric lied because his father was a publishing president! "Why can't you be on TV like Brian's dad?"

Stress comes from all sides. Whether based on facts or feeling, the pain of it is real to the children caught in its vise. Stress can make them strong, or stress can make them weak. How the adults in their lives steer the course makes the difference. And in that matter children are helpless.

CHILDREN ARE WHAT PEOPLE SAY

"Children live up or down to their labels," says Elaine Barbour, 1978 National Teacher of the Year. In one such study two groups of students, both of equal ability, were assigned to teachers who were told that one group was bright and one group slow. All conditions such as curriculum, length of school day, and evaluative criteria, were similar. At the end of the test period, however, the teachers had graded those students identified as bright with high marks and those identified as slow with low marks. In other words, the teachers created the learning ability of their students.

How often this practice stereotypes children in regular, not test, school situations cannot be measured. I can say from my own experience, however, that it occurs continually. It is a rare teacher who accepts each year's class as if each child had been born anew on the doorstep. In most cases they have checked their IQ and past records and in September begin predetermined to have each child live up to the teacher's expectations. In some cases it is not even the record, but the subjective and often prejudiced opinions of last year's teacher that set the course for the new year.

Another study conducted by John Pratt at Sheffield City Polytechnic in England revealed that teachers tend to label students not only on past performance, but on socioeconomic factors. He showed first that the stress a teacher feels in dealing with a child affects that child's work negatively. He then went on to show that teachers feel greater stress in dealing with children from the lower classes than with those from the middle and upper. His conclusion: that teachers automatically turn lower-class children into poorer students.

We know that children who are abused by their parents grow up believing themselves unworthy of better treatment. The streets swarm with dropouts whose parents have convinced them they are "bad." Juvenile detention homes see a continual flow-through of young people who acknowledge, "I'm no damn good." Night courts are filled with prostitutes, many of whom, unloved by fathers who, too important or too uncaring, ignored their little girls into rejection. Inmates in adult prisons come with backgrounds of repeated beating, sexual abuse and neglect. Social outcasts are not born; they are molded by society.

Children grow up mirroring the image of others. They have no other way of knowing who they are, for they cannot peer inward until they know how they look. In fact lovable, because they are unique little beings in this conglomerate world, they are fascinating, needful, ever-changing. They look out at the faces of people, and in those faces see reflections of themselves. When the mirror is clear, they see their own loveliness as it is. But when the mirror is distorted, like a funhouse mirror, the image comes back distorted. Tragedy lies in their being unaware that the fault lies with the mirror, not with themselves. Babies can withstand the reflection of a faulty mirror for only a short while; all too quickly they believe that the negative image is what they truly are.

Six-month-old Noah proves this to me every day. He waits for my reaction to see how he feels. When I smile at him, he bursts into joy. If I frown, his lower lip curls and he looks as if he is about to cry. My smile tells him he is beautiful and wonderful and loved; my frown rejects him.

We see this in older children as well. Darcy, three, drops an ashtray and spins around to see her mother's reaction. Her mother remains calm, reassuring, suggesting they pick up the pieces together. "Everyone makes mistakes." Darcy learns that what she is and what she does are different: she may *do* a mistake, but she *is* loved. Had her mother scolded, turning on Darcy with anger, the little girl would have learned a different and highly distressing lesson.

Selma Fraiberg in what I consider the best book ever written on children, *The Magic Years*, says, "The child who is made to feel worthless and degraded for his childhood offenses will come to believe in his own worthlessness and unlovability, and out of this degradation of the self come the mental cripples and outcasts of our society."

What are these offenses for which children are made to feel worthless, offenses committed long before the mugging and murder that make headlines? They cry as babies . . . and are not picked up. They soil new clothes . . . and are called dirty. They break a glass . . . and are clumsy. They express their anger . . . and are naughty. They weep . . . and are crybabies. They receive a poor report card . . . and are dumb. They rebel . . . and are bad.

No wonder the recidivism rate at juvenile institutions is as high as ninety-five percent: there is no hope for a child who thinks there is no hope. No wonder adopted children struggle through an identity crisis far more painfully than natural children: there is evidence that their parents rejected them. My son Chris shies away from art work. I am not surprised: when he was eight years old his third-grade teacher destroyed a painting he made for me, saying it was ugly. I myself still break out into a cold sweat at the sight of numbers because I was raised believing I had only verbal skills. And millions of parents all across the country create far more destructive and dangerous self-images than those.

"Treat people as if they were what they ought to be, and you help them to become what they are capable of," wrote the poet Goethe. Clear the mirror, he is saying, so that children can see themselves beautiful, as they were born. When they see themselves as ugly, then the stress that should spice their life mounts to the *dis*tress that chokes them. They become Wednesday's children.

TRUST—A CHILD'S RELIEF FROM STRESS

The antidote to distress is "the child's trust of himself and of those who are most immediately concerned with his upbringing."

Psychologist Zvi Kurzweil arrived at that conclusion after years of work with children in and out of stress. Where there is trust, he says, there is always someone with whom the strangling tensions of stress can be released.

The adults in a child's world are his only hope for trust. Who else is there? His mother at whose breast he finds comfort. His father in whose arms he finds strength. Grandparents, closer in days past when the extended family nurtured all members, but still in evidence today to bestow special favors and love. Relatives and friends who come and go with regularity. Teachers—in day-care centers for infants, for toddlers, for the growing legion who attend nursery schools and kindergarten at the start of their twelve-year stint of schooling.

These, plus adults on the periphery, make up what Edmund Husserl called as far back as 1915 *Lebenswelt*—a child's world. Those working with children have long realized the vital role adults play in shaping a child's life. What the adult *does* in the present becomes what the child *is* in the future.

Dr. M. J. Langeveld, the Dutch psychiatrist who reported on "The Favorable Assimilation of Profound Psychic Shock," concluded, "Everyone who is associated with the child contributes to his lifeworld. . . . The only way of making the world fit for human beings to live in is to wage a constant struggle for the greater responsibility and the profound humanity and maturity of every individual." In short, a struggle for *trust*. When children can rely on the adults in their world to be responsible, to be humane and to be mature, then they can rely on them with trust.

The *Lebenswelt*, unfortunately, is no utopia. On a grand scale the disasters into which children are hurled rip trust out by the roots. Dr. Langeveld tells of a ten-year-old boy who saw his father bleed to death in a concentration camp when the Nazis cut off his hands. In three years the child was totally unable to move his hands. The trauma of his experience so undermined his trust in the world that his body refused to function in it. His hands hung limp by his side.

Only by restoring his trust was she able to restore use of his hands. This she accomplished by urging and easing him into joining her in activities that required hands—rowing a boat, beating a carpet, etc. As he gained security with her, he gained security with his hands, and in time could use them alone. An interesting footnote is that years later he married—of all things—a harpist!

To children, disasters have no degree. A parent who dies of cancer or a coronary attack causes a trauma as debilitating as one who dies in a plane crash or a concentration camp. Death betrays children. It takes away parents on whom they believed they could always rely, who would always be there. "What right did you have to leave me?" a child feels as the rest of the family grieves. And worse still, she wonders, "What did I do to kill her?" Death takes away trust in herself.

Death, however, is not the only betrayer in the world of children. Parents betray them every day—parents who love them, parents who want them to be happy, parents who would gasp, "Who—me?"

Dr. Rita Harper of North Shore University Hospital on Long Island believes that postnatal isolation in the sterile obstetrics wing can cause the first betrayal. Those first few days after an infant is thrust from dark, wet snugness into a bright, crisp world are traumatic, she believes. "They can affect the long-term relationship of baby-mother," she reports. If a newborn infant could speak, would it not cry out, "Mother, where are you?" Changing practices in hospitals indicate that the infant's cry is being heard.

Growing children often find themselves in isolation as alienating and stressful as that of newborns. A few years ago when I was spending a week with my daughter and her year-old Darcy at the beach, we met Karen. She was eight, bright, pretty, eager to be friends. Always dressed like a fashion plate, she peered in our window by seven each morning and was happy to down the cold coffee cake and canned orange juice we passed off as breakfast. Once she walked down the beach with us as, Darcy in backpack, we sloshed in the surf and wet sand, but after that she refused. We rarely saw her parents head-on, although their room was only a few doors from ours.

At first we found Karen charming, but slowly a horror story unfolded. Karen was shooed from the room as soon as she awoke so that her parents could sleep late. Her mother, shining from head to toe with suntan oil, lay on a chaise on the terrace from noon until five. Her father watched TV and drank scotch. "He's cuckoo at the end of the day," Karen told us. We never saw either of her parents play with her on the beach or go down to the water. They once gave her a kite, but the string was so knotted that she couldn't fly it. We never even heard them talk to her, except to call her to get dressed for dinner.

Karen's parents betrayed her trust long ago, and now she had no one. She picked up strangers as she went through life, longing for contact, but she could not sustain it: behavior patterns developed as a result of her distress blocked her way. She whined each day as we left to walk on the beach, yet she would not accompany us: "I'll get sandy." She nagged manipulatively: "I wish I had a balloon like Darcy's." She played sick with headaches, invisible scratches and complaints of not being able to sleep. She was even devious in hurting Darcy and pretending it was an accident.

Karen on the surface was an out-and-out brat. A pest. We could have disliked her, as I am sure some people did, if we had not glimpsed beneath the surface of her behavior into the core of her pain. Like a child whose parent dies, Karen was crying out, "Mother, Daddy, why did you leave me?" Her disaster was worse than death, for her parents were there to reach out to and not to touch . . . to speak to and not be heard . . . to love and be ignored.

At age eight she was trying to cope. Her defense mechanisms were showing, however, as they succeeded less and less. We have not seen her since. She is eleven now, and I wonder what has happened to the hurt within her. Has it exploded? Has it been buried deep under her feelings? Has it found someone to share and help it go away? Or is it weeping still under the mask of a pesty brat? Her parents may never know.

We all know Karen in various forms with a multitude of names. She is Helene, with overindulgent parents so afraid of her disfavor that they give and give in whenever she frowns. Helene cannot trust them: she *controls* them. Karen is also Peter, whose parents fight. He hides under the bed as they scream, and sometimes he hears his father's hand slap or hears a dish crash into the wall. He cannot trust his parents: he expects them to *kill* each other. Karen is Wilma, whose parents divorced when she was one and a half, and her mother took a full-time job. Wilma has been in day care for three years with eight different "teachers." She can't trust her mother; she rarely *sees* her. Karen is Eugene, whose father brags about his accomplishments and punishes his failures, one of which at age ten is wetting the bed. He can't trust his father: he doesn't *accept* Eugene.

Karen is furthermore all the millions of children in school starting each year with new hopes and promises and sliding quickly into the old familiar roles of failure and self-hate. Children turning to their teachers for help and being given extra homework . . . for reassurance and being punished . . . for understanding and being met with indifference. Deprivation comes from many corners of the *Lebenswelt*.

Do we need statistics to prove the destruction that trustlessness wreaks? Over half of the prostitutes in a major city come from broken homes. Ninety percent of teenage runaways feel they have no communication with their parents. Fifty percent of a group of children suffering from depression were found to have been separated from their mother between the ages of six months and eight years. Almost one hundred percent of alcoholics, drug addicts and compulsive eaters are people whose self-trust was lost as children at home, in the classroom or on the street. In my own experience, I have been appalled at the high incidence of early sexual abuse among female inmates at the federal prison where I served as counselor.

Pondering the endless experiences of children that can lead to a lack of trust and a lifetime of pain, many of them unavoidable, we wonder how and why anyone grows up with the ability to cope. Surely each one of us has suffered unbearable and prolonged hurt: death of loved ones, insensitive teachers, divorce, fighting parents, failure, shame, cruelty. Why aren't we all Wednesday's children?

The difference between coping and non-coping, most psychologists agree, is the presence of a "significant other" in the lifeworld of a child. M. T. Haslam, a British consultant in psychology, highlights this in a recent issue of the *International Journal of Social Psychology*. Infants in a study he conducted, when transferred to strange surroundings *without* their mothers, displayed great signs of stress—prolonged crying. On the other hand, infants transferred to the same surroundings *with* their mothers showed little stress; they continued to sleep, eat and lie in content wakeful states. In other words, the event that could have been traumatic was saved by the presence of a person in whom these infants had developed trust— their mother.

In line with this observation, some psychologists who work with children of divorce urge the court to keep babies with their mother and to forbid all but the shortest paternal visits unless the mother is present.

When parents fail and teachers fail, when there is no one in a child's life to whom he can turn in trust, he becomes the child of woe to whom strangers throw lifelines. Child-abuse centers, psychiatric wards, juvenile rehabilitation centers attempt to undo the damage. In most cases they fail. The children grow up and, if they are lucky, reach for other lifelines thrown to them: a suicide hotline . . . a priest's center for runaways . . . a church van parked in Times Square for prostitutes . . . rehabilitation centers for addicts with names such as Odyssey House, Phoenix House, Project Return.

Had the parents of these children been alert to the stressors burdening their children, how different the course of their lives might have been! The signs were there to be seen, even in the very young, but parents did not recognize them. They ignored them or shrugged them off as behavior problems.

SIGNS OF STRESS

What are the signs of stress? How can parents tell when their children are working hard to cope with stressors of which they themselves may not even be aware? Hans Selye in *The Stress of Life* lists thirty-one such signs for adults. I have selected from his list fifteen most applicable to children under stress. While each in itself may be meaningless, taken together groups of signs form a syndrome of stress with which a child may be unable to cope.

Parents should hear children calling for help when they observe several of the following signs:

1. General irritability, manifested in either aggressive or indolent behavior
2. Impulsive behavior
3. Inability to concentrate
4. Loss of a sense of joy
5. Fatigue
6. Nervous tics

7. Nervous laughter
8. Stuttering
9. Grinding of the teeth
10. Insomnia
11. Hyperactivity
12. Frequent urination
13. Loss of or excessive appetite
14. Nightmares
15. Accident-proneness

Dr. Selye's theory that people are born with only limited amounts of adaptation energy was discussed in Chapter I. Bodies and emotions, he believes, can cope with traumatic situations up to a certain point, and then no more.

I experienced this physically firsthand some years ago when I was visiting a brilliant teacher on an Indian reservation in Minnesota. I had left home with a sore on my wrist but I ignored it, though it hurt, because I had work to do. The red area filled with pus—my body's defenses fighting to heal. They were inadequate, and the infection spread outward until what had been a quarter of an inch was now four times that size—inflamed, swollen, throbbing. Still I foolishly ignored it, aware that the nearest physician was forty miles away and determined to complete my assignment.

My body continued to fight the infection, yet within a day a red line began to crawl up from the point of the infected wrist. As it reached higher, my body put up an even fiercer struggle with all its defenses: I developed a high fever; I grew weak and spent. My state of mind fought too, finally making me agree to go to the doctor. Upon examining me, he ordered me immediately into the hospital, had me hooked up to intravenous antibiotics and had my arm bathed round the clock. For several days I lay still as my body kept up the fight for my life. Had I waited too long, used up too many of my defenses before receiving aid? That was the question. My rising temperature and the crawling red line on my arm answered, "Perhaps." But antibiotics and wet compresses sent reinforcements, strong enough when joined by my own defenses to battle back the infection. Fever subsided; the red line crawled back. In time the ugly sore on my wrist healed, with only a small round mark where the original sore had been. I was fortunate. I had not expended my adaptation energy. But if I had not received help in time, I might very well have died.

Young people under emotional stress are reaching the limits of their adaptation energy every day. Whether they will exceed the limit given them at birth, run out of ability to cope, depends, as it did with me, on the help they receive. If they go on alone for too long, it will be too late for help.

This book is a fervent attempt to get parents and teachers, grand-parents and friends and uncles and aunts and all adults who create the *Lebenswelt* to know how to help their young people before adaptation energy runs out, to enable children to live in trust and love and fulfillment, so that they in turn may build a world of trust and love and fulfillment. They are the parents of the next generation; they are the shapers of the future.

In order to offer help, adults must be able to recognize the adaptive behavior children use as coping techniques, which are as many and as varied as the children themselves. Often they are so deceptive that they pass for laziness, shyness or hostility.

In *Adaptation to Life,* George Vaillant classifies adaptive behavior on four levels, ranging from the most destructive ones, which he labels "psychotic," to the most constructive ones, called "mature." Although he is discussing adults, the defenses he lists apply to young people as well. I include his classifications here so that adults may view their children's behavior as he interprets it, and view their own as it affects their children.

Psychotic Defenses — (Common in children under five years old)
1. Delusions, usually of persecution, about the real world: "I can't go to bed because the witch will be there."
2. Denial of external reality: "My daddy gave me a new dress . . ." when she has no daddy.
3. Distortion of external facts: "I can beat up any boy in my class . . ." when he is small and weak.

Immature Defenses — (Common in children ages five to fifteen)
1. Attributing one's own feelings to others: "Mary is afraid of the teacher . . ." when the child herself is afraid.

2. Fantasy and retreat to resolve conflict and find gratification: "I'm not me, I'm Cinderella . . ." which she does not really believe.
3. Directing bad feelings toward others into self-reproach and physical complaints: "I have a stomachache . . ." when he hates school.
4. Aggressive feelings expressed indirectly: "I can't get good marks . . ." when she is punishing her parents.
5. Acting out in order to avoid one's own feelings: Temper tantrums . . . drug abuse . . . stealing to cover up unhappiness.

Neurotic Defenses — (Common in children and adults)
1. Intellectualizing wishes in order not to act on them: Rationalization . . . overabsorption with work to avoid relationships.
2. Repressing a painful thought: Memory lapses . . . inexplicable naïveté . . . not hearing or seeing selected sounds or sights.
3. Redirecting feelings from a cared-for object to a safer one: Phobias . . . practical jokes . . . prejudice . . . overattention to a pet.
4. Behaving the opposite of what one knows is wrong: Hating a loved person . . . loving an enemy . . . caring attentively for a person by whom one longs to be cared for.
5. Dramatic and temporary change of character to avoid pain: Sudden lack of worry . . . safe emotional expression through acting . . . sudden religious fervor.

Mature Defenses — (Common from ages twelve up)
1. Vicarious pleasure through giving to others: Charity work . . . paid service to others . . . personal offers of help.
2. Humor: Not sarcasm, but games and play and laughter in the face of what might otherwise be unbearable.
3. Suppressing problems and pain through conscious effort: "I'll think about it tomorrow" . . . "I'll live through it."
4. Anticipating and planning for future problems: Physical planning and mental preparation for hospitalization, divorce, travel, new job, death, etc.
5. Sublimating feelings: Football to work off aggression . . . writing poetry to express feelings caused by a broken love affair.

"The sons-of-bitches in the world," George Vaillant writes, "are neither born that way nor self-willed. Sons-of-bitches evolve by their unconscious effort to adapt to what for them has proven an unreasonable world."

Most children find the world—or at best, *some* of their worlds—unreasonable. Like adults, they seek survival in the chaos of their stress through defense mechanisms. Adaptation. Coping. Like the evolutionary cell, some survive. Like the dinosaur, others fail. Unless parents perceive, interpret and understand their children's adaptive behavior, however, there can be little hope for survival.

In my discussion of adaptive behavior in this book, I have not used George Vaillant's classifications, informative though they are. As a psychiatrist, he has probed into the relationship of a person with himself; as an educator and counselor, I have drawn conclusions from my observations and research on a person in response to those who respond to him. Rather than Vaillant's psychiatric terminology, I have used the everyday language of everyday behavior—the fight, the flight and the resignation.

I have isolated five different kinds of behavior which signify children's attempts to cope with stressors. They are the following:

Aggression
}   Fight
Self-destruction

Escape
}   Flight
Apathy

Playing the Game } Resignation

A chapter is devoted to each of the five in turn. It may be remarked that apathy is really one form of escape and that self-destruction is merely another form of aggression. That is true. However, there is so much apathetic behavior and so much self-destructive behavior among children that I have chosen to deal with each separately.

I urge child-involved adults in reading these five chapters to drop labels, stereotypes and preconceived interpretations of their children and their children's actions. I plead with them to look at their children anew—to see what their children, as they react to stress, are trying to tell them.

PART TWO

◆

Signals of Stress

Rock-a-bye baby on the tree top,
When the wind blows, the cradle will rock,
When the bough breaks, the cradle will fall,
And down will come baby, cradle and all.

CHAPTER IV

❖

Aggressive Behavior

Punch and Judy
Fought for a pie;
Punch gave Judy
A knock in the eye.

AGGRESSION AS ADAPTIVE BEHAVIOR

"Why," asks the Indian poet Rabindranath Tagore, "when a man is struck, does he defend himself?"

"Because he has life," he replies. "A stone can bear all sorts of blows quietly."

Children are not stones. When they are attacked, they fight back. The most unsteady toddler will swat a child who grabs her toy or throws sand at her or hits her. As children grow, they continue to fight back—with fists perhaps, or fingernails or kicking feet. These kinds of defenses we seem to understand. Although we may not approve, urging children instead to find alternative, less violent means of evening the score, at least we understand.

The legion of understanders thins out, however, as the defenses of children turn in unexpected and unacceptable directions. For instance, Tommy's kindergarten teacher could understand, despite a

bruised shin, that he had kicked her because she had dragged him
away from the block corner where he was playing. Similarly, when
an inner city junior high girl slapped her teacher, the community
rose to her defense, understanding that the teacher had pushed her
into a wall: an eye for an eye, a tooth for a tooth.

Yet when a boy in Texas shot and killed his teacher, people saw
no relationship between his act and the failing mark he had been
given the previous day. Was there anyone to understand? In the
mind of the boy, his teacher, just as surely as the other teacher, had
pushed him against a wall—not with his hand, but with an even
more lethal weapon: a bad mark. The boy struck back, not with a
kick or a slap, but with a bullet. Whether he deserved the failing
mark or not bears as little importance as whether the girl deserved
to be pushed into the wall or whether the kindergartener deserved to
be dragged from his blocks. The only reality that mattered lay in the
minds of the three young people, who, not being stones, defended
themselves.

It is important to emphasize here, at the outset of this discussion
on aggressive behavior, that *understanding* an action is a far cry
from *condoning* it:

Understanding speaks in a voice of compassion: "I see why he did
it."

Condoning speaks in a voice of acceptance: "He couldn't help it."

These children *could* help it. The child did not have to kick his
teacher; the girl did not have to slap her teacher; the youth did not
have to shoot. They had alternatives which they did not use, perhaps from ignorance, perhaps from choice. In either case, adults find
themselves unable to change the course of aggressive behavior in
young people until they begin to understand and reach into the
causes that lie beneath it. Behavior is a language: aggressive behavior is frequently the language of stress beyond coping. Dr. Zigmond
Lebensohn, a Washington, D.C., psychiatrist, hears this language in
the act of assassination. Following the attempt on President Rea-
gan's life by John W. Hinckley, Jr., Dr. Lebensohn commented that
an assassin is often a person "who is alienated from society, who
feels like a zero, is wanted by no one, and can't get a job." He is
clearly profiling a person unable to handle the stress of nonentity.

It is too late for us to alter the behavior of John Hinckley, Jr.: the damage is done. Where, when, we do not know—somewhere twenty years ago and more when, according to the New York *Times*, he was "a quiet child who lived in the shadow of his older brother and sister." It is not too late, however, for the children in our homes and in our schools, where the damage may just be beginning.

Let us LISTEN to what their behavior is saying . . . understand why they do what they do.

Let us ANSWER their cry for help . . . help them handle their stress . . . teach them another language of behavior.

Gregg Sanders at fifteen killed his parents with an ax and then jumped off a water tower to his death—a crime so horrible that one could only read the newspaper account gasping for breath. The boy apparently had everything to make him happy—a good home, concerned parents, an expensive private school education. He was attractive, a better than average athlete, a B student. Against what did he feel the need to defend himself as he reached for an ax?

The answer may lie buried in newspaper accounts:

"He was under pressure from his parents," neighbors said.

"He was pushed into making A's because he always had to live up to his sister," a classmate explained.

"We used to tease him and call him 'Diapers'," added another.

A third remembered, "When he got off the school bus, the kids would ask why his mother wasn't waiting for him."

What did Gregg Sanders strike back at? Perhaps at overdemanding and overprotective parents . . . and at himself as a failure.

If Gregg Sanders horrifies us, Willie Bosket chills us beyond the limits of credibility. He too was fifteen when he robbed and killed two subway passengers. When one raised his hands in surrender, Willie shot him in the face. He put a bullet through the head of the other because he had only thirteen cents.

"He gets his kicks out of blowing people away," explained his older cousin. His only other kicks turn out to be watching television, reading Mickey Mouse comics and playing cards for dollar bills.

"He's a cold-blooded killer," said the prosecutor at Family Court.

Yet was he a cold-blooded killer when he was born in the ghetto? Was he a cold-blooded killer growing up with no father and a mother away from home every day? Was he a cold-blooded killer when he was first arrested at the age of nine for robbery? He quit school at ten. He worked as a handyman around the neighborhood for a time. He found a gun on the street after a man in a fight dropped it and ran off. He kept the gun, and nobody objected or worried or tried to take it away. Once his mother asked him where he got it.

"Sometimes he thinks we don't love him," his sister says.

Was Willie Bosket a cold-blooded killer, or was cold-blooded killing the voice with which he screamed for help?

What about Brenda Spencer, a California sixteen-year-old who shot nine children and a policeman and killed the school principal? Neighbors used the words "crazy" and "terrible" to describe her. But no one considered her crazy or terrible enough to try to help when she was caught over and over again for shoplifting. No one expressed concern when she burned a cat's tail or when she took drugs and walked around stoned. No one asked questions when her father gave her a .22-caliber rifle. And no one reached out to comfort her when, in her struggling early teens, her mother and father got divorced and she went to live with her father.

Was Brenda Spencer terrible and crazy? Or was she hurt and lonely, aching for the mother other children had? It was, after all, nine children she shot to prove she could "do something big that will be on television and everything." Distorted cries for help always sound crazy and terrible when nobody answers them.

A recent study at Yale University issued the following statement in a report: "Violent youngsters rarely perceive themselves as provocateurs. Rather, they interpret most interpersonal encounters as potential threats against which they have to protect themselves." Here the Yale scientist furnishes proof for the Indian poet: people *do* defend themselves when struck. The Yale study in fact found that almost eighty-two percent of the violent young people studied showed symptoms of paranoia—the mental syndrome in which they perceive themselves as being persecuted and attacked by outside forces. Despite what the world calls them, they do not see their own acts as aggressive.

We must, therefore, while never *accepting* the behavior of Gregg and Willie and Brenda, or of the thousands and tens of thousands of children and young people whose behavior we label aggressive, begin to glimpse method in their madness. Cold-blooded killers do not step full-grown, like Athena from the head of Zeus, into the world. They develop slowly and painfully in homes, in classrooms and on street corners. They tell us through their actions—first in small voices, later in louder ones and finally, in screams of violence —that something is amiss. Cold-blooded killers are not born; they are home-grown in the soil of our deafness and blindness.

A study conducted for the Vera Institute of Justice by Paul Strasburg, New York's Commissioner of Juvenile Justice, reinforces our need to search beneath the surface of behavior. Although psychosis in violent delinquents is relatively rare, he claims, "rage, low self-esteem, lack of empathy and limited frustration tolerance are typical of violent youths." Are not these, then, the attackers against which aggressive children and teenagers defend themselves—rage, low self-esteem, unfeelingness and frustration? Is their violence born of rage? Their rage born of frustration? And their frustration born of love-lessness and a sense of failure?

PROFILE OF VIOLENCE

RAGE

Where does such rage come from that it leads children to maim and kill? Rage can stem from specific sources—as specific as a sick brother or sister. For instance, researchers J. Barbour Aply and I. Westmacott found that twenty-seven percent of children whose siblings suffer from congenital heart disease act out their stress. Similarly, C. M. Binger and associates discovered that up to fifty percent of those whose siblings have leukemia evidence behavioral and other stress-related problems.

Seriously ill brothers and sisters channel parental attention away from children. They deplete family income and energy. In addition, sick siblings demand all-out pity and care—even by the children who feel shelved because of them. So they, torn between love and jealousy, grow to hate themselves out of guilt. Their behavior problems cry out what they themselves dare not articulate.

On the other hand, rage can stem from general sources—as general as an irremedial condition like poverty. Is it really so difficult for the white middle class to see city ghettos as fertile soil for rage which, early on, erupts in violence? Is it so difficult for them to imagine anger bred in cramped quarters, filthy streets and the cold that comes from nonfunctioning boilers? Anger nurtured by pimps and drugs and street fights? The anger of "latchkey children" alone all day while their mothers earn food money caring for other women's children? The anger taught in schools resigned to failure, in prison by police resigned to crime?

From this source comes seventy, eighty, ninety percent of the street violence that plagues American cities, because from this source grows rage. In the infant's voice it whimpers against the rat bite that bleeds at night; in the voice of a child it speaks softly, stealing a bicycle, grabbing a wallet; but in the voices of youth it shrieks in mugging and beating and murder. Then it becomes a statistic, as the rage of others to come echo their cries for help.

FRUSTRATION

Frustration leads to rage. We verify that within our own experience. The frustration identified by Paul Strasburg is inevitable among children cut off in a hundred different ways from the mainstream of their peers. They may be slow learners who cannot keep up with the others—cannot read what they read, cannot verbalize as they do, cannot catch on to games, cannot get jobs. Or they may be the gifted, equally isolated by a maturity and curiosity their peers cannot grasp. No wonder, explains Henry Collis, Director of Britain's National Association for Gifted Children: "an unusually difficult pupil may just be suffering from frustration."

In even greater numbers are delinquents born of frustration— those children, bright or slow, who from birth have reached out for love and been rebuffed. They have been neglected by parents who do not care, overprotected by parents who think they care, held up as status symbols by parents who care only for themselves. Many a young violent offender's head has beaten against such cold walls.

LOW SELF-ESTEEM

From frustration and rage, therefore, evolves self-loathing so acute, hurting so painfully, that young people cry in violence. Thirty

girls in a Detroit high school felt so inferior to a classmate more attractive and smarter than they that they beat her up and seriously
injured her by stabbing her with pencils.

Our personal experience and history books, in addition to socio-
logical studies, indicate that men of small stature feel inferior to tall
men, at least in the Western world with its stereotypes of manliness.
As a result, they may overreact with shows of strength, with the "little man" syndrome. For instance, John Sorge, who was a mere 5'3",
reinforced his self-image by raping women and escaping the police
for years. Lord Byron, both short and lame, proved himself less
crudely: he subdued his women through seduction. Napoleon embla-
zoned the pages of history and the countries of Europe with the big
feats of The Little General. And, of course, there are the aggressive
and determinedly successful business executives who are no more
than 5'5".

Children also lash out against the hurt of feeling unacceptable
when they think love has been denied them. Adopted children rank
high in behavior problems, and children of single parents, and
orphans. Teenagers ran to Haight-Ashbury in droves a decade ago
when their parents rejected their lifestyle . . . and them. Richard
Herrin ran no further than Scarsdale to murder the girl who turned
him down.

Lack of Empathy

A look at what Paul Strasburg terms lack of empathy adds to our
understanding of aggressiveness. Tests among chimpanzees have
shown that baby chimps fondled by their mothers grow up as social
creatures, while those singled out to grow up in isolation become antisocial. In other words, chimpanzees learn to love by being loved.
So do children.

I shared a panel with psychiatrist Dr. Arthur Kornhaber some
time ago. Like Paul Strasburg, he finds a strong relationship between youth violence and lack of feeling. He points a finger at television. Children, viewing TV up to forty hours a week, sit amidst
the comforts of a soft chair, a bag of pretzels and a Coke—secure
and physically satisfied. Simultaneously on television they see people being chased, shot at, robbed, beaten, tortured, murdered, raped,
hanged and physically abused in a creative assortment of ways.

Blood flows, flesh tears, screams of agony pierce the room. Yet the little viewers remain comfortable, munching their goodies, happy observers in a world of mutilation.

"How can they develop feelings for people," Dr. Kornhaber asks, "when their association with pain has only pleasant sensations?" A good question.

Non-personhood creates lack of empathy. Whether children feel that they themselves have been depersonalized, unschooled in loving, or whether they look at others, anesthetized as they are by violence, as being depersonalized, the result is the same. These children lack feelings.

A television documentary last June brought viewers in touch with a group of young violent offenders—rapists, murderers, assaulters. The show was called "Youth Terror: A View From Behind the Gun." If readers need reminding of Paul Strasburg's four sources of youthful violence, they need only hear the words of the young people on the show.

THEY SPOKE FROM RAGE:

"Crime pays. We're not going for the shit jobs our parents do."

"My father's a drug addict. My mother's an alcoholic."

"Sometimes when they hit me, I laugh. But sometimes I make myself real tight."

THEY SPOKE IN FRUSTRATION:

"After you get all the money and everything, you got the same old pain."

"I wouldn't mind going to school if I knew how to read, but the teachers aren't going to teach you."

"If you can't read, you chew a pencil and act like a fool and talk."

"I can't read. I can't get a job or nothing. If I was a judge, I couldn't even read the papers."

THEY SPOKE TO RAISE THEIR SELF-IMAGE:

"I saw a Jewish boy and cracked his head. It felt real good."

"I alone have cost this city ten thousand dollars."

"They raised us like animals; we act like animals."

"It's a way of getting known, of getting a reputation."

"It makes you feel important."

"I love the streets. We have our little subjects running around that we can terrorize."

"I want to be somebody. I don't know what, but I'm going to be somebody."

THEY SPOKE WITH A LACK OF EMPATHY:

"I see something I want, I take it. Then I go back and get something else I want."

"I get a thrill out of breaking heads—all that blood."

"I hit them with a baseball bat or throw coffee in their face and then kill them. I wanted to show a guy he was a punk—I put his hand under a car and crushed it."

LESSONS IN VIOLENCE

Evolution teaches us survival, and the defense mechanisms of these young killers speak eloquently for Darwin's theory. Since the gentle arts will not help them survive in their world, they acquire the less gentle arts that will. Actually, even the most "civilized" of us select for easy learning those skills most needed for immediate survival. We learn to walk and talk before we learn to read; we learn to grab before we say "please."

Violence is a primitive defense, learned young and used by our evolutionary forebears long before *Homo erectus* tried it about 3,000,000 years ago. As animals teach their young to fight off predators, so do we. The Puritan ethic, which burdens most of us, however, fills us with too much guilt and shame to allow us to admit our violent strain. We sublimate it, therefore, in more acceptable forms. Yet the fact remains that the young of our species learn violence—great imitators that they are—from their elders, as deliberately as young cubs from their growling lioness mother.

They begin their lessons at home when parents yell at them, fight with each other and actually hit their children—we use the euphemism "spank." In many homes this is a daily occurrence, excluding those homes in which thousands of parents batter their children into injury and death.

Children soon leave home for school, where in well over half of the states in the nation physical punishment is not only *used* by

teachers, but is legally endorsed. Like capital punishment, it is creeping back into the laws of additional states—ironically enough, as a
way to cure aggressive students!

The sports world, apotheosized in homes across America, provides
equally dramatic lessons in violence. Muhammad Ali is a hero . . .
and football's Mean Joe Green. Fathers and mothers urge their own
small heroes to victory, yelling, "Kill 'em," from the sidelines till
they are hoarse. In compliance, football, hockey and lacrosse—
among the roughest of sports—form teams among ten-year-olds, who
tear their hearts out, often along with their shoulders and kneecaps,
to make Mommy and Daddy proud.

Coaches toughen up their teams from elementary school to college: an Arizona State coach led his team to victory by cursing them
when they failed. An Ohio State coach led his by striking them with
his fist. Neither team complained: they learned to be more aggressive.

Then, of course, there is the greatest teacher of all—television.
After years of silence in the face of TV violence, the American Medical Association finally spoke out, releasing some shocking statistics.
By the time children graduate from high school, the doctors pointed
out, they will have watched an average of 15,000 hours of television
—4,000 more than they have spent in classroom learning. In the
course of those hours they will have witnessed 18,000 murders, not
to mention countless other crimes—from being run over by automobiles in shows like "Charlie's Angels" and "Kojak" to paddlings,
slammings, squashings and entrapment in seemingly harmless car-
toons like "Bugs Bunny" and "Tweety."

"Studies of children," the AMA reported, "have shown diminished emotional sensitivity to media violence and an increase in
the ability to be violent with each other." Learned violent behavior
is retained, they claim, for long periods of time. In short, human
cubs are taught their lessons well. Aggression becomes their defense.

While it is important to keep in mind that violence is a weapon
used to ward off attackers, it is equally important to know that it
can be detected long before the weapon draws blood. Aggressive
cries of children under stress are audible from the cradle. All adults
need to do is listen.

An infant cries to defend herself from hunger . . . and the breast
in her mouth brings peace. An infant screams to defend herself from

pain when a stomachache knots her tiny intestine . . . and warmth on the stomach brings relief. An infant cries to defend herself from the fear of loneliness as she lies in spaceless dark . . . and her mother's arms and the gentle sounds of love comfort her.

But sometimes no breast is given—"We have to get her on a feeding schedule."

Sometimes there is no warmth for a stomachache—"She's just fussing."

And sometimes Mother's arms do not reach her in the dark—"Let her cry herself to sleep so she'll learn."

Then defense behavior takes over. Cries for help cannot go long unheeded without reaction. Infants are too unsophisticated to manipulate: when they cry, they need help.

So do all children need help when they cry. If nobody hears and reaches out to them, their cries become louder and more violent. Adults around them can detect violent behavior in four different patterns:

Physical Violence
Verbal Violence
Defiance
Destructiveness

Singly, almost any of these is normal in the early stages. When carried out in conjunction, in two or more manifestations of violent behavior, however, they call for parental attention. Similarly, any of these evidenced only occasionally is expected from children. If violent behavior persists over a prolonged period of time, however, and especially if it intensifies, parents must be concerned. The child, let us remember the poet's words, is not a stone: his actions are fighting off attackers. The responsibility of the adults in his world is to identify those attackers and seek out what they may be.

DEFENSIVE AGGRESSIVENESS IN PRESCHOOLERS

PHYSICAL VIOLENCE

Victor was a darling little boy, blue-eyed and smiling. He sat in his carriage as his mother wheeled him, drawing chuckles and praise from passers-by. But if another child approached, either on foot or in a carriage, Victor, still smiling, reached out and bit him. Sometimes he drew blood.

Angelic on the surface, Victor was actually raging inside at having to live up to his parents' image of the sweet little boy he pretended to be. He vented his rage on other children because he was too "nice" to vent it on his parents. How many older Victors we see explode in a flow of blood, as we remark in amazement, "I didn't think he would hurt a fly."

Scratching, kicking, pulling hair, pinching, hitting—these are variations of Victor's behavior. So is what kindergarten teachers see so often—grabbing toys from other children or tearing up what they have made. Happy children are social creatures most of the time; they play and let others play. It is unhappy children who lash out. Yet their behavior is not "mean" or "naughty," calling for punishment. It is a sign of their misery, calling for adult caring that will find its cause.

VERBAL VIOLENCE

When Ashley was small, he shouted "No" to everything, screaming, yelling, throwing temper tantrums. It was the best way he could devise to get attention from his parents, who were away from home most of the time.

Dottie found another way: she talked incessantly. Whether her mother listened or tuned out made little difference—Dottie still talked, rarely bothering to listen to replies. Dottie began compulsive talking when her little brother was four months old. For her it was a way to compete, and since it worked, she kept it up.

Rhoda used name calling instead. Whatever she heard her thirteen-year-old brother say to her in anger, she imitated when he crossed her path. "You sun pitch," she would curse, with the solemnity of an ancient tribesman issuing a nature incantation.

Some children use nonsense sounds as invective—it can be very irritating! Others whisper so softly that no one can hear. Still others stifle all sound, merely going through the lip motions of speech. The extent of their success can be measured in the decibel level of their mother's reaction.

Some children are more direct, articulating their feelings without hesitation. "I hate you," they shout. Three-year-old Carrie used to cry out in her stress, "I wish you were dead," long before she knew that "dead" was anything more than out of sight. Like her, most children use verbal violence because they are either uncomfortable with physical violence or afraid of the consequences of using it.

DEFIANCE

Defiant behavior begins early. It can be as blatant as refusing to eat or get dressed in the morning, or as subtle as dawdling. Laura played with her cereal at the breakfast table every morning to the tune of her mother's nagging for speed, so that her father could drop her off at nursery school on his way to work. She knew she had her mother in a bind because although her mother wanted her to eat the cereal, she also wanted her out of the house so she could go back to bed. Dawdling bespoke Laura's sense of rejection loud and clear.

Toilet habits, children quickly learn, are the most powerful weapons of defiance next to eating. Coaxed by overeager mothers, they refuse to learn. I have seen a child asked by his mother whether he wants to "go potty" shake his head and then deliberately wet his pants as he stands in the living room, glaring at her during the act. At the other extreme, I have seen children stay constipated for days rather than have a bowel movement in the toilet and give their mother that satisfaction.

Defiance is quiet aggression. Often it is so quiet as to be totally speechless, as we see in the sulking child who refuses to answer a question. Instead of bloodying the attacker, it cleanly drives him mad. For instance, Father asks, "Do you want to come to the store with me?" No answer. "Do you want to come to the store with me?" Still no answer, but inside, "That will teach him not to ignore me as he did this morning." A wise father hears what the silence is saying. Others merely grow angry and scold—and the silence grows louder.

DESTRUCTIVENESS

My son Eric chewed everything in sight when he was little—his shirt collar, his gloves, his jacket, everything close and chewable. One day his grandmother, tired of seeing him with holey gloves, dragged him into the nearest store where she bought him a new pair. Before she was out the door with him, he had chewed off two fingers.

In a conference one day, I asked Eric's teacher whether she had any kind of musical band for the children. "We did," she replied, "before Eric ate up the drumsticks." She proceeded to explain to this horrified young mother that Eric's chewing might be a sign of stress. Oh wise teacher!

"Would Eric have any reason for extra stress right now?" she asked.

He would indeed—a baby sister, crawling into trouble at every moment, who diverted my attention. Eric felt not only neglected but replaced, and tried to protect himself aggressively. Thanks to a sensitive teacher, I was able to reschedule my time with hours set aside just for Eric and me. His stress was relieved, and his gloves lasted. Many parents are not so fortunate in a child's teacher as I was.

Destructive behavior goes on many tracks. Some children have a penchant for breaking toys, dishes, glasses. Others tear up clothing. I know a toddler who could not be stopped from crayoning on walls and furniture; another who fiercely uprooted his mother's plants. Done once, done occasionally, these acts signify nothing more than curiosity and testing. But done repeatedly and purposefully, destructive behavior is a signpost of distress.

Even more indicative of trouble is the aggressive acting out which leads to the destruction or mutilation of animals. Parents should be concerned over the child who joyfully crushes ants underfoot; a coping child will sit and watch them for hours. Parents should be concerned over a child who throws stones at birds or teases the pet dog or cat. Allie would offer their cocker spaniel food and then snatch it away as the dog began to eat. She also pulled the cat's whiskers to hear it spit.

Woody loved animals, especially Chico, his grandparents' chihuahua. With his divorced mother working, the little boy spent a good part of each day at his grandparents' home. One day they saw Woody walking into the bathroom with Chico in his hands.

"What are you doing?" asked his grandmother.

"Going to put him in the toilet and flush it," Woody replied without malice. At two and a half he was unable to identify his feelings of hurt. All he knew was that he would feel better if he got rid of the little dog that he and everyone else loved.

These then are four ways in which small children use aggressive behavior to rid themselves of pain. When adults in their lives are sensitive enough to suspect a problem churning beneath their behavior, such children can be helped—usually with speed and ease. When, however, adults either overlook or punish it, aggressiveness continues. It becomes magnified, more violent, more difficult to deal with. By the time children reach elementary school, they are crying louder by acting worse.

DEFENSIVE AGGRESSIVENESS IN SCHOOLCHILDREN

PHYSICAL AGGRESSIVENESS

Fighting is the obvious way to strike back at attackers—as eleven-year-old Susan did. She was a bright, pretty girl in a family that cared—but doted on her older brother. Susan failed to feel the caring: she felt second-rate. Since the only reality that affects a child is her internal reality, not what the rest of the world may see, Susan *was* second-rate. In self-defense she began using her fists—anywhere, on anyone. Her brother, amused, gave her daily boxing lessons which she applied more and more eagerly as she won his praise. Soon she was the terror of the neighborhood, and parents began refusing to let their children play with her. Her own parents merely shook their heads, hoping she would outgrow it.

Stealing is another common expression of defensive aggression. It is a means of physically lashing out without actually hurting anyone. Blood does not flow. Stealing in schools has become so prevalent that locker companies are kept busy trying to invent foolproof locks. Still, children figure out ways. They watch classmates open their lockers and then memorize the combination, or they slip keys from pockets. Some children, even as young as six, pilfer coins from Mother's purse or from Dad's trousers as they lie across the chair waiting to be worn. Teachers have been so frequently ripped off that many wear belt purses or leave money at home. With prize possessions stolen from even pre-primary grades, Show and Tell has become Show and Take.

Distressed children, as we have reiterated, do not like themselves. They often, therefore, seek to assume aggressive roles so that they can be someone else. From these attempts spring roles familiar in every classroom—the clown and the bully. There is little that is funny about the child who clowns: he is in fact, like the circus clown, wearing only a painted face. He throws an eraser, cackles like a hen, crosses his eyes, asks inane questions—all to draw attention that he cannot draw more constructively. When his classmates laugh, as the teenage killer said on television, "It makes the pain go away." But only while he performs. Does he win the sought-after prize of peer approval?

"We feel sorry for him," a fifth-grader explained to me.

"Then why do you laugh?" I questioned.

"Because it makes him feel better."

The class bully is the clown sans weapons. Feeling incapable of meeting fair competition among his classmates, he blows himself up to become the biggest and the strongest. If he cannot win a place through friendship, he will win it through fear. Saul did, and it helped him forget that he was a slower learner than most of his classmates—and far slower than his sister. Unfortunately, his parents made no effort to translate his behavior into feelings. If they had, they could have built up Saul's self-image by minimizing academic competition and helping him shine in an area where he could excel —sports. Instead, his mother applied disciplinary measures, while his father merely shrugged his shoulders sighing, "Boys will be boys." So Saul's cries went unheard—until he got into the drug scene and dropped out of high school.

Girls find less obvious ways to bully: they form cliques which rank in pecking order. Hearts are broken with a rejection. Year after year I saw this happen in successive sixth and seventh grades. Sensitive to the pain of the outcasts, and devastated by the need of the "in" group to hurt so viciously, I talked to a group of mothers whose daughters were particularly adept at excluding others. They responded with the old familiar refrain, "Girls will be girls."

VERBAL AGGRESSIVENESS

Nonphysical children find abundant verbal outlets for their urge to strike back. Obscenity, for instance, is a powerful weapon, especially when it traumatizes the people on whom it is being used. An angry fourth-grader will look straight into his mother's eyes and yell, "Shit," in the hope of shocking her. If she gasps and turns ashen, the child has discovered a sharp weapon.

I remember a little boy who came armed with four-letter words into an elitist private school where teachers' prejudices were showing. The little boy knew well how to attack his teachers. "Mother fucker," he would throw at them, awaiting the looks of horror, which inevitably led to their dragging him to my office.

One day as a sputtering teacher departed, leaving the boy still shouting at her, I put my arms around his shoulders, drawing him close. "Mother fucker," he continued to shout. Turning his head to look into my face, "Mother fucker," he screamed. Then he buried his head in my chest and wept. I was never successful in getting the teacher to understand his barrage of obscenity, but I hope I was able to get him to understand her prejudice.

Name calling, even when less profane, is verbal aggressiveness. "Fatty," "Four Eyes," "Dummy," "Teacher's Pet," "Goody-good,"— these can slash a child to ribbons. Other names reflect social hostility: "Nigger," "Honky," "Jew," "Queer." Where do they learn how lethal such names are? As Rogers and Hammerstein said, "You've got to be taught to hate." They learn from adults.

Innocuous teasing often includes name calling and turns out to be not so innocuous. Two brothers I know used to call their little sister "Frog"—a charming animal, unless you happen to hate being called one. She did—so the name stuck for years, as the boys chopped her down with a monosyllabic blow.

Other kinds of teasing might be considered physical aggression— poking, untying a belt, pulling a ponytail. Karl found a way to drive his father crazy: as he read the newspaper after dinner, Karl would throw his metal airplanes against it, crying, "Coming in for a landing." A wise father would have required no phrasebook to translate his son's words as meaning, "Please talk to me. I need you." But Karl's father got angry each evening and sent Karl to his room.

Young children can be verbally aggressive, as toddlers are, through compulsive talking. One little girl, considered rather quiet in school, talks nonstop at home—while her mother is cooking, while her mother is reading, while her mother is on the phone, even while her mother is talking to her. She talks most of all when her mother nurses the new baby. Another asks questions: "What is that?" "Why is this?" "How does this work?" "When is that happening?" "Where is something?" An adverbial drum roll. Throwing out questions, she never stops to hear an answer.

Habitual lying is another kind of verbal aggression. There are many kinds of lies. Billy inflated his ego by telling stories of things that never happened. He convinced his teacher that his father had died; then he reversed the situation, convincing his father that his teacher had died. Francie, afraid of losing parental love, lied when she did anything wrong. A diabetic, she was forbidden to eat sweets; yet when her mother left freshly baked brownies on the table, she quickly stuffed five of them down and swore she had not. Had she been less naïve, she might have looked in the mirror first and noticed chocolate all over her mouth! Jennie liked to get her older brother into trouble; she poked holes in the toothpaste, and when her father squeezed the tube, a handful of sticky worms squirted into his palm. In answer to her father's raging, Jennie calmly insisted, "I saw Eddie do it."

DEFIANCE

As school begins, teachers place in the hands of children a most potent means of defiance—homework. Like the animal bone first held by a hominid five million years ago, homework is a weapon with untold potential. Millions of homes across the country are turned into nightly battlegrounds as children attack, wielding their assignment books.

"Have you done your homework yet?" comes the charge.

"No," resounds the counterattack.

"Do it."

"Later."

"You can't watch TV till it's done."

"I don't understand it. The teacher didn't explain."

"Bring it here. I'll help you."

And so a good evening is overturned while parents either fight to get Junior to do his homework or surrender and do it themselves. Homework is a double-edged sword, enabling the attacker to strike at both home and school in a single blow.

Equally effective defiance appears in the form of piano lessons, practicing for which—or, rather, not practicing for which—can goad parents into a total frenzy. Paul outdid himself in inventiveness: he turned the piano over to his sister and took up the drums instead. Only masochistic parents can nag for drum practice!

Some children defy their parents by not communicating.

"What did you do in school today?"

"Nothing."

"How do you like . . . ?"

"It's O.K."

"Why did you do that?"

Silence.

Even small children learn to do this ably. When Patty's father continued probing to learn what she had done in school each day, she finally announced, "It's my school, not yours." Patty's father did not counterattack.

Children often seek the forbidden in defiance. Two sixth-grade boys urinated on the lawn of a girl classmate as she looked out the window. A group of girls defecated on a church kneeling bench. One child strips while her mother has company. Another refuses to bathe. I know a teenager who pretends to bathe when forced into the bathroom, even going so far as to running bath water to fool his parents. Another confessed to me that he urinates in the washbowl when he is angry, but he flushes the toilet so his parents will not suspect.

Less dramatic methods of aggressive defiance are seen in children who sulk and in those whose first response to any suggestion is a forceful "No." It is not uncommon for younger children to regress—to begin bed-wetting again or to talk baby talk—after the birth of a sibling. Teachers see regression in lapses of effort after a child has tried, improved his work but received little acknowledgment from home. Like poison, defiance can be an unbloodied attempt at self-defense.

DESTRUCTIVENESS

A ten-year-old boy, a newspaper reported, was accused in Family Court of arson after setting fire to a classroom wastebasket during recess. He was a child with severe learning disabilities, facing repeated failures day after day. Sent to a juvenile detention institution for processing and then for eighteen months to a boys' home for correction, he was punished severely for his attempt "to make the pain go away." Perhaps upon release, he was another Willie Bosket. Our system of corrections does little to correct.

Destruction of property is one of the loudest cries for help that a child can emit. Educators realize that the amount of graffiti on school walls correlates directly with the attitudes of students. Gouged desks, broken sinks, torn books, battered walls speak loudly of the failure and frustration within, as a walk through most urban schools attests.

New York subways, painted nightly, scrawled on daily, echo with more than the sound of train tracks. "Cool Luke" is painted in foot-high letters. "Here Comes Ed the Red"; "Watch Out for J. F."; "Ben Rough, Ben Tough"; "Sam," "Dick," "George"—names written on walls and doors and windows for the riding public to admire. Names that make a kid know by writing them that he exists.

Subtler kinds of destructiveness should concern parents as well. When a child consistently tears her clothes or loses toys or breaks windows, the tendency is to call her careless. Repeated "carelessness," however, adds up to a way of lashing out. A mother I know found the front seat of her car circled with marks from the cigarette lighter; she found initials carved on the piano; she found her daughter's underpants cut with scissors. Individually each bit of evidence meant little more than a child's curiosity in action. Together, however, they painted a composite picture of a little girl under stress.

Children who destroy a loved object seem to be crying out in extra-loud voices: they are destroying themselves. A little girl may tear up her doll's clothes, or even her doll itself, to alleviate the pain of guilt—and imagined guilt hurts as much, we must remember, as guilt real and deserved. Six-year-old Lois bashed in the faces of her two favorite dolls a few months after her mother died. Feeling that she was somehow responsible, she had been able to cope with her guilt for a short while, but then it had overpowered her and forced a way out.

When Elsie was eleven, her prize possession was a bride doll, whose long titian hair she enviously combed, restyling it with combs and barrettes and ribbons. One day Elsie's mother found the doll, not standing on the dresser as usual but crumpled in a corner, her once long hair lying cut on the floor. She picked up the doll and saw, in the straggly cropped hair that remained, the image that Elsie must have seen every morning as she faced the mirror.

"But Elsie is beautiful," her mother wept.

The only answer is, "Not in *her* mirror."

Ross loved his dog and cut the tip off his tail. His parents said it was all right because he cried over his "mistake." He lost things too—his allowance, his football; later, as he became a teenager, tickets to hockey games that his father gave him. The last I heard, he had run his sports car into a tree and was hospitalized with a broken leg. I still wonder what stress signals he had sent his parents as a young child before I knew him. What cries had they failed to hear?

Through the elementary school years of children, the stressors that underlie their behavior can in most cases be dealt with easily. Adults may be able to relieve situations that cause extreme stress by altering their own behavior or attitudes. In addition, they should be able to help their children identify stressors and guide them toward more constructive coping. In some cases short periods of outside help may be called for—not for the child alone, but for the whole family whose dynamics may be creating the stressful situation. Generally, the care and concern a child feels when parents attempt to help with any or all of these methods is in itself supportive enough to help him over the rough time of stress.

When little children become bigger, however, when they leave the relatively protected world of preteens to enter junior high and high school as adolescents, the problems they carry with them become bigger as well. The unhappiness of a ten-year-old does not suddenly vanish when she becomes fourteen; insecurity, self-hate, anger, feelings of failure follow her—growing even larger and blacker.

Unfortunately, adults, frightened by the growing severity of their children's stress signals, are less apt to interpret them as pleas for help, and more ready to see them as behavior problems and delinquency. As a result, they are less willing to offer help and more eager to exact punishment. How seldom we hear, "We must be doing something wrong; let's find out what it is." How often we hear only demands for retribution:

"The trouble with schools is, they're not tough enough."

"You ought to lock up those kids and put them away."

"Stop talking and give the kids a good beating."

The futility of such phrases is attested to by the increasingly antisocial behavior of the young people on whom punishment and pressure are used. Just as a parent cannot make a child do homework by locking the door to his room, neither can parents or teachers or judges or jailers make a teenager behave as they demand by any kind of force. Parental beatings do not convert an offspring to gentleness; suspension from school does not turn a troublemaker into a student; a prison sentence does not rehabilitate an angry teenager; a locked cell does not prepare him to function in society. The only way a get-tough policy could really curb crime would be if every violent offender could be incarcerated for life. We have neither the facilities nor the finances—and I would hope we have not the heart—for that.

When adults observe aggressiveness in older children, just as in younger ones, they must *not allow* it; neither must they merely *punish* it. They must—we have said it before—*understand* it. Only then will they have the material from which to build new attitudes, new lifestyles, new behavior. This is not soft talk—it is pragmatic talk, for there is no way, short of getting at the source, that enables society to eliminate the end result.

Youthful violence persists because two mistakes are made:

1. Some people understand and condone it.
2. Other people refuse to understand it and punish.

Neither way works. That is why we must resort to a third way:

3. Understand the source of the behavior and relieve the stress.

In earlier chapters of this book we have tried to show children's reactions to stress. In later chapters we shall offer suggestions for relieving stress. At this point, however, we shall continue to point out the signposts of stress.

DEFENSIVE AGGRESSIVENESS IN TEENAGERS

Physical Aggressiveness

Six teenage boys beat up former ice-skating champion Dick Button as he jogged through Central Park, clubbing him with tree branches and baseball bats. This was no lone offense: they had been up on charges of assault, robbery, burglary, attempted rape and sexual abuse many times before. At that stage of their lives they appeared to be pretty hardened criminals; yet, long before they met Dick Button in the park, they had given signals of stress. Their parents had received the signals too:

— They had been booked on many "minor youthful offenses."
— One mother referred to her son as "a stupid boy who hung out with the wrong kids."
— One admitted, "I have a difficult time controlling him. I can't even get him out of bed in the morning."
— Another mother confessed, "I can't control him at all."
— Neighbors detected signs: "Him and his friends would always be sitting around the halls and spitting at the building."
— They were known to sniff glue and drink.

All the signs were there. The boys had been scrawling them across their lives for years, but no one paid any attention. Adults saw, but they shrugged their shoulders. I do not know what happened to the six boys: they probably received sentences of a year or so in prison, and then what? As a police officer said of Willie Bosket, "They're putting him away for eighteen months. In eighteen months and one day, someone on the street will be dead." How many others will be clubbed when these boys are turned loose?

Young people cry out against their stressors in far less destructive ways before they resort to beating and mugging and murder. They shoplift; they snatch a purse; they carry knives long before they dare use them. They form gangs in school, fighting for leadership. They drive cars wildly. They get drunk. They smoke pot, swallow pills, sniff cocaine and angel dust, shoot up heroin.

Just as small children are given the weapon of homework to attack with, so teenagers are given a lethal weapon too: sex. No crime short of murder—and maybe not even that—expresses hostility as graphically as rape.

Why does a boy rape an eighty-three-year-old woman?

"She didn't have but twenty-eight cents."

Why does a boy rape a four-year-old girl?

"In school they taught us sex, but they didn't tell us nothing about love."

Why does a man rape his wife?

"She is such a bitch."

Rape is the expression of rage. Seduction is its smoother relative, and bisexual at that. Girls and boys scream their misery by tallying up sexual successes like trophies. Tens of thousands of pregnant children each year have babies or abortions, and all the sex education that Mary Calderone dreamed of will not stop it. Those girls *want* to become pregnant—to get even with their mothers, to show their fathers, to prove something to themselves. Or, most pitiably, in the words of a thirteen-year-old in a foster home, "I wanted someone all my own."

Any of these aggressive acts, sexual or otherwise, is a sign written in bold letters: "I am hurting. Help me." When no one reads the signs, the letters become bolder and the signs more visible. A snatched purse becomes a stolen car. Shoplifting becomes burglary. A knife carried for effect comes unsheathed. Fights become mugging and murder. Drinking and drug abuse become addiction. Gangs become terrorists. No one can miss the signs now, but is it too late? Certainly in the prison system as it exists today it is too late to help youths who have reached this point.

Verbal Aggressiveness

TV's Archie Bunker was the prototype of verbal aggression. He shouted abuse at long-suffering Edith and at his son-in-law. He threatened to throw out a friend who, he learned, was gay. He wrote letters to denounce a liberal politician. He excoriated blacks and Jews, Poles, hippies and career women. He never actually hurt anyone, retracting his threats before the half hour ended. By the next week, however, his verbal arsenal was filled once again.

I was interested to read in a television magazine one day that the background of the character created to be Archie Bunker was provided with motivation for his behavior. Archie, according to his creator, was rejected by his father, who preferred and favored his brother. In this light the character makes sense, and we can imagine him growing up hurt and guilty, as many real-life children of our acquaintance have.

People used verbal aggression long before Archie Bunker taught them how. Even young people demonstrate it as gossip and rumor that they spread among their peers. Who can ever forget the little girl in Lillian Hellman's *The Children's Hour,* destroying the lives of her two teachers. Teenagers demonstrate aggression in their bragging, in their threats, in their verbal karate chops. The high school student who humiliates his teacher is demonstrating it. The one who lies demonstrates it . . . the one who hurls prejudice . . . and the one who defends himself with sarcasm. These young people are knifing and mugging and raping just as surely as their more physical brothers and sisters, only they have learned to use more socially acceptable weapons.

DEFIANCE

René Dubos explained in *So Human an Animal,* "Rebelling is not the same as defining a cause that would improve the quality of human life or formulating a constructive program of action." Teenagers tend to defy the world by rebelling *against* rather than by defining *causes* for. It is a normal process as they emerge from childhood into adulthood. Some adults, however, never complete the transition: I know a forty-year-old who is still fighting the system, any system. As a result, he cannot hold a job, a wife or even the respect of his children.

So-called hippie dress and long hair were the "in" ways of youth rebellion during the sixties. Adults were horrified at first, but then they pulled the rug from under their children: they adopted their lifestyle. Men in the mainstream began wearing longer hair and beards; women, the layered, baggy look. Blue jeans became so "in" that they now sport designer names from high fashion. It is nearly impossible to be defiant when the enemy disarms you.

Yet, young people continue to invent ways to lash out. Who

could have anticipated "streaking" before the naked figures of their own children raced across campuses and through city streets? Who would have believed the sight of bare behinds stuck through a car window stopped in traffic before seeing them in the adjacent lane? Protest marches came as a surprise during the Vietnam War, as did anti-nuclear demonstrations afterward. Through all the creativity, tried and true means of defiance grow in intensity—drugs, drinking, truancy and running away from home. As the generation of grand-parents exclaims, "I'd hate to start raising kids in this day and age."

DESTRUCTIVENESS

The nation's annual cost to repair school vandalism is over half a billion dollars—more than the amount spent on textbooks in every school in the country. In New York City alone, a quarter of a mil-lion windows are broken in a single year. Though staggering, these figures do not end the horror story: in a single year, arson accounts for the destruction of close to two hundred thousand structures, amounting to a billion dollars in damages, not to mention the cost in lives. It is estimated that anywhere from twenty-five to seventy percent of these fires are set by youthful arsonists—an average of half a billion dollars' worth attributable to children!

What drives so many young people to such destructive behavior? They are often "nice" children, accepted children, children whose parents smugly feel they would never do such things. But then Si's mother did not know he shot frogs with his .22. Jack's parents did not know he tore down the flag at school. Penny's parents did not know she slashed car tires. Whose parents know they break store windows or rip aerials from roofs?

Destructiveness is usually a secret act—teachers have trouble even discovering who writes the four-letter words on armchairs. Cynthia Wilkerson's parents might never have discovered her bomb-making if she had not been seen fleeing a burning house in Greenwich Vil-lage. Yet even from dark and hidden corners, destructiveness issues a loud cry for help.

Before leaving the subject of aggression, there is an interesting point to note: girls have traditionally been less aggressive than boys.

The cultural roles into which they are cast from birth makes this observation a foregone conclusion. Whatever aggressive behavior girls have manifested has for the most part been more verbal than physical: they tattle rather than push; they gossip rather than punch. As teenagers, they wear provocative clothes rather than fight for sex; they forge checks rather than snatch purses.

Times are changing, however. The woman's movement, alerting us all to equality of the sexes, is bringing women's aggressiveness out of the closet. This appears to be true in the bedroom, where an increasing number of men are growing impotent under newfound female initiative. It is true also in the professional world, where the aggressive fields of business and politics are inundated by women competing with men. Not surprising, therefore, is the fact that in the area of violent crime also, women are assuming more active roles. The past decade or so has produced the following statistics:

Female aggravated assault   up 134%
Female burglary   up 246%
Female robbery   up 306%
Females carrying weapons   up 391%

There are even cases pending in court at this moment of female rape.

So much for young people's defensive behavior couched in the guise of aggression. Let adults not be misled: no matter how violent it looks, it is still an attempt at defense. Perhaps children have forgotten, or have never really known, exactly what they are fighting back at. Most assuredly they are unable to articulate the hurts. But the hurts are there nonetheless—deep, embedded, eating away at what might be healthy and productive.

It is easy to understand the baby's cries and know they stem from need, not naughtiness. My plea is for adults to interpret as well the cries of older children.

CHAPTER V

❖

Self-destructive Behavior

Ring-a-ring o' roses,
A pocket full of posies,
A-tishoo! A-tishoo!
We all fall down.

SUICIDE — THE ULTIMATE SELF-DESTRUCTION

Michael Wechsler is the subject of James Wechsler's moving book *In a Darkness*. Bright, creative, sensitive, attractive, he possessed all the qualities that mothers dream of in their sons and hope for in the sons of others whom their daughters marry. Yet something was wrong.

One day Michael almost walked into a moving car.

Later, when he was old enough to have his own car, he smashed it up.

He bought a motorbike, but he ran it into a bus. "I wish I hadn't lived through it," he said later.

He got heavily involved in drugs.

He swallowed a handful of sleeping pills one day and had to be rushed to the hospital to have his stomach pumped.

He was hospitalized five times.

He dreamed of cutting himself with knives.

He developed phobias—became afraid to cross the street or to go on subways (long before transit terrorism made everyone afraid).

He shoved his hand through a window.

He played at strangling himself—with ties and the shaver cord and with the strap from his guitar.

He poured out unhappiness in his diary: "I really feel like a failure," he wrote.

One day Michael took an overdose of barbiturates and died.

When a young person kills himself, a question always surfaces: Why? Why did Michael Wechsler take his life? Why, in fact, has teenage suicide risen over two hundred percent in recent years, become a national epidemic? According to Scott Spencer in his *Harper's* article entitled "Childhood's End," fifty-seven young people like Michael Wechsler attempt suicide in America *every single hour!* Fortunately, only a small percent of them succeed—if a young person's suicide can ever be considered successful!

While suicide ranks tenth among the leading causes of death of America's general population, it ranks second among young people. Accidents rank first. Even this rating does not paint the enormity of the problem, for many teenage deaths that are reported euphemistically by guilt-ridden parents as accidental are in truth suicides. It is far more accurate to face up to the shocking reality and admit the truth: more young Americans are killed by suicide than by any other cause.

Our country is not alone. Japan and Germany, both countries in which the educational system exerts pass-or-perish pressures upon students, see teenage suicide far surpassing ours. At the other extreme, easygoing countries such as Italy and France evidence a far lower suicide rate among their youth.

While generalizations can be dangerous, there is an indicative one to be made from statistics on the kind of young people that commit suicide. Past records paint them as white, middle or upper income, better than average students. Let us contrast this composite picture with the one that statistics paint of typical young people who commit *murder*. They are, the record tells us, black, low-income, school dropouts. The exact opposite.

What does this say? That suicide, like murder, is an act of aggression. The young black raised in a ghetto and the young white raised in a suburb—helpless, hopeless and lonely—both lash out in despair. The ghetto black is alienated by the syndrome of poverty; the middle-class white, by pressures for success. Both feel loveless. Both feel inadequate. Unable to cope with their ensuing frustration and rage, both attack.

There is, however, one difference. Brought up amidst ghetto hatred and violence, the black child strikes *out*; filled with guilt and self-doubt, the white child strikes *in*. Homicide for one; suicide for the other. An alarming increase in crime is reported by the media in graphic detail that keeps us quaking in our homes at night, yet the past decade has seen twice as many suicides as homicides every single year. The difference is that suicide rarely makes headlines unless the last name is familiar—Newman, Peck, Linkletter, Moore.

In effect then, Michael Wechsler, gentle and bright, suffers the same agony as Willie Bosket the "hardened criminal." In a struggle for survival, both kill. Only, Willie lacks empathy and blows off a person's head without feeling, while Michael's intense sensitivity puts an end to his pain in never-ending sleep. Two prevailing theories are put forth to explain aggression turned inward into self-destruction.

WHY SUICIDE?

1. One theory is that the young suicide, raging as he may be against those who wrong him, feels too much guilt to attack. He may be a child overprotected from birth, doted on, waited on, used, in his parent's words, "to have the things I never had"—the spoiled brat grown up. His wishes instantly gratified, he does not learn to work or to want or to wait. His is instant satisfaction, which, like too much candy, cloys. He reaches no goals; he finds no contentment; he is miserable.

On the other hand, he may be the superachiever—an A student, president of the student council, newspaper editor. Whereas he used to get dollar bills for his achievements, now he receives parental praise and pride. As his accomplishments are displayed by his parents, he begins to forget he is a person. Worse still, he believes his parents have forgotten. He feels rejected, unacceptable, a failure.

These young people can only hate those who have cheated them of what all children deserve and expect—fulfillment. Who has done this to them? Their parents. Yet, nice people do not hate their parents—especially when parents have given them so much, have been so proud of them. Nice people love their parents. And so guilt sets in, bringing with it the dilemma of love and hate. Dilemmas are insoluble, and guilt can be unbearable. The only way out is self-destruction.

The suicide note of a seventeen-year-old boy reveals the aching guilt that drove him to hang himself with a clothesline from the shower. "I can't understand anything," he wrote. "I don't know why I'm doing this except I feel too bad to do anything else. I hope you won't hate me."

Lianne lost sight of the fact that she was primarily a person. Lianne's father was dead, and her mother ran the home with the singular purpose of an autocrat: Lianne would have the best she could afford; Lianne would work hard; Lianne would succeed. And Lianne did—at everything except achieving herself. Finally, too exhausted to struggle further, she took an overdose of sleeping pills.

Her mother found an explanation on a page of her diary: "I see myself dancing on a stage, only I have nothing to say about what steps I am doing. My mother is up above me holding that wooden thing with the string attached. I don't even want to dance."

Despite that image, her mother, even years later, cannot accept the fact that Lianne took her life. "She had everything," she says. To her Lianne did—she had beauty, brains, a star-studded future. Her mother cannot see that her daughter lacked the one thing that would have given worth to all the others—her sense of self. With that she would not have had to rage against her mother by raging against her own sense of guilt. Could it have been otherwise? Yes, if her mother, instead of equating Lianne's worth with her success, had accepted it as intrinsic to Lianne, regardless of success or failure.

2. Another theory put forth to explain suicide in terms of self-directed aggression begins with the realization that young people identify with the object of their love. Young children *are* their mother and father, assimilating their values, their attitudes, even

their mannerisms. When the maturing process is restricted by barriers such as overprotective parents or unresolved emotional problems, children fail to grow up. They have no choice but to remain extensions of their parents. They will not, as we discussed in an earlier chapter, go through the now famous identity crisis.

Dissension with parents, therefore, becomes inner conflict. Anger and hatred directed toward parents, who are by birth and growth love objects, become anger and hatred toward themselves. When they think in the violent terms of aggressors, "I could kill you," they kill. Only "you" means "me," and they kill themselves. This about-face in the direction of violence has led some psychologists to refer to suicide as "murder in the 180th degree."

Several hours before attempting suicide, Edna acted out a textbook lesson in psychology, although she was conscious of nothing more than the private hell through which she was struggling. She had had a fight with her mother over a boyfriend of whom her mother did not approve.

"I don't want him here anymore, and you are not to see him outside."

"You're a bitch," Edna screamed. "You have no feelings," and she ran off, banging the door to her room behind her. An hour or so later she sought her mother out in the kitchen and apologized. She went out, returning with a package from the hardware store. She kissed her mother on the cheek, went into her room and quietly closed the door.

Less than an hour later, her mother found her almost unconscious body in a pool of vomit. She had swallowed two boxes of rat poison.

Often with teenagers, the love object with which they identify is not a parent, but another young person. Adolescent love, sometimes a subject of amusement to adults, is no laughing matter to the boy and girl caught in its grip. They are dead serious—and sometimes, when the relationship ends, dead.

For teenagers form relationships with an intensity that all but ingests the love object. Parents are aware of this; they see their adolescents become mirror images of the boy or girl with whom they go steady. They adapt their dress, read their books, listen to their music, become fans of their sports, study together and talk on the telephone as ceaselessly as parents allow. When classmates announce that Jim and Carol are "an item," they epitomize the whole relationship: teenagers in love are a single unit.

When, therefore, that unit splits up, when one half of it falls *out* of love, the other half lashes out in hurt and anger. Only it cannot lash out at the former love object because that love object has become a part of the other half itself. It must lash not *out*, therefore, but *in*, attacking the rejected one, not the rejecter. The young lover kills the object of his love—himself.

A few years ago I received a letter from a college freshman who had tried to kill herself by slashing her wrists. "The day I made an attempt on my life," she wrote, "I had been on the phone with a very special male friend. Our conversation was upsetting and he had been very cruel. Before hanging up, I told him I was going to kill him, but he didn't believe me."

The young girl put down the receiver with the single determination of destroying the boy who had hurt her. But having so closely identified with him in a love relationship, she *was* the boy. She attempted to destroy herself.

Ambivalence shadows all of us during our lives: we want to live while at the same time we want to die. Fortunately for most of us, the former prevails, and the spark of life that cannot be reignited is extinguished, not by our own hands, but by sickness, accident or old age. Fantasies of death may tip the scale at times, but the life force usually overcomes.

Suicidal young people, like the rest of us, waver on the brink of ambivalence. Even as they court death, the life wish beckons them back. It has been observed, for instance, that young lovers fished out of the Thames River in England have scraped fingers from clawing to get out.

Dr. Edwin S. Shneidman, Professor of Medical Psychology at UCLA, puts it this way: "Until he dies, a suicide is begging to be saved." His very act is a gesture displayed for the world to heed. In the light of this thinking, an attempted suicide is a cry for help; a completed suicide is a mistake.

The girl who wrote me from college was motivated by reading an article I had written on teenage suicide. "I felt like you were trying to reach me," she said, "something I had never felt until I screamed with pain from a bleeding wrist. It is funny—people listened to me after that." Her suicide attempt was successful in enabling her to reach her goal: to make someone hear. Luck was on her side as well, for the attempt did not end in the mistake of death.

EARLY SELF-DESTRUCTIVE CRIES FOR HELP

The tragedy is that someone had not heard her cries before she resorted to a razor across her wrist. She had emitted them, loud and clear, as all suicides do. A young person does not just suddenly take her life; she hints at it a thousand ways. But just as adults in the *Lebenswelt* overlook the signs pointing to homicide, so do they even more ignore the signs toward suicide.

Yet, according to Dr. Shneidman, "Before his death [the teenage suicide] leaves a trail of subtle and obvious hints of his intentions. Every suicide attempt is a serious cry for help." The slit wrist, the bullet shot, the overdose of sleeping pills, the noose—these are the end results of unheard cries.

"What all suicide victims have in common," explains Dr. Calvin Frederick, former assistant chief for the Center for Studies of Suicide Prevention, National Institute of Mental Health, "are intense feelings of *loneliness, helplessness* and *hopelessness.*" That should sound familiar to us. These children are not strangers: they are Wednesday's children, unable to cope with their problems, screaming in pain.

Their distress, Dr. Frederick goes on to say, "is usually brought on by family problems, but all kinds of problems—the failure to make good grades or to be accepted into a school group or an argument with a friend—are magnified in their small world." We have listened to this explanation before. We have listened to the children's cries before. Now, perhaps we will hear them in the last final cry of death.

WE KNOW THESE HELPLESS CHILDREN.

We know Harriet packing her suitcase every two years or so to be driven to other foster parents—a child without attachments, without a home. We know Phil, relentlessly pushed by his father to make it into Harvard. We know Harry, whose alcoholic mother embarrasses him at school. We know Liz, terrified to tell her mother about her stepfather's sexual advances. We know Ethel, the "dumb" one in the family. Trapped in situations from which they see no way out, these children in their helplessness have called for help, but no one noticed. Their final call stifled their cries forever.

WE KNOW THESE HOPELESS CHILDREN.

The hopelessness of young suicide victims resounds through a poem given to me some years ago by a fifteen-year-old girl, who wrote it by hand on lined notebook paper:

> *Did you ever really love a boy*
> *And know he didn't love you?*
> *Did you ever feel like crying*
> *And think what good would it do?*
> *Did you ever see him walking*
> *With his head down low?*
> *Did you ever whisper, "I love you,*
> *But I'll never let you know?"*
> *Did you ever look into his eyes*
> *And say a little prayer?*
> *Did you ever look into his heart*
> *And wish that you were there?*
> *Love is fine but it hurts so much,*
> *The price you pay is high.*
> *If I could choose between love or death,*
> *I think I'd choose to die.*
> *So when I say don't fall in love*
> *You'll be hurt before you're through,*
> *You see, my friend, I ought to know,*
> *I fell in love with you.*

Although hopelessness comes in many forms, they all have one aspect in common—a sense of eternity. The young man will *never* return the poet's love. The son will *never* do well enough to please his parents. The daughter will *always* shake in fear as her parents fight. The child will *never* have a father to love him. The girl will *always* be overweight and ugly. Feeling that the condition of misery is changeless, these young people relinquish dreams of the future. In their hopelessness they obliterate themselves in order to obliterate the inevitable anguish of tomorrow.

Parents found this note beside the bleeding body of their son: "I love you, but there's just no point to going on when you'll never accept me." He was a homosexual.

Never is a long time in the life of a teenager—too long to endure. Michael Wechsler understood this as he asked the question:

"It's a feeling of hopelessness, creeping, casual but sure;
   How much more, Dr. Freud, can I endure?"
Barbiturates answered his question.

WE KNOW THESE LONELY CHILDREN.

"Youth is much lonelier than old age," wrote Anne Frank in her diary, sensitive in her darkened hiding place to the loneliness of all young people. A special person can fill the void of a teenager's life— a "significant other," in the terms of psychologists: a lover, parent, best friend, sometimes a teacher, counselor or grandparent. That one person alone can keep the scale of life-death wishes in balance, supporting the young person through stressors otherwise unbearable.

I heard a four-year-old say to her mother the other day, "You're even a better friend than my best friend." With that mainstay in her life, she will not be lonely.

Yet sometimes the significant other is taken out of the life of the one who needs—through death or moving away or a broken love affair. Then loneliness overwhelms. "When I am alone, I stop believing I exist," a young girl wrote in an effort to explain the emptiness she felt upon breaking up with her boyfriend. Feeling nonexistent, she needed to take only a short step to the razor blade and eternal nonexistence. In her loneliness she was already dead.

Adults left behind in the wake of teenage suicide are traumatized by the impact of the tragedy. They feel as helpless, hopeless and lonely as the young people who took their lives. They cannot find meaning to the act. Yet eighty percent of teenage suicides give warning—in cryptic terms, perhaps, but as surely as the handwriting on the wall gave warning to King Belshazzar. *Mene, mene, tekel, upharsin*, wrote the mysterious hand at the king's feast. When Belshazzar failed to comprehend the meaning of the words, Daniel was called in to translate.

A young college boy wrote a suicide note to his father: "I tried everything, but nothing seemed to help." What had the young boy tried prior to driving his car off a cliff? What suicide notes had he written in the mysterious hand of Babylon that his father did not interpret? Where was the Daniel who might have saved his life?

All of us can be Daniels once we learn the language of adaptive behavior through which distressed children speak. One of the most easily translatable is the language of self-destruction, but we must attune our ears to pick it up. Michael Wechsler's life is the story of a boy in agony screaming for help that could not be given—for Michael's stressor was incurable schizophrenia. His years of self-destruction, however, parallel those of thousands of children who *can* be helped when adults learn what their behavior means.

PSYCHOSOMATIC ILLNESSES

In the days of the family doctor, psychosomatic illnesses were treated as a matter of course, even before the terminology became a part of the doctor's working vocabulary. He knew his patients, their family dynamics, the stresses under which they lived. If a child had repeated headaches, he did not have to send her for the equivalent of a brain scan; he talked to her. Better still, he listened to her. He called in her parents; he phoned her teachers, talking and listening to them as well. He diagnosed and prescribed for her in human terms.

In today's age of specialization, however, it is more difficult to do this. A sore foot sends us to a podiatrist; a skin rash, to a dermatologist; an upset stomach to an internist. Therefore a child with repeated headaches is likely to be treated for headaches before her physician undertakes to isolate the stressors that may cause those headaches. If she is fortunate in her choice of physician, she may receive counseling. If she is truly lucky, she may find herself in the same kind of treatment the old-fashioned general practitioner gave—family therapy. The realization that a child both creates and solves her problems, not alone, but in a family system, has given birth to the spread of this kind of treatment. Although family therapy is being practiced more often, tragically it is not *sought* often enough to save the health and the lives of hundreds of thousands of young people in our country.

Psychosomatic illnesses, adults must remember, are real. They are as real, as painful, as destructive as influenza or tuberculosis. The only difference is that the latter may be brought on by a virus or bacteria, while the former are brought on by stress. In most cases psychosomatic illnesses develop subconsciously; the child does not will them to appear. Although she may say in her stress, "I'll hold my breath till my face turns blue," she will not say, "I'll hold my breath till I get a headache." The headache comes on its own when beckoned from subconscious depths to help solve a problem. It is the body's plea for help.

While forty percent of Americans suffer from chronic stress-related headaches, this is far from the most debilitating psychosomatic illness from which children suffer. Dr. William Liebman in his *Clinical Pediatrics* article "Recurrent Abdominal Pain in Children" claims that about fifteen percent of all children suffer from psychosomatic stomachaches. He further points out that forty-four percent of them are carrying around burdens of parental turmoil, while thirty percent of them suffer from the pressures of achieving. Colic in infants may be a precursor of future stomachaches, an even earlier stress signpost. In the words of the famous Dr. Karl Menninger: "The stomach mirrors the emotions better than any other body system."

Other psychosomatic illnesses related to the stomach also appear with frequency: vomiting, constipation, diarrhea. When my daughter was young, one of her friends vomited whenever stress became too much for her to cope with—even the stress of something pleasant. The youngest of five children, highly pressured toward achievement, she lived in a state of such constant tension that the slightest added stressor pushed her over the edge. Never once did we have her stay overnight without her vomiting either before going to bed or later during the night.

Constipation follows many a distressed child through life. John, now a man in his fifties, has been constipated as long as he can remember. "I can remember as a kid sitting in the corner of my room," he says, "listening in terror to my mother and father scream at each other. I would hear glass break and things thrown against the wall. And I would pull myself in as tight as I could—my arms and legs would tense until the back of my knees and my hands

would go numb. And I could feel my whole insides shutting off."
John has been X-rayed, medicated, given enemas and laxatives
throughout his life, but no one has ever treated his constipation as
the symptom of stress it is. How much pain his parents could have
spared him by settling their conflicts with reasonable instead of hostile arguments. Marriage counselors daily guide couples in this direction; that failing, they find divorce a less destructive solution.

When diarrhea is chronic and stems from nonspecific causes
rather than from something ingested, it is considered psychosomatic.
Dr. Esther Wender at the University of Utah Medical Center found
in her studies a strong correlation between this kind of diarrhea and
behavioral problems among children—specifically, insomnia, crying,
irritability, temper tantrums and lack of empathy. However, in all
my years of working in schools, I have never heard a teacher consider diarrhea or any other illness as a possible correlation to a student's behavior problems. Furthermore, I have only rarely heard a
parent or a doctor contact a teacher in order to investigate a child's
physical problem in relation to possible stresses in school.

Psychosomatic illnesses, some say, act as substitutes for psychological manifestations of stress. Therefore, children who appear emotionally stable may still be suffering stress symptoms as severe as
those of the most difficult behavior problems. They may afflict a
child with asthma, which, according to physician Alexander Meijer
of Hadassah University in Jerusalem, correlates highly with an over-
dependent mother-child relationship. Even earlier, the stress symptom may appear as eczema, which is common among children who
later develop asthma. While it was originally thought that the skin
and respiratory ailments appeared in the same person because of a
physical weakness, it is now generally accepted that their common
bond is one of stress.

Ulcers may be a psychosomatic symptom. We have long accepted
ulcers as a sign of stress in adults—particularly in self-pressured business executives—and we now learn that they are becoming more
common in young people as well. Dr. Norman Mauroner, Associate
Professor of Psychiatry at Louisiana State University, finds ulcers
alarmingly prevalent in children—especially in boys aged six to
twelve. He further finds them related to home problems created by
the immaturity of fathers and feelings of inadequacy of the mothers.

These boys for the most part do not act out their stress, but tend to be "good" children—neat, punctual, earnest, striving to retain their parents' love.

Dentists, also becoming more aware of the effects of stress, find children's mouths rife with telltale signs. Britain's Dr. Marshall Midda, a leader in the field, reports an increase in the following mouth problems which he relates to stress:

— *Canker sores:* ulcerations on the soft red flesh of the mouth. They may start with itching and develop rapidly into painful sores lasting about two weeks.
— *Trench mouth:* ulcers of the gum. Originally found among soldiers during the First World War, from which it derived its name, it now appears with growing frequency among college and high school students under competitive pressure.
— *Bruxism:* grinding and clenching of teeth. This occurs most often at night when even sleep brings no relief from stress. Also, teachers notice it, usually by the grating sound, during examinations.
— *Cheek and lip biting:* Even children as young as two and three injure themselves this way when trapped in stressful situations.
— *Split gums:* Older children will sometimes split their gums with their fingernail, drawing blood and keeping their mouth in a continual state of soreness.

I have presented only the most common and evident psychosomatic stress signs. There may be hundreds more, each unique to a child. As medicine and psychiatry interact more closely, other diseases begin to emerge as stress-related, cancer and diabetes among the most recently recognized.

Perhaps the most encouraging aspect of the new merger of body and mind sciences is the emergence of holistic medicine. This not new, but reborn, field sets forth the principle that since stress can cause disease, positive feelings can cure them. Norman Cousins, Dr. Lawrence LeShan and Dr. Carl Simonton, among others, attest to their success with holistic medicine in recent books. In time, Wednesday's children may be able to rid themselves of illnesses and join their happier Sabbath day peers. Until that time, parents and teachers who observe recurring patterns of sickness in children must not alone relegate them to a physician, but must investigate them as significant signs of stress.

While non-coping children cry out subconsciously through psychosomatic illnesses, they also emit cries with the conscious intent of self-destruction.

ANOREXIA

Anorexia is self-inflicted starvation. The sufferers are usually adolescents, and ninety percent of them are girls. They tend to be overachievers striving for acceptance; perfectionists never reaching a goal. Anorectics become morbidly obsessed with food, losing twenty-five to fifty percent of their body weight in their relentless effort to be thin. One anorectic girl speaks of her self-hatred upon eating a saltine cracker: "I felt so guilty, as if I had soiled myself with a substance that would never wash off. I stuck my finger down my throat and vomited, but I still felt smeared with filth."

Some psychologists feel that anorexia is a young person's way of punishing her parents, who may be overprotective or may be pushing too hard. Others believe that it is a struggle to ward off approaching maturity in order to avoid the sexual battlefield—the wasted body of an anorectic girl will not develop breasts or menstruate. Still others see anorexia as an attention-getting effort to retain parental love as a baby. Whatever the explanation, anorexia is an attempt to gain control over a situation so stressful that the child caught in its grip feels helpless. The anorectic controls her parents through her fleshless body.

OVEREATING

The opposite of anorexia is compulsive eating, the enormity of which is attested to by America's glut of best-selling diet books. Compulsive eaters, like alcoholics, cannot help themselves: they eat to escape stress. They overeat, hate themselves, then overeat again to erase their guilt. Fast-food shops beckon young people with pizza, milk shakes, french fries and double burgers on every street, so that even when they try to avoid eating, the odds are against them. Parents offer little help. They nag and create greater stress. They put them on fad diets, expecting miracles, and force them to fail. They send them to summer diet camps where they win praise for losing a few pounds and develop guilt complexes when they regain them over the winter. As the cries of compulsive eaters resound louder, their bodies swell up bigger, and the only diet to work for them will be cutting down on stressors.

Accidents

Bonnie was constantly hurting herself. As a little child, she was full of cuts and bruises; as she got older, she broke bones—her ankle, once when she fell from a tree, her sternum while playing basketball in school, then three fingers and the little toe on each foot. She broke two bicycles in crashes and once knocked herself unconscious running into a wall.

Stress in Bonnie's life came from many directions: her parents fought openly; her mother was competitively glamorous; her father, a successful physician, worked long hours that excluded his daughter; her younger brother was retarded. She had no close friends although she was attractive in a sexy way and popular with boys. However, she could not cope with the accumulation of stressors in her life, and with no one to turn to, she did the best she could.

The best for her was gaining attention that looked like love; being accident-prone gained her that attention. While she did not deliberately fall and hurt herself, her carelessness pushed her. People healed her wounds; yet they failed to heal her distress. And so, still seeking relief, she fell harder and harder. Her parents picked her up from a final push in her wrecked automobile. Far earlier they might have lightened her load of stress by questioning her accidents instead of shrugging them off with, "There goes Bonnie again!" If their lines of communication with her had blocked, they could have provided a significant other in a friend, relative, teacher or therapist. Unfortunately, they never looked beneath the broken bones and body bruises.

Risk Taking

Self-destructive children are often daredevils. They deliberately put themselves in dangerous situations, as if defying fate to do the job for them. A twelve-year-old girl I know, highly competitive with an older sister, followed the pattern of the accident-prone child described above. Additionally, however, she sought out danger. Her mother found her one day walking along the top of a foot-wide ledge around the roof of their twelve-story apartment building. Not daring to shout, her mother called her gently, and when she jumped down, grabbed and spanked her.

On another occasion her mother saw her walking across a thinly ice-coated pond. She rushed to throw her a rope and then punished her again after pulling her in. This child did not need spankings: she needed coping skills to help her through what she felt was a losing battle with her sister.

SELF-MUTILATION

Children destroy their bodies in a multitude of ways which psychologists identify as signposts to stress. *They bite*—their fingernails, their lips, their tongue, the insides of their mouth. As their inability to cope becomes more extreme, they may actually bite their flesh. I have seen teenagers with teeth marks on their arms or with the sides of their fingers chewed raw.

They tear at themselves — They pick the heads of pimples; they rip the cuticle of fingernails till their hands are red and swollen; they scratch through the skin on their cheek or chest or thighs.

They pull themselves apart — They twist and pull their hair so vehemently that bald spots appear; they pull off toenails, causing a constant inflammation as they become ingrown. I heard of a girl who sat and pulled out her eyelashes during exams at school.

They cut their bodies — With scissors, razors, knives, they slash themselves or poke holes in their skin with pencils, forks and compass points.

They inflict burns — They may hold their hand in a candle flame or set their clothing afire with matches.

INGESTING POISONS

"He eats everything in sight," a young mother complained the other day about her baby as she snatched a cigarette butt from his hands. While it is normal for babies to satisfy their oral needs with any available object, by the time they become toddlers they usually have outgrown the need. If the habit hangs on, parents should question the possibility of undue stress.

Children are known to make themselves sick by eating pencil leads, paint chips, cartridges of ball-point pens. X-rays of children's stomachs have shown an assortment of ingested objects as diverse as paper clips, pins, aluminum foil, coins and eyebrow tweezers.

By the time a child reaches adolescence, the poisons he ingests, while not appearing in X-rays, are far more lethal. Cigarette smoking, which twenty-five years ago may not have been considered self-destructive, today leaves no doubt. The fourteen-year-old daughter of a friend of mine, deep in a depression, smoked several packs a day despite her parents' pleas and warnings. "I don't care what I do to myself," she retorted. Not until five years later, after extensive psychotherapy which restored her feeling of self-worth, was she ready to live and stop smoking.

Drugs, admittedly dangerous, but readily available, allow easy trips to self-destruction. Alcohol abuse begins with an occasional beer or glass of wine and ends up in alcoholism and vital organs eaten away. Marijuana, not so innocuous as once thought, is smoked by as many as twenty percent of high school students regularly and by fifty percent on an occasional basis. Angel dust, LSD, mescaline, amphetamines, barbiturates, cocaine, heroin—teenagers recognize these killers by these and other names. They do not fill their system with them heedlessly when they become drug users: they are well aware of the destination of their trip.

GESTURES

The most significant cry for help heard from self-destructive children is the suicide gesture. Although all the cries we have discussed above are gestures of a sort, they are less graphic. A parent may misinterpret a child's anorexia or nail biting, even drug abuse, failing to relate it to a death wish. A real suicide gesture, however, cannot be misinterpreted. Even though its message is often ignored, it does not come across garbled.

Claire was an unhappy girl in her teens, finding the problems of adolescence difficult to handle. She went to her mother one day, holding out her left arm and laughing.

"Look what I did," she said lightly. Her mother saw across her wrist a red scratch mark, as if from a pin. Not knowing how to react, her mother also laughed.

"Great," she replied, imitating her daughter's flippant tone, "a slashed wrist. Very funny."

"I think so," Claire said as she left.

Three weeks later Claire slit her left wrist with a razor. Yet even as she was on the brink of making her death wish come true, the life wish triumphed: she telephoned her mother at work, screaming for her to come home. Fortunately she came in time to rush Claire to the hospital, save her life and begin to recognize her emotional needs. Had she recognized them sooner, she would not have laughed at Claire's scratched wrist.

"I don't think you're really laughing," she might have said to open a dialogue . . . or, "You must be feeling awfully low to pretend slashing your wrist like that."

Reassured that her mother understood, Claire might have been able to talk, rather than act out her misery.

Not all suicide gestures end so fortuitously. Chuck held a pistol to his head in front of his mother. Hysterically she screamed for his father, who after seeing the gun was empty attacked Chuck for his selfishness in so upsetting his mother.

"I was only kidding," Chuck explained sheepishly.

That night Chuck loaded the pistol and pulled the trigger.

Lettie's father was too busy to include her in his life: he had business trips and weekend meetings and an attaché case full of papers to read at night. He missed the Father-Daughter dinner at school.

"What would happen if I slept for a hundred years?" Lettie asked him as he went to bed.

"You'd be Sleeping Beauty," he tossed back, not looking up.

Several days later, after he left on a business trip, Lettie swallowed a full bottle of her mother's sleeping pills. Her mother found her in time because Lettie threw her comatose body against the door. Her mother, hearing the thud, investigated.

Lettie phoned her father from the hospital. "Why did you do such a thing?" he asked, appalled.

Lettie did not answer. Although her mother had heard the thud of her body against the bedroom wall, neither she nor her husband could hear the sound of their daughter's longing for her father's love. A psychiatrist, required by the hospital to examine Lettie, heard the sound, though, and although he could not change Lettie's father, he was successful in helping Lettie see that her father's lack of affection was *his* problem, not *hers*.

T. S. Eliot calls hell oneself: "Hell is alone," he says. Self-destructive children must agree with him since they seek to eliminate that self which cannot cope with life. They do not decide on whim, however, and in one fell swoop eliminate themselves. On the contrary, they leave a trail of clues far less subtle than those in an Agatha Christie murder mystery. It takes no Hercule Poirot to recognize the hints as evidence; yet parents, teachers and other adults in the child's lifeworld fail to pick them up, even when those hints are dropped before their eyes every day.

The "Help me" of children continues to echo unheard. Stitches repair the flesh of their body; a tourniquet holds back their blood, but no balm heals the open wounds of their life. When they finally resort to suicide, even then they are uttering a cry for help—the last and loudest. They kill themselves for life, not for death.

Who can predict the timing of that final cry? Seven-month-old infants have been known to die of depression. A five-year-old Japanese boy took his life after failing to be accepted in the kindergarten for which his parents had him compete. A nine-year-old threw himself in front of an oncoming train; no one could explain why. A pregnant twelve-year-old gassed herself in the kitchen after her parents called her "dirty."

Thousands of children keep trying to cope with the unbearable, tearing themselves apart both physically and emotionally in an effort to get someone to hear . . . to understand . . . to help.

In the face of death, adults usually hear. But then it is too late to help their helplessness. It is too late to bring hope to their hopelessness. And it is too late to fill the void of their loneliness. That could have been done years ago—or one split second before.

CHAPTER VI

◈

Behavior of Escape

Little Boy Blue, come blow your horn,
The sheep's in the meadow, the cow's in the corn;
But where is the boy who looks after the sheep?
He's under the haystack, fast asleep.

A child psychologist speaks with three-year-old Lucy:

PSYCHOLOGIST: How did you get here today?

LUCY: On the bike. My mommy rides it, and I sit on a special seat in the back. [She is animated.] I have a bike, but it's too little to come this far. When I'm big, I'll get a big bike like Mommy's.

PSYCHOLOGIST: You look very pretty today.

LUCY: I know. [She smiles.] I'm wearing a dress. Mommy said I could pick out whatever I want, and I like this dress best. It's green. That's my favorite color.

PSYCHOLOGIST: I see you are wearing beads too. Are they yours?

LUCY: Oh no, no, no. They're Gammy's [her grandmother's]. She lets me wear them to be fancy. I'm going to wear them when I get married [all excited], and I'm going to wear her rings too. Ten rings, one on each finger. And I'm going to have a cake.

PSYCHOLOGIST: A tall wedding cake?
LUCY: Yes, this tall. [She lifts her arm as high as it will
                go.] And Mommy and I will be on top. Our whole
                family will be on top—Gammy and Grampa and
                Ben and Sally and Bobby and Bill and Erica and
                Shel [aunts, uncles and cousins]. Our whole family.
PSYCHOLOGIST: What about Daddy? Will he be on top too?
LUCY: And the cake will be white and green and pink
                with flowers all over.
PSYCHOLOGIST: Will your daddy be on the cake too?
LUCY: Inside the cake will be chocolate, and everybody can
                have a piece. You can have a piece.
PSYCHOLOGIST: You haven't answered my question: will your daddy
                be on top of the cake too?
LUCY: I can't get married till I'm big, though. I have to
                be six.

Lucy is an incredibly articulate three-year-old, able to express her
thoughts with joy and excitement and to share the give and take of
dialogue. Yet whenever Daddy is brought into the conversation, she
does not hear. Three times the psychologist attempted to elicit a response from the child concerning her father; each time she adroitly
evaded.

Lucy's father abused her sexually. While she was too young to realize what he was doing over a period of about a year, she resisted
and cried whenever he came near. Although her parents are now
divorced, she living with her mother and receiving psychological
help, she continues to carry the burden of her father's behavior.

The burden is too heavy for her. The only way she keeps from
crumbling under its weight is by pretending it is not there. By not
acknowledging her father's existence, she eliminates the pain he
caused her. Like Little Boy Blue, three-year-old Lucy is "under the
haystack, fast asleep." She is running away from reality. Yet it is un-
likely that Lucy will grow up to be Wednesday's child since her
mother is sensitive to the problem and is seeking help for it.

Not all children are so fortunate. For many, avoidance of the
stressors that confront them goes undetected so long that escape becomes their lifestyle. They are eternal fugitives, running from them-

selves, seeking darker and more secure hiding places in order not to detect where they are.

FLIGHT FROM PAIN

Hans Selye in his writings on stress points out the "fight or flight" method of coping. In the two previous chapters, we have discussed fight—aggression and self-destruction—as a child's fists-on method of handling pain. Escape represents the other way—flight. There are probably as many escape routes from the pain of stress as there are children pursued by stressors. Let us examine some of their methods of defense through escape.

MAKING IT GO AWAY

The easiest way to blot out the disagreeable is to close one's eyes. I found myself doing this one evening while watching the film *The Deer Hunter* on television. So brutal were certain scenes that, unable to cope with the horror they aroused in me, I covered my face with my hands, asking my husband to tell me when it was over.

Children use this technique constantly in handling uncomfortable situations. At the simplest level, they do what I did—close their eyes. Adam was painfully shy at two and three, having been raised on a farm where he rarely saw people other than his parents. Visiting his uncle in the city, he was taken on walks and into shops, passing strangers every day. Unable to face people, he began covering his eyes with his hand whenever he went outdoors. Occasionally he would peek out between his fingers to see whether anyone was approaching. If not, he might risk a few seeing steps; if so, he let his small hand make the stranger go away.

Lucy used the same technique with somewhat more sophistication. She blocked her father out of view under persistent attempts by others to bring him in, not with closed eyes, but with closed ears. If she refused to discuss her father, he did not exist.

Battered children may try to escape the complex agony of physical injury, parental rejection and personal guilt by refusing to admit anything is wrong. Teachers questioning repeatedly bruised children receive only a series of excuses: "I fell," or "I ran my bike into a car." Similarly, children cover up the shame of alcoholism in the family or of marital discord or financial troubles: it is easier to cope with such problems when, like Adam and Lucy, they close their eyes.

Brett discovered a different way to erase his problems. He built an emotional wall around himself that allowed no one in and not even himself out. Like a feudal lord in his fortress, Brett kept the world at a distance because the world he knew was unsafe for small boys. His mother had died when he was five, and his father had hired a series of baby sitters to care for him, none remaining very long. His father, busy climbing the executive ladder, gave him little time; when he remarried, he gave him even less.

With no one to turn to, Brett felt frightened and alone. But abandonment when he craved love was too big an ache to endure; so Brett made the ache go away. He withdrew behind his battlements, determined that no outside force would penetrate his feelings again. Numbness knows no pain.

The tragedy of Brett, like that of most children who wall themselves off from emotion, is that he grew up inside his castle and never emerged, even when it was safe. Brett has had two unsuccessful marriages and three children with whom he has only a cursory relationship. He is a lonely man and does not even know it. He feels nothing at all.

Many stressors too painful to bear are pushed from sight by children behind walls of their own making. While autistic children are usually recognizable, cut off as they are from communication with the outside world, the Bretts in our lives easily slip past our notice. They, after all, speak to us and listen to us and, quiet and nonviolent, go through the motions of daily life. Since they cause little trouble, we are apt to overlook the fact that they are no longer with us in an emotional way.

An eleven-year-old gifted child, considered a troublemaker by his teachers and a loner by his classmates, suffered the pain of being different, which in the world of children often means isolation. In order to avoid the pain, he pushed it away, along with his teachers and his classmates. He expressed his withdrawal in a poem:

And so I built myself a wall,
Strong and solid, ten foot tall,
With bricks you couldn't see at all.

There the boy remained, safe in his fortress, while the pain-producing people of the world lived on without him. Until . . .

And then came Sir,
A jovial, beaming, kindly man,
Saw through my wall and took my hand
And the bricks came tumbling down,
For he could understand.

Sir, great nameless man and teacher that he was, read the stress signposts along the escape route this young boy had taken, followed them and released him from his prison. Sir did what we plead with all adults to do: he understood.

Procrastination is another way children find to make a problem go away.

"Have you done your homework?"

"Are you dressed for church?"

"Did you clear the table?"

"Are you in bed yet?"

To these queries the non-coping child repeatedly answers, "In a minute." The minute drags on until the question is asked again . . . and again . . . and again. Stalling is a no-fail way to avoid facing a stressor.

By stalling, not only does a child avoid an unpleasant task, be it homework, church, household chores or bedtime, he also avoids confronting a larger problem: his feelings toward his parents. The act over which he is procrastinating may not be the issue at all. It may more realistically be desire for greater control of his life . . . feelings of inadequacy . . . resentment toward his parents and desire to punish them. By putting off the task assigned him, he is able to evade the larger issue with which he feels inadequate to cope. In short, procrastination can be a diversionary tactic.

The mind serves human needs effectively, and there are few better ways to erase life's problems than by forgetting them. My husband brought this fact home to me years ago. When taking a psychological test required for a job application, he was asked to list four important events of his childhood.

"I couldn't think of a single one," he told me that night.

"What do you mean? You couldn't think of any childhood event that was important?" I asked.

"No," he said. "I couldn't think of any damn childhood event at all."

On that day, twenty-five years after the childhood he could not remember, my husband learned that he had totally blocked it out. His had not been a happy childhood, but he did not know how unhappy it was until he came face to face with the device he had used to survive it: escape.

Children do this to a lesser degree every day for a similar reason—to enable them to cope. They forget to hand in homework or to bring notebooks to class or to take their assignment pads home at night when school is a defeating experience for them. They forget to go on errands that make them uncomfortable. They forget social activities if they expect to have a bad time. They forget a dentist appointment if there is a ball game after school.

I am not talking about pretend forgetting, where a child lies his way out of a chore by saying, "I forgot." I am talking about honest-to-goodness forgetting, a trick of the mind to eliminate the unpleasant. I have seen children forget the name of a teacher in whose class they sit every day. I heard of a little girl who forgot the name of her brother after he died. I knew a ten-year-old boy who every single week forgot that he was to go to his father's house after school on Friday, not to his own home where he lived with his mother.

Sometimes children make the stressors in their lives go away by turning them into something else—music, for instance. My daughter used to sit down at the piano and play, not always well, but passionately for an hour or so when she was in the throes of high school. Both of my sons wrote poetry to drive off their hurts. Truman Capote began his writing career as an emotional escape, explaining it this way: "I always felt that nobody was going to understand me, going to understand what I felt about things. I guess that's why I started writing."

Sometimes young people turn their stressors into dreams, even as adults do. When they cannot bear to confront a reality, they may find themselves working through it in one of the game-playing guises our mind delivers in a dream.

Gloria serves as a good example here. At fifteen, she felt like a washout, pale in comparison to her popular, bouncy sister, growing more and more pale the more her sister bounced. Inside she yearned to scream out, "I'm here. Look at me," but outside she meekly filled the role of introvert to which she had been assigned.

Then she began having a recurrent dream: she was lying in a casket on a tilted platform. Her family and friends stood around, sad that she was dead, placing flowers and jewels around her on the platform. Only she was not dead. She longed to yell out to them that she was alive, but she was afraid of embarrassing them. So she remained still, playing the part of a corpse.

The dream plagued her. Night after night she dreaded going to sleep, knowing she would have to relive the frustration of her dream. Finally, with the help of a therapist, she gained insight into the fact that she was using the dream to act out pain too unbearable to face in real life. She realized that even though she was not like her extroverted sister, she was a living, breathing person with assets to contribute to the family and to her peer group. Her parents could have guided her toward that realization earlier by expressing more support and enthusiasm for her own unique talents and personality.

Even young children frequently escape difficult situations through dreams, converting their stressors into animals, witches and monsters. What they may be pushing from their consciousness is lack of love from a parent, a sense of inadequacy, too much competition, sexual fears, guilt or a dread of their own power, among others. Whatever it is, the stressors are too overwhelming to be met head on; dreams form a temporary escape hatch.

Finally, young people are apt to turn their stressors into fears, even into phobias. A first-grader who walked with his older brother to school each morning developed a school phobia after the birth of a baby sister. He was afraid of meeting monkeys on the street that would jump on his back and tear at him. Actually, although he was excited about the new baby, he was jealous of her, resenting his mother's being with her all day while he was at school. The monkeys he feared were his own anger, which raged to tear the baby apart. Unable to admit the ambivalence of his love-hate feelings, he got rid of them through his phobia.

Terry's father kidnapped her from nursery school one day, overriding a court order that gave her mother custody. When he returned her the next day, the little girl ran and hid in the corner of a closet.

"There are bad wolves out there," she insisted. Of course there were—for her. They were her father, whose erratic behavior had so frightened her that she could not accept it. Fathers do not scare children: wolves do.

Children's fears should always be taken seriously, never shrugged off or laughed away. We know there is no bear in the closet. When a child, however, knows there *is* a bear in the closet, that bear is real.

When Jesse was two, he suddenly developed a fear of thunder. It soon extended into a fear of rain, which he associated with thunder. At the first drop he would scream, and even his mother's enfolding arms could not assuage his fear. No one understood what had happened to bring on so violent a fear so suddenly.

It was not until almost a year later that Jesse was able to express himself. He had seen a tree branch swept to the ground by a storm. "The tree lost an arm in the storm, didn't it?" his father had commented. Not giving his statement another thought, he was as confused as everyone else over the onset of his son's fear.

But the little boy had lived in terror during even a light spring shower that like the tree, he too would lose an arm. How much easier life would have been for all of them if he had only defined his fear! He could not, though; the dread being too great for him to handle, he could only push it off on the rain. How much easier life would have been for all of them if his parents had only been able to interpret his behavior!

MAKING YOURSELF GO AWAY

Some children escape problems not by making their stressors go away, but by making themselves go away: they simply leave the scene. Most of the time, departure is so subtle that even their parents remain unaware of their absence, and therein lies the trouble.

Sleep is an easy exit for those who find life too painful to face. Even newborn infants, distressed from difficult births or separation from their mothers, are reported sleeping far more than their newborn neighbors whose births have not been traumatic or whose mothers spend time with them. The latter, apparently content, lie in what doctors call alert wakefulness, while the former seem to escape their stress through sleep.

While stressed preschool and school-age children do not often use sleep as an escape (in fact, they tend to become insomniacs if they use sleep as a defense at all), occasionally a child will find this works. Claudine, for instance, whose home life was unstable and destructive, tried to cope by taking long naps. Even at four, she slept two hours in the morning and as long as three in the afternoon. When she entered morning kindergarten she had to relinquish the safety of her nap, but slept the afternoons away. While she was clearly sending out an SOS, her mother not only failed to hear it, but actually encouraged her long naps, which gave her free time. If consulted, a child psychologist would have suggested that she limit the nap to about an hour.

The happiest teenagers can sleep till noon on weekends, much to the annoyance of their parents. The unhappiest can sleep all afternoon as well. Neil testifies to that. Although he had been a happy child during his early years, by the time he reached his teens, social pressures became too much for him to cope with. Having put on thirty pounds, he did not join boys in sports and was considered unattractive by girls. Instead of developing his own interests when he was excluded from his classmates' activities, he moped, following his parents around the house, listless and bored. Instead of sensing his hurt, however, his parents turned on him in their frustration. So Neil escaped to his room, where he slept away what he could not face—weekend after weekend after weekend.

Television is the next best thing to sleep, for children can become absorbed in it with total passivity. Not Lucy, whom we met earlier: she watches "Romper Room" going through each activity with the teacher and the class; she watches "Mr. Rogers," guessing what color sweater he will don, talking back to Lady Elaine and shouting out answers to questions. Television is no escape to her; it is involvement, for she is a child born on the Sabbath day.

To Wednesday's children, however, whether preschoolers or teens, television is a narcotic. Slouched down in comfortable chairs or lying on the floor, children watch and do not watch at the same time. The late Dorothy Cohen of the Bank Street School of Education once told me, "If parents realized that their children had a box of heroin in the living room, they would throw it out. The television set is more numbing and more dangerous; and not only don't parents throw it out, they put it in their children's room and close the door."

Teachers see a relationship between turned-off students and turned-on television, attributing poor marks to time overspent on TV. I think they have the process reversed. Young people do not become poor students because they watch too much television: on the contrary, they watch too much television because they have become poor students. Their feelings of academic inadequacy and their resulting lack of interest in studies send them to television for escape. On the other hand, good students, finding personal satisfaction in their studies, have no need to run away to the TV set.

Unfortunately, teachers communicate their beliefs to parents, who, grasping at any miracle to convert their F children into A students, hang their hopes on television.

"You can't watch television till you've done your homework," becomes the war cry.

Or, "No more television till you pull up your marks."

Having taken action, parents feel better, but the result is rarely improved marks or more arduous homework habits. Why? Because television was not the problem in the first place. The problem was stress within the child, which neither parents nor teachers saw beneath a poor school record. Since an overworked television set was no more the problem than a cough is in pneumonia, limiting hours is about as effective as cough syrup.

While we are on the subject of school, let us briefly examine the other side of the coin. *Some children use an immersion in studies rather than an avoidance of them as their escape.* For instance, Leslie, seeing no more of herself than her thick eyeglasses and stringy hair, gave up competing socially with her classmates. In her mind the cards were stacked, and she refused to submit herself to the hurt of being left out. Instead she took herself away from the battleground by plunging into academics like a fanatic. She used free periods and lunch hour, when her classmates gathered, to study; she spent weekends at her desk; she skipped class games after school; she dropped extracurricular activity. True, she ranked first in her class, and she put on a good show of scorning her classmates' social life; but she was lonely and bitter, a deeply unhappy girl.

Playacting is another effective way for children to avoid dealing with stressors: they make themselves go away into someone else. Little Lucy loves to playact. She held a small book her father had given her when she returned from a visit with him the other day. When her mother asked to see it, Lucy slid right into a role.

"Now I'm going to show it to all the children," she announced in her teacher voice, holding up the book. Her mother leaned over to look. "No, it's not your turn yet," she said patronizingly with a little smile. "First Jennifer. Then you." And so she continued her school scene, evading the conflict between two lives, until her mother suggested a bath. Then she was Lucy again, all laughs and splashes in the tub.

Playacting has the ability to take all of us away from our troubles. Thousands of struggling actors enjoy bit parts in regional theaters far away from home and family. Overworked homemakers and business people spend long rehearsal hours in amateur productions. Children audition for school plays, heart in throat and life on the line. Those who are cast in parts have an escape: they can lose themselves and become anyone from the Pied Piper to Hamlet.

Those who are not cast may still escape by casting themselves in roles in the drama of their everyday lives. One girl may play the siren, another the sympathetic listener. One boy may put on a macho act, another become the hippie. Just as surely as though they were treading the theater boards, they are running away from whatever hurts by assuming the role of someone else on the proscenium of their lives.

While the make-believe of role playing can well serve as escape, it is only temporary because the child is aware of his game. Lucy was pretending to be a teacher, and she knew it, dropping the role as soon as the bath water ran. When playacting extends beyond the realm of reality, however—that is, when the actor no longer knows he is acting—the actor enters a world of fantasy.

Sometimes it is difficult for parents to tell on which side of the brink their children are hovering. Casey is an example of both sides. As a little boy, he developed imaginary friends—Monty and Klug— who lived in his closet. They emerged to attend kindergarten with him, where they turned out to be extremely disruptive members of the class.

When Casey threw blocks, he announced, "Look what Monty did."

When Casey pushed a child, he scolded, "Go to the corner, Klug. You are a bad boy."

Casey reported his imaginary friends' antisocial behavior in minute detail at home, often punishing them by relegating them to the closet for an entire day. So realistically did he include them as part of the family, that when I was visiting there one day I almost stepped on one of them. "Don't walk there," Casey yelled at me. "Monty's playing marbles." I walked around him.

Yet, throughout his relationship with Monty and Klug, Casey knew what he was doing: he was not fooling us and he was not fooling himself. He was using his friends, as author Selma Fraiberg says, "to personify his Vices like characters in a morality play." Casey had developed a conscience, and to prevent its hurting he avoided accountability for his misdeeds by attributing them to his imaginary friends. It was a workable coping device.

However, Casey, unlike most children, hung on to Monty and Klug through first and second grade. In third grade Klug vanished, but Monty became even more real—so much so that Casey's mother actually believed there was a child in his class by that name.

"It's not your old friend Monty?" she asked.

With sincerity Casey replied, "Oh no, this Monty is a real boy. It's funny he has the same name."

Monty tore Casey's papers and excluded him from a birthday party. Monty would not even talk to Casey on the telephone. Then one day Casey cut his finger and, unaware that his mother had seen him do it, he said, "Look what Monty did to me." And Casey's mother knew that her little boy had lost himself somewhere between make-believe and fantasy. Only later with outside help did she learn the reason—that Casey found it impossible to cope with his feelings of rejection as an adopted child.

Daydreams, like imaginary friends, can be constructively used as a coping technique. We are all familiar with James Thurber's Walter Mitty, the insignificant little man who scaled the heights of heroism in his imagination, winning both girl and glory. His daydreams, like those of many children, enabled him to endure his own self-image. Dr. Jerome Singer of Yale and Ellen Switzer, in their recent book *Mind Play*, claim that children who daydream are a great deal happier than those who do not.

Even adults use daydreams positively, developing ways to take mind trips to pleasant places that give them a ten-minute respite from the harassments of the working day.

When daydreams replace reality, however, they become destructive. For instance, John Wilkes Booth, raised in the shadow of a famous grandfather, father and brother, dreamed of acclaim resounding to drown out theirs. He found that fame when he leaped on stage after he had assassinated the President.

Recently two teenagers built a reincarnation fantasy, embellishing the image of their return after death with such adornments that they too forgot reality. They drove a car into a brick wall. In less dramatic language, children who dream of school achievement instead of striving to achieve it and children who dream of peer success while withdrawing to isolation and children who dream of contributions to the world without setting goals—they too drive into brick walls. While Walter Mitty amuses readers, young people who find a strong self-image only by escaping into fantasyland and becoming someone else are not amusing. They are dangerous to themselves and to others.

Each year tens of thousands of Wednesday's children find daydreams inadequate: they escape their conflicts by actually running away. They run from small towns and the discipline of home to independence in big cities like New York "where the action is." The action for them turns out to be pimps, prostitution and crime. Or they run from loneliness to life on a commune where, when group living creates its inevitable hostilities, they find disillusionment. Or they run from cynicism to join cults where, according to contributor Thom Shanker writing in an Anti-Defamation League Bulletin, they seek "an element of being born again or starting over." For them rebirth eliminates family, friends and past life.

Runaways are the most tragic escapees of all, for whether they cut

off family ties by order of the cult leader or through their own
shame at what they have done, they become lost, wandering souls.
Their parents, halfway around the world or the country, suddenly
empty in their empty homes, rarely realize that their children have
been running away for years.

ESCAPE THROUGH SEX

In his book *Teenage Sexuality*, psychiatrist Aaron Hass reports the
following:

— That forty-two percent of the boys and girls in his study had
  experienced sexual intercourse by the time they were sixteen.
— That thirty-three percent of thirteen-year-old girls consider it
  acceptable for boys to fondle their breasts.
— That twice that number—sixty-six percent—of fifteen-year-old
  girls consider it acceptable for boys to fondle their breasts.
— That seventy-eight percent of fifteen- and sixteen-year-old girls
  approved of touching a boy's genitals.

Let us add to this the findings of Dr. Robert Hatcher of the Gyn-
ecology and Obstetrics Division of Emory University School of Medicine:

— That more than a million girls aged fifteen to nineteen become
  pregnant each year.
— That over thirty thousand girls under fifteen become pregnant
  each year.
— That together, this means that ten percent of all U.S. teenagers
  get pregnant every year.

In the light of these facts, it is obvious that sex is a major preoccu-
pation of America's young people. They see movies like *Pretty Baby*
and *Little Darlings* in which teenagers like themselves play sex
games, and they determine, "I'm going to have fun too." They listen
to sexual innuendos on television and sing along with them as their
records blare. They know something pretty exciting is going on out
there; yet they live under the moral stress of parents who act as
though sex does not exist. What can they do but escape into a world
where very little else exists!

Sex is the escape of the lonely. What surer sign of love can young people cling to than arms wrapped around their naked body? When Nell's mother expressed revulsion upon learning that her daughter had been having intercourse regularly with her boyfriend, Nell articulated the feelings of many young people:

"Even in the back seat of a car with my skirt over my head, I get more love and respect from him than I ever got from you."

Sex is also the escape of failures. "I feel like somebody when I'm inside you," a young man told his girl. He was not sharing the sexual embrace; he was using it, and he was using her as well. He could find no more effective way to obliterate his failures at school, the disgrace he brought his parents and the anger he felt toward himself than through sexual intercourse. Nell could find no more tangible way to convince herself of her female identity than to feel a fetus in her womb.

Every year about 700,000 teenage girls become pregnant unintentionally. Sex education is available to them; contraceptives are dispensed free of charge. They do not want babies, yet they still become pregnant. The reason has to be given in psychological, not in intellectual terms, for the majority of these girls know better.

First, they get pregnant because in the escape world of their sexual fantasies, "nice" girls do not plan to have sex. It just happens as they are swept away by romance. No amount of contraceptive knowhow will outweigh the yearning for love that these girls feel. They will continue to run away from the misery of their lives and of themselves into a sexual dream.

Second, young girls get pregnant because they want someone who is all their own. Parents—even the best of them—have to be shared, and few sexually active girls report their parents among the best. Boyfriends come and go, but a baby belongs forever. In an article in the *Journal of Clinical Psychology*, Dr. R. Dean Coddington reported on a study of pregnant girls aged fourteen to nineteen. Almost half of them had just lost a grandparent; a fifth of them, a parent. Thirty-nine percent had a hospitalized parent; twenty-eight percent, a hospitalized sibling. Twenty percent had recently faced the death of a parent.

Dr. Coddington reported findings of a similar study conducted by Rosenthal and Rothchild of teenage girls referred for abortion.

Thirty-five percent of them had lost a close person within the year. It appears evident in the light of such studies and from our own experience that a large number of teenage girls suffering the loss of a significant other in their lives run to a boy and to the hope of a baby.

ESCAPE THROUGH DRUGS

Heather is an attractive college freshman today. Four years ago she was an alcoholic. An extremely shy girl, she had been overshadowed by a dynamic mother and under-loved by a passive father. She hardly dared answer a question in class for fear of error; she declined invitations from her classmates—the few that were extended—certain that she would dress and speak and act incorrectly. Self-conscious and self-hating, she went unsmiling through the routine motions of living.

But Heather discovered a way to cope. If she downed a few jiggers of rye in the morning, she could face school without dread: her teachers even commented upon her cheerier "Good morning." If she tried a few more after school, she could face a lonely evening without wishing she were dead. Her parents were pleased at the disappearance of her depression.

Soon, however, the efficacy of two shots of rye diminished, and Heather doubled the dose. She also filled an empty vitamin pill bottle, carrying it in her purse to drink at lunch. By the time Heather's parents realized what she was doing, she was drunk a good part of the time—passing out at night, waking with hangovers and blacking out whole sections of her day. At fourteen Heather was an alcoholic.

She is not a lone case in the United States in the eighties. Teenage problem drinkers number over a million, the majority starting in junior high school and some far younger. According to the Texas Commission on Alcoholism, "There have been some children under the age of ten admitted to state hospitals."

Edmund G. Addeo, author of *Why Our Children Drink*, attributes teenaged drinking to four main reasons:

— Because parents set an example of drinking in the house.
— Because peers drink and the pressure to be one of the group is strong.

— Because young people find drinking an easy way to rebel against adult authority.

— Because drinking teenagers are in a state of "anxiety, insecurity, extreme self-consciousness, with a lack of self-confidence and a strong self-image."

Here we have a description once again of Wednesday's children, escaping themselves through alcohol.

While alcohol is the nation's Number One drug, marijuana runs a close second, with close to a third of teenagers smoking it more than occasionally. The fact, however, may be even worse than the statistics indicate for in the words of Dr. Robert L. DuPont, former head of the National Institute on Drug Abuse, "Far from being the fad it was in the 1960s and 1970s, we will see drug abuse as one of the enduring problems of human existence."

What the name of the drug is matters far less than its availability. Marijuana is grown in window boxes; cocaine is served at fashionable parties; hallucinogens are cultivated from do-it-yourself kits; uppers and downers are bought over drug counters; inhalants come in paint and glue cans and in the gas tanks of automobiles. Even heroin can be found in the schoolyard.

Surprisingly, the increase in alcohol use among young people has not resulted in a decrease in drug abuse. The National Institute on Drug Abuse reported the following increases within a five-year period:

Marijuana:	Young people	100% increase
	Adults	50% increase
Cocaine:	Young people	400% increase
	Adults	100% increase
Heroin:	Young people	100% increase
	Adults	0% increase

Angel dust, one of youth's major drugs, cannot even be measured by increase since it was practically nonexistent until three or four years ago. It now heads the danger list.

Like alcohol, drugs are reaching down into elementary schools: children as young as eight and nine carry joints during lunch; two fifth-graders killed themselves recently sniffing glue; twelve-year-olds are a common sight in drug rehabilitation centers. A four-year-old preschooler was heard playing "junkie" with his friend.

Why are young people turning to drugs? In the light of increasing pressures in their lives, we hardly need ask the question. "Abused drugs make people feel good," says Dr. DuPont. "They are powerful reinforcing substances."

Young drug users echo his words:

"I begin to feel I'm the greatest man on earth," says one.

"Drugs relax me," says another, "like when I'm all keyed up."

"I'm going to have a good time when I pop a few pills," explains a third.

Or simply, as one puts it, "It gets me away from all this shit."

When what is now called the New York State Division of Substance Abuse Services questioned young people about their motivation for drug taking, they tabulated the answers into twenty-two separate categories ranging from "To get high" and "To be cool," all the way to the other extreme—"To get down" and "To hurt someone." "As different as all these reasons seem," the report stated, "there is one common thread. People usually take drugs to change the way they feel: to feel better; to feel happy; to feel nothing; to forget; to remember; to be accepted; to be sociable. To be something different from what they are."

We could summarize the tabulated reasons and the conclusions of the report itself into two words: to cope. Young people take drugs in order to cope with stresses they consider unbearable otherwise—"to deal with some kind of internal pain," in the words of Harvard Medical School's Dr. Lester Grinspoon.

ESCAPE THROUGH ILLNESS

The subject of coping through escape is not complete without a brief look at hypochondria. Not to be confused with psychosomatic illness, which manifests itself in *physical symptoms*, hypochondria comes from the mind with only *imaginary symptoms*. Yet it accounts for twenty million hospital visits a year and fifteen billion dollars in medical costs.

While the typical hypochondriac is an adult female, anyone who has raised children or taught them in school has met younger counterparts. They are high school girls who have imaginary cramps so severely every month that they stay home. They "know" their leg is broken when they fall. They self-diagnose cancer with the release of the latest report. They read *Death Be Not Proud* and develop a brain tumor; *Love Story*, and have leukemia.

While hypochondriacs may display no physical symptoms of illness, neither do they actually lie to feign them. They *think* they are sick because they *need* to be sick. "To be sick is to find a haven in a demanding, pressure-filled world—a compelling invitation," writes *Medical Dimensions Magazine* editor Bernice Kanner Mosesson in *Working Woman*. So the young hypochondriac, unable to handle the pressures of school, of her peer group, of her parents and siblings, imagines illnesses into which she can sink.

Then, instead of having to achieve in the classroom, she relaxes in bed. Instead of having to compete socially, she surrenders herself to her friends' sympathy. Instead of having to meet parental demands, she becomes a baby again, catered to and cared for. And instead of vying for place with a sibling, she wins by default.

With life overpowering them, Wednesday's children feel impotent; it is only a short step from there to feeling sick. Jocelyn felt she was talentless, but she found it easy to develop the diseases her physician father discussed at home. She limped around with sprained ankles, wore slings on strained arms and even spent a week in bed having convinced her father she had mumps. Paige used a different tactic: she came down with the symptoms her classmates had. She survived colitis, mononucleosis, ulcers and pleurisy and was working into a bad case of lead poisoning when she learned that her friend was vomiting from pregnancy instead!

An old Yiddish proverb defines the greatest pain as that which you cannot tell others. Wednesday's children feel the greatest pain, and the poultice they apply for relief is escape. Yet running away, whatever the form it takes, is no panacea; for though their remedy may dull the pain temporarily, it does not eradicate it. Their wounds will continue to fester until the adults in their lives learn the art of healing and care enough to practice it when their children's gash first appears.

CHAPTER VII

◆

Behavior of Apathy

Sing, sing, what shall I sing?
The cat's run away with the pudding string.
Do, do, what shall I do?
The cat has bitten it quite in two.

THE WALKING DEAD

"What do you want for breakfast?" Jessica's mother asked as her daughter slouched over the table.

"I don't care."

Her mother made a few attempts to whip up enthusiasm. "How about pancakes?" No response. "French toast?" No response. In disgust she poured the usual bowl of Cheerios, put them before Jessica and went into her room to finish dressing.

She dropped Jessica off at school—a half hour early so she could get to work in time—where Jessica sat in the hall alone, staring at the wall, with whose cracks she had become familiar over the preceding year.

A taxi took her home after school, where the maid gave her milk and cookies while she watched soap operas on television. When her mother returned, Jessica was watching the evening news without even realizing it.

"What did you do in school today?" her mother asked vigorously.

"Nothing."

"Oh come on, you did *something*," she teased.

"We never do anything," was Jessica's only reply. In frustration her mother picked up the evening paper while her daughter wandered into the kitchen to see what was for dinner.

Jessica is bored with school. She is bored with her classmates too. "They're no fun," she complains.

She enjoys a new toy or game only for the first few minutes after opening it, then lays it aside to gather dust. Her uncle took her to the circus, but halfway through she had seen enough and nagged to come home.

Jessica is five years old.

Eric Hoffer, the people's philosopher, points out that when people are bored, it is not with the world, but with themselves. Jessica substantiates his thought, for although each day's newness brings an array of wonders to stir the soul, Jessica's soul beholds them lifeless. So dormant and dull lies Jessica's soul that it bores even her.

But Jessica is only five years old. With only five years on earth—a mere two hundred and sixty short weeks—life should still dawn with the thrill of novelty if nothing else. The gamut of emotions with which a five-year-old might respond is an adventure in itself. What a combination of wonders awaits her: not only a red morning sky, but her incredulity at seeing it . . . not just a baby doll that cries, but her instinct to nurture it . . . a loud "No," from her mother, along with her own sudden rage . . . fear of the dark and the comfort of nearby voices . . . the painted smile of a clown and her own real laughter. To a five-year-old life should be a four-star movie with scene after scene of action-packed drama to involve her, with tears and giggles, screams and shouts of joy.

If Jessica's mother found her daughter more interesting than her job, if she offered the little girl more stimulation than television, if she herself responded to life with enthusiasm, perhaps then Jessica could rejoice. But Jessica's mother is lifeless too.

Children come into the world equipped with life's greatest asset—

curiosity. Long before they can talk, they seem to ask themselves eternal questions: How? What? Where? Who? Why? When? In searching for answers, they learn to taste and crawl and wiggle their toes and smile and cry and hide in their mother's arms. They discover. They grow. They respond to every minute of their living.

Seth is seven months old. When I hold him, his hands and his eyes explore my face with intensity. "What is that?" he seems to ask, poking my chin.

"Why does this move?" . . . as he grabs my lips.

"Will that come off?" . . . as he twists my nose.

"How can I get rid of this?" . . . as he pulls my hair.

And then with a cry of triumph he has my eyeglasses off, waving them in the air with the look of all those for whom learning suddenly dawns. "I know, I know," he shouts in the foreign but intelligible language of babies.

His three-year-old sister Nancy is equally curious. When she comes to visit, she heads for the bedroom and my top dresser drawer, before which she stands waiting for me to give the nod. Then she has it open, and with the hushed expectation of Howard Carter discovering the tomb of Tutankhamen, she commences to explore.

She pulls out strings of beads, circling her neck with them until she is top-heavy. She finds bracelets and rings, commenting in a running patter of, "It's beautiful. May I put it on? I'll be very careful."

She uncovers a stray earring and announces, "I'll find the other, I know." Perfume . . . a misplaced bankbook . . . two stamps . . . a stick of chewing gum . . . hair combs—she finds uses for them all as her little hands carry out the orders of her busy mind.

At last she unearths a yellow box, running to me with, "May I?" while her head bobs up and down to encourage my affirmative. She places it on my bed, smoothing the spread around it before lifting the lid. Then slowly, barely breathing, she uncovers the box, pausing intermittently to gasp at its contents. Of course, she has seen its contents before—on every visit—yet the wonder of what lies within has not faded.

In both hands she holds a tiara, somewhat bent and tarnished, glittering with very fake diamonds. In front of the mirror she places it on her head, and suddenly she is no longer my three-year-old friend, but a queen of regal bearing.

The poet Carl Sandburg believed that "the greatest to which man can achieve is wonder." Nancy finds everything around her a constant source of wonder. It excites her, be it the five-day-a-week experience of school or the first-in-a-lifetime Macy's Thanksgiving Day parade. Her own responses to life's events excite her as well—even the familiar ones that she anticipates, like her awe over my tiara—because Nancy loves herself and loves life too exuberantly to be bored. "Ho-hum," does not lodge in her vocabulary.

Nancy is a Sabbath day child. She is alive and curious and happy, despite the combined traumas of her father's recent death and her being transplanted to another city. Secure in her mother's love and in her place in the extended family of grandparents, aunts, uncles and cousins, Nancy copes. She does more than that: she joys.

Jessica, on the other hand, is Wednesday's child. She does not search the corners of her life for the hidden treasures they hold: she is no adventurer. She does not thrill to the colors and noises of fun; she does not recognize them. Nor does she reach to someone she loves to feel the spontaneous warmth of a hand, the security of an arm around her, the nest of a lap; she is indifferent. "He who can no longer pause to wonder and to stand rapt in awe is as good as dead," Einstein once said. Jessica is dead. At five years old.

On a rainy day not long ago, Jessica followed her mother listlessly around the house, whining, "What can I do?" Miles away, Nancy grabbed the afghan from her bed, dragged a chair over to the window and wrapped herself up. "Isn't it warm and cozy?" she asked rhetorically as she snuggled down. That is the difference between apathy and life.

To Jessica there are no wonders, for she has closed the safety valve of her senses. She found that living hurt, with a mother too busy to give her love and a father too eagerly giving love to other women to make room for a wife and daughter. It hurt so much that she turned herself off. The sights and smells and sounds and tastes and touches of life, swirling as they are around her, ricochet like bullets against stone. Jessica has become impenetrable.

Psychologists have a name for the defense mechanism Jessica uses, at least when it reaches the clinical stage. Depersonalization, they call it—"a particular change in awareness of the self, a change in the awareness of the external world . . . a lack of feeling." People use it, particularly children, when their life trauma becomes too much to bear.

Dr. Aida McKellar of Baylor's Department of Psychiatry reported on a young Lebanese boy who demonstrated total indifference to his environment. Having been torn from his family and friends during the Lebanese civil war, he became depersonalized as a way of surviving anguish. By cutting off all his feelings, he was able to cut off the pain and panic of his tragedy.

"Acute stress is an important cause of depersonalization . . . It is a response to overwhelming calamity," writes Dr. McKellar in the *Southern Medical Journal*. The Lebanese boy's calamitous situation jolts us; yet we do not have to single out a war orphan to feel the impact of a child's tragedy. Hundreds of thousands of American children awake to tragedies every morning, carry them around all day and hide under covers at night in a struggle to push them off into the dark.

These are not the tragedies of war or catastrophes that stir the nations of the world, but tragedies within families, and nobody knows. These are the tragedies of being unloved or of feeling unloved, and to a child there is no difference . . . of neglect or of overprotectiveness, both of which destroy a child's feeling of worth . . . of failure, which erases identity with its stereotype, and of success, which does the same. Yet, unlike the Lebanese boy, the children caught in these tragedies are expected to get through a normal day: eat breakfast, attend school, do homework, coexist with parents and brothers and sisters, complying with social demands. How can they do it?

Dr. McKellar gives us an answer. "Depersonalization," she writes, "is a performed cerebral response which serves as a primitive protective device called into action when fear and anxiety threaten to overwhelm the individual." In other words, under the stress of his unbearable situation, the Lebanese boy's mind knew that he could not cope: the fear he felt and the sense of loss were too extreme for him to handle. His brain, therefore, like a *deus ex machina*, sent a defense mechanism to ensure his survival. It eliminated his terror; yet, unable to be selective, in the process it was forced to eliminate his feelings altogether.

Even as removed from the horrors of war as we have been, we are able to comprehend the self-protective device the Lebanese boy used. Ironically, however, we tend to overlook a similar device used by our own children when they also suffer from stress too severe to handle. Granted, in most cases they do not actually resort to depersonalization in the psychological sense, but they resort to the next best thing, or the next worst thing: a state of apathy. They too, unselectively, smother all feeling.

Jessica is the lost Lebanese child; she is countless children in families across our own country. They too have been torn from their parents, by hostility or divorce or lovelessness. They too live in dread —of another parental fight, another beating, another sign of rejection. And they too are disoriented in a world that makes no sense. They see nothing to laugh at; they dare not love; and it hurts too much to cry. Therefore, they call repeatedly upon their *deus ex machina* to help them survive by making them feel nothing at all.

Although it would be impossible to examine all the sources from which a child's apathy might stem, let us here look at some of the major ones.

SOURCES OF APATHY

PHYSICAL CAUSES

Children who are sick usually lack energy. We ourselves know that with a bad cold or a case of flu, all we want to do is lie down and be left alone. Similarly, we cannot expect—nor do we expect—a child with measles, chicken pox or whatever to be bursting with zest. Yet parents and teachers will often nag and prod a listless child who has an illness that is just as virulent, but less visible. For example, children suffering from anemia or low blood sugar appear apathetic. Mononucleosis, frequently undiagnosed, saps a child's energy. Hormone imbalances and glandular malfunctions drain a child's pep. Since these conditions do not proclaim themselves with red spots, however, parents and teachers easily overlook them.

Tommy, for instance, sat in school all day staring out the window. His teachers called him lazy and punished him with extra homework assignments. His parents nagged him to complete them. "I don't know what to do with that boy," they sighed, and they were right: they did not know what to do with him. What they did was scold and prod and punish. What they should have done was take him to the doctor, who would have discovered a serious thyroid deficiency. Tommy's metabolism was too low to supply him with the energy required to perform routine daily tasks. The school nurse finally forced the issue.

Millions of children around the world suffer from malnutrition. Their deep eyes stare lifelessly at us in newspaper photographs as they stand naked with distended bellies. They spend lives, not of wonder, but of waiting—for a piece of bread from the Red Cross, milk from UNESCO, a handful of rice from CARE . . . and waiting too for death. Photographs of our own undernourished children appear less often—children from Appalachia, of the Southwest's migrant workers, of the Deep South's tenant farmers. They too stand with hollow eyes and bloated bellies, for in this vast land of ours hundreds of thousands of children live below the poverty level, indifferent to everything but their hunger.

Although we can undoubtedly understand their condition, how aware are we of our own teenagers? Recent studies have uncovered the fact that half our country's adolescents eat an imbalanced diet. Pizza, hamburgers, french fries, Cokes and candy bars take the place of required nutrients. A skipped breakfast, lunch and dinner on the run forfeit time for digestion. So masses of our own "privileged" children also suffer from malnutrition, though obviously not so acute a malnutrition as that in Third World nations. Still, debilitated and continually drained of vigor, these young people slow down emotionally and intellectually as well as physically.

Exhaustion is another factor in apathy. Millions of husbands who, returned from a hard day's work, slouch silently before a television set are living (well, *almost* living) proof of this—certainly to their wives, who complain of faded romance and fun over and gone. But are these parents tolerant, or even aware, of their children's fatigue?

David Manning, a teacher in West Hartford, recently conducted an informal survey among high school juniors and seniors in six Connecticut schools. He found that seventy-seven percent of the boys and girls work at part-time jobs, averaging twenty hours each week. When this time is added to the hours spent in school, these students put in a twelve-hour day. "Only students with uncommon talents or with unusual pluck are willing and able to tackle several hours of demanding homework assignments following three to four hours of often tedious drudgery at a part-time job," wrote Mr. Manning in the New York *Times*.

"As physical and mental fatigue creeps in from a steady diet of twelve-hour stints of school and work," he observed, "youthful effervescence gives way to languor." Are America's teenagers turning off from exhaustion? If seventy-seven percent in West Hartford are, what is the statistic in other cities? Will it be fifty percent in Detroit? Eighty percent in Pittsburgh? Forty-five percent in Los Angeles? If it averages only twenty-five percent nationally, we are still relegating a quarter of our sixteen-, seventeen- and eighteen-year-olds to exhaustion and indifference.

Younger children do not usually hold down jobs, but they work hard all the same. Those who belong to our eager middle class are rushed from school to lessons in tennis, dance, ice skating, piano, even good manners! And they begin their homework after dinner at seven or eight. A twelve-year-old seventh-grade boy whose head was drooping told me the other day, "I've been up till two o'clock every night this week studying for exams."

If they are rural children, they help their father with farm chores. In the ghetto, they can be seen hanging around the streets till midnight waiting for working parents to come home. Driving through cities, I see mothers dragging toddlers through twenty-four-hour supermarkets and ten-year-olds stuffing dirty clothes into all-night laundromats. And in homes in all kinds of communities there are children sitting up late watching television with their parents in the living room or alone in secret in their beds.

Physicians tell us that infants require twenty-two hours of sleep a day; preschoolers about fifteen hours; elementary schoolchildren, at least eleven; and adolescents, no less than nine. Yet children in most American families are not getting the sleep they require. In their fatigue, they can only drag themselves through the routine of a day, with no energy left over for what David Manning calls effervescence. They are doomed to apathy.

EMOTIONAL CAUSES

There was an old song that went as follows:

> *I would climb the highest mountain,*
> *Span the mighty desert wide,*
> *I would swim the deepest ocean,*
> *Just to have you by my side . . .*
> *I'll be over tonight if it doesn't rain.*

While the song writer envisions himself as Romeo in the depth and breadth of his devotion, he obviously lacks Shakespearean commitment. Romeo went all the way to the tomb for the sake of his love, embracing poison, blood and immortality. The ardor of the young man in the lyrics dissolves in a drop of rain. His caution reminds us of the high school student who acknowledged, "I believe in God . . . if there is one."

Commitment is the pledge of Sabbath children, believing in themselves, getting involved in the business of life. It may be Darcy bossing her nursery school classmates around "because that's not what the teacher said to do." Or it may be Ruth Ann volunteering at an old-age home on Sundays. Or Chris sticking with the basketball team even though he is only a third-string bench warmer. Commitment is caring.

Wednesday's children are afraid to care—about people or happenings or themselves. Rather than make a commitment, they wander aimlessly through their days, unattached. It is safer. Carlos is an example. He attends school regularly, getting by with a minimum of work; but he belongs to no clubs and participates in no extracurricular activity. When questioned, he replies, "Oh, they're nothing." If he could answer what he really feels, he would change it to, "*I* am nothing." Nothing is *how* he feels alongside his dynamic twin brother; so he has made "nothing" *what* he feels for survival's sake.

Hans Selye refers to the aimlessness that stems from lack of commitment as "a social disease which has reached pandemic proportions." The cure, he says, is finding purpose in life. Yet absence of feeling precludes finding a purpose because, like a damp blanket, it smothers fires that could ignite a search. "To feel emotion is at least to feel," wrote Archibald MacLeish. "The crime against life, the worst of all crimes, is *not* to feel." He was right. Children who cannot commit themselves are in effect criminals—murderers of their own potential.

Apathy may also result from a fear of vulnerability. I remember, from my days as a school principal, a little boy in second grade who did poorly academically. Periodically his father would drag him into my office to see what I could do to improve the situation. As the father ran down the list of his son's failings, tears would well up in the little blue eyes and spill down his cheeks.

"Stop that crying," his father would order. "You look like a baby."

By fourth grade the little boy, bigger now, was no longer crying. He was still doing poorly in his studies, and his father was still dragging him in to me for a solution. There were no tears, however. Not even tears held back behind the blue eyes. There were no smiles either. The little boy had simply stopped daring to feel.

I remember another child, somewhat older, who showed righteous indignation when her teacher accused her of copying a paper, which I am convinced she did not do. Her mother met with us and, seeing her child, said through tight lips, "I don't care how you feel. Put a smile on your face."

I heard her mother use the same line several months later when she called for her at school on a day when most of her classmates had been invited to a party. The child's face was contorted in pain.

"Why didn't she ask me?" the child sobbed.

"Smile," her mother ordered in a whisper, "and they'll think you don't care."

Since the girl left school at the end of that year, I do not know what happened to her. I can bet, however, that now at the age of eighteen she is so afraid of her emotions that not even she knows how she feels. If she feels.

"To live is to run risks," read the title of an upcoming sermon I saw outside a church one day. Or, as Fletcher Knebel, coauthor of *Seven Days in May*, phrased the same thought: "To be human is to be vulnerable." Edmund Muskie ran a risk the day he openly wept as he was campaigning for President, but the little blue-eyed second-grader will never grow up fearless enough for that. Christ showed the world his humanity when he raged against the money changers in the temple, but the little girl who had to disguise her feelings will never dare respond with such force.

Apathetic children may be, as Mark Twain put it, "safe from the turmoil of life." They are, alas, in their safety also invulnerable to life's joys.

SEVERED COMMUNICATIONS

Picture yourself set down in a foreign land, surrounded by people speaking a language unintelligible to you. What will you do? At first you will try to communicate. "English?" you will ask. "Do you speak English?" You may speak slowly and very loudly; yet people will pass you by, unaware even of the question you are posing. You may resort to charades, body language that speaks for you. People stare as if you are crazy, and shrug their shoulders or laugh and go their way.

Frustrated now, you may grab a passerby by the arm or run in and out of stores seeking help. If you do not wind up with a black eye or a night in jail, you will probably realize the hopelessness of your situation and simply abandon attempts to communicate. Resigning yourself to the inevitable, you are no longer angry or frustrated. You may not even feel helpless any longer. You get on with what you have to do by yourself, and you do not feel anything.

Such is the condition of children who for a variety of reasons do not communicate with the outside world. *They may be infants lacking a mothering figure,* children in institutions, those with a series of surrogate mothers or those left alone for large segments of the day. Lying first in their cribs, later in their playpens, alone and unnurtured, they have no association with a person who creates for them the sensation of pleasure. They feel no hands fondling them, hear no soft voice cooing in their ear. They do not rock in comforting arms or laugh at a smiling face. They play no games of peekaboo or pat-a-cake. Since nobody brings them joy, they have no reason to be attracted to the outside world. To them it is passionless, and passionless they grow up.

On the other hand, *noncommunicative children may be products of what author Malcolm Cowley calls "Me-ness."* Overindulged, instantly gratified, granted license at will—or at whim—they have never formed a relationship with the world out there. They have remained what babies are: the center of their own universe. But the satisfactions of Me children are of short duration. Unfulfilled, Me children grow disillusioned. Disillusioned, they grow apathetic.

That is what happened to Cliff. A spoiled child, he was surly, never seeming to enjoy even those things he demanded of his parents. He neither made friends nor built inner resources for his solitude. Throughout elementary school, his parents acted as though Cliff's happiness lay just around the next present or the next trip or the next new jacket. By the time he was in high school, however, they began to realize that there was no happiness ahead for Cliff. Listless and bored, he had cut himself off from everything: he barely spoke to his parents, went nowhere, enjoyed virtually nothing. He has been seeing a therapist for two years now, but she says she is not sure she will ever get through to him. Cliff may have cut off his response to the outside world permanently. Cliff would have been far happier without a store of material possessions. Learning to wait would have brought more satisfaction; learning to give would have brought more love.

When children are forbidden, for reasons of safety or plain Puritan cleanliness, from venturing into the world around them, they lose touch with it; they lose sight, hearing, smell and taste as well. The resultant loss of excitement is inevitable, since children thrill to the world only by immersing themselves in it. Crawling in the mud, jumping in rain puddles, finger painting, feeding oneself, using the toilet, baking a cake—all these can be messy. They can also be learning experiences. Walking, cutting paper dolls, going to school alone, pouring hot cocoa, climbing trees—all these can be dangerous. They can also develop skills and self-confidence.

With heart in mouth and prayer on lips, many mothers are willing to endure the dirt and risk the dangers in order to afford their children an opportunity to grow up. When they do, their children learn to connect with the outside world both physically and emotionally: they live and they feel. They are the Darcys and Noahs and Nancys and Lucys of the earth.

Some mothers, however, are too fainthearted or, perhaps, too neurotic to give their children such an opportunity. "You can't go there. You can't touch that," echoes through their lives. I had never actually seen such children close up until my neighbor's granddaughters, ages three and six, came over to play with my daughter Amy years ago. It had been raining, and the backyard was awash with mud puddles. Armed with spoons, pots and muffin tins, Amy led the others out the back door to an adventure in mud pies. When I checked fifteen minutes later, Amy was elbow-deep in mud, one cheek brown where she had smeared it and a rock lined with cupcakes by her side. The other two, however, were merely sitting apart watching, as clean and fresh as ever.

"Don't you girls have spoons?" I questioned.

"We don't want to get teetee," the little one answered.

"But mud isn't really dirty," I began to explain. The two little girls looked at me, got up and walked home gingerly across the lawn.

The girls spent the summer next door with their grandparents. I never saw them dirty. I never saw them climb the rocks or trees in our yard. Amy and I thought we could seduce them by having them join us in cooky making one day—but the dough was too sticky and the colored crystals of sugar stuck to their fingers, so they decided to watch instead.

"It's more fun to eat them," the older girl explained.

The two little girls had lost long before that day, and they continued to lose as they grew up neat, clean and unexcited. Amy is a young woman now—"a little sunburnt by the glare of life," as the poet Elizabeth Barrett Browning might say—but with feeling, with zest, with joy!

Obviously, *a language disability also cuts off communication from the outside world.* A child may not hear because of deafness and may not speak because of a cleft palate; both these disabilities are easily identified, as are many other obvious obstacles to communication. However, reading specialist and author Priscilla Vail feels that countless numbers of children suffer from a little-detected problem called "receptive learning disability." Although these children hear perfectly well, they have trouble processing the words they hear into meaning.

They go into the world, therefore, only partially understanding what is happening, and that limited understanding comes mostly by sight and repeated experience. They know Mother comforts them, but they do not know whether "Eat your banana" is more or less reassuring than "I love you." Hearing words all day, they cannot easily sort out which ones are important to them and which superfluous. Explains Mrs. Vail, "If language is threatening because a child can't understand it, she blocks it out, literally as a survival technique."

Becoming noncommunicative, therefore, in order to survive, the "receptive language disabled" child begins to show "an apparent lack of interest in stories and the adult verbal world." She will "probably draw away from adults"; she will seem "uninterested."

"Without trust," the author writes in *Independent School*, "the child has little energy left . . . so much is drained off in self-protective activities." Although Mrs. Vail quotes no figures, she alludes to far greater numbers of children suffering the lack of communication and ensuing apathy of receptive language disability than anyone has ever imagined.

To summarize, it is important for children to communicate with their world in order for them to feel. Yet, when the pain of feeling grows too intense, then their recourse is to sever lines of communication and feel nothing. Like a lobotomy, apathy is a high price to pay for the commodity called ease. Anne Sexton wrote:

> The joy that isn't shared, I've heard,
> dies young.

So does the child.

SENSE OF FAILURE

At the basis of all our discussions of stress lies a child's sense of failure. We have seen how it can make him lash out against those he perceives as his tormentors; we have seen how it can turn him against himself in self-destruction; and we have seen how it can drive him to flee reality by escaping into more blissful realms. Not surprisingly, therefore, we shall see how a sense of failure can also deaden a child.

Many husbands and wives live for years indifferent to each other. Once loving, each may have been hurt so repeatedly by the other that feeling has died. They do not hate each other; they are no longer even angry. They simply do not feel. Children go through a similar process: they start life loving parents and siblings and friends and striving for requital. When they meet repeated rejection, however, or scorn or coldness, they eventually give up. In the unbearable pain of their failure to win love, they stop loving. "I couldn't care less," becomes their byword.

A similar process takes place in school, from which up to thirty percent of the students may be truant on any given day. Tens of thousands drop out completely. Shocking as the statistics may be, they are understandable when we probe below the surface to see who these truants and dropouts are. They are not individuals, but numbers in school records. They are our youth, not interested enough to participate and not interesting enough to be noticed. While they may have entered school with hopes for learning, their failures have been passed down year after year, and they now face each day and each year hopeless, awaiting the inevitable.

Then one day they do not face school at all.

"What do you do all day?" I asked a young truant.

"Nothing, just hang around."

For him there is little difference: whereas he was dead *in* school before, he is now dead *out* of school.

EXPERIENCE OF LOSS

When Skip was four years old, his father brought home a boxer puppy which Skip named Junior. It was his, all his, and it helped offset the birth of a little brother two months later. Junior slept on the floor by Skip's bed, and once when Skip had chicken pox Junior had to be dragged away for outdoor duties. Junior saw Skip off to kindergarten and then to regular school every morning, greeting him on the porch as he returned. Though Skip had friends and school activities to involve him as he grew older, Junior never lost his place of honor as Skip's best friend.

Then one day when Skip was ten, Junior disappeared. Skip searched the neighborhood for him; his mother phoned all over town; his father ran ads in the local paper. But Junior never reappeared. At first Skip lived in anxiety with nothing else on his mind, jumping up every few minutes to peer out the window, even creeping downstairs at night to see whether Junior was at the front door. He cried himself to sleep and wept openly when his classmates at school questioned him. Skip's heartbreak was a consequence his parents well understood.

What happened next, however, left them baffled. Skip stopped talking about Junior, stopped running to the window and door, stopped crying at night. "He has accepted it," his mother told his father, but Skip also stopped seeing his old friends, cut phone conversations short, fell behind in schoolwork. Although he still attended Scouts, he did so perfunctorily. Nothing interested him any longer; he wanted nothing, asked to go nowhere. He simply existed.

Skip's parents grew impatient with him, unaware that he was in a state of mourning as deep and real to him as any adult's over a lost family member. Emotionally exhausted by grieving for Junior, he had no energy left to reenter his once-active life. Drained by grief, he was without feeling. Instead of parental impatience, he needed understanding talks to help him grow through his loss rather than withdrawing into protective apathy.

While the loss of a dog seems small to an adult as he looks around at the mass human death and suffering caused by starvation, war and natural catastrophe, to a child it is enormous. His loss, after all, touches the center of his world, whereas all the rest are so many statistics in a news report. Supportive parents are in a position to guide a child through a period of mourning, helping him emerge stronger and more confident to handle love and, if necessary, loss again.

However, when parents fail to understand their child's grief trauma, they may edge him toward non-feeling for the rest of his life. Nagging him to "Cheer up," or forcing him into activities for which he is not yet emotionally ready will burden him with additional pain. In self-protection, he may retreat altogether.

Many children of our transient society retreat from their feelings. Uprooted through military life or upward social mobility or professional ladder climbing, families in the past several decades have not been settlers, but movers. Children make friends and leave them as often as every two or three years. Although they may try to keep relationships alive through letters, phone calls and promised visits, friendships wilt and fade. With them goes trust, for when children balance the joy of friends against the pain of separation, the latter often overbalances. Eventually they abandon the idea of friendship, for although not having a friend hurts, losing a friend hurts even more. It is safer to feel nothing but the most casual acquaintanceship. Settling for safety is the story of apathy.

The coping devices we have discussed earlier in Chapters IV, V and VI are not too subtle for detection, despite the fact that they are often overlooked. Aggression is noisy; self-destruction bleeds; escape acts weird. Apathy, on the other hand, is barely noticeable. Since at home it may appear in the guise of boredom or fatigue or simply silence, parents tend to ignore its significance. Since at school it may appear as lack of interest and industry, teachers settle for labeling it as low effort.

Yet, apathy is as lethal as murder and suicide, and children driven to apathy as a means of coping with hurts are as tragic as victims in death. Perhaps more tragic, for their attempts to cope are the height of irony: they make themselves dead in order to live.

The naturalist John Muir might have been defining the plight of apathetic children when he wrote, "Most people are *on* the world, not *in* it—having no conscious sympathy or relationship to anything about them—undiffused, separate and rigidly alone, like marbles of polished stone touching but separate."

CHAPTER VIII

❖

Playing the Game

Jack be nimble,
Jack be quick,
Jack jump over
The candlestick.

SUCCESS GAMES

The Mother Goose books we leaf through in childhood and later read to our own children portray a happy Jack. Smiling he was in days past as, dressed in lace-collared blue velveteen suit, he leaped across the tiny flickering flame. Smiling he remains as, updated in denim jeans, he continues to jump through the years. We can with little trouble imagine proud faces of parents in the wings and hear their cries of, "Good boy, Jack," sound through generations.

Jack jumps. He jumps when his parents are watching. He jumps when his parents are otherwise absorbed, shouting perhaps at his highest leap in the hope they will turn and see. He jumps when he is tired. He jumps when he is bored. He jumps as the flame licks against his foot, burning his heel where no one can see.

Were we able to interview Jack, asking him why he jumps, he would probably answer, "I like it." Were we able to delve more deeply into his secret thoughts, through drugs or hypnosis or therapy, asking, "Why do you jump when you hurt and when your heart longs to be elsewhere?" he might answer instead, "It is worth it."

I know a boy named Michael who jumped for the first twenty-one years of his life. He was the best student in his class. When the rest of the kids stayed late after school for a ball game, he left to do his homework, and he skipped weekend parties when papers were due. His dad bragged to his friends about Michael's marks, and when Michael was there to hear and feel the pat on his shoulder, he nodded modestly, pleased. Michael applied to Harvard, where his dad had gone, and was accepted, starting his freshman year with a bang that resounded through four years, and even at graduation, where he received Magna Cum Laude and wore his Phi Beta Kappa key.

Then something went wrong. Slated for law school after the summer of 1977, Michael did not head for Cambridge but, knapsack on back, took off for California. For almost a year he did not contact his parents, and then he wrote a letter. "Dear Mom and Dad, I don't want you to worry about me. I am O.K. I have a job I like, which I plan to keep for the rest of my life. For the first time I am happy." Michael was assembling parts at a tool and die factory. He still is. His mother flew out to see him after receiving the letter and returned admitting, "He really *is* happy." His father has neither visited nor written him, pretending he has no son—until friends ask, "Whatever happened to Michael?"

"He's running a business on the West Coast," he answers and quickly changes the subject.

You probably know children who jump over candles. Do you know Samantha? She stayed pretty and clean in her starched, ruffled dresses and curtsied when she said, "How do you do?" Her mother curled her hair and entered her picture in a children's contest. When she failed to win or even receive Honorable Mention, her mother explained that the judges had been "fixed." Samantha did not understand but liked the sound of it since it meant she was still the prettiest and best and pleased her mother.

Samantha is a junior in high school now, screaming back at her mother every morning as she dons her torn blue jeans and oversized flannel shirt.

She says, "I'm not pretty any more, and Mom can't stand that." What she feels is only slightly different, but far worse: "Mom can't stand *me*."

If Samantha's and Michael's parents had been able to love them as individuals instead of using them as status symbols, all could have been more fulfilled. But Michael's parents—his father, at any rate— and Samantha's in no way understand what they have done to their children; in fact, until Michael rejected law school and Samantha donned blue jeans, they were unaware of having done anything to their children. They were proud, both of their children's accomplishments and of their own image projected through their children.

Naturally. All parents are. However, not all parents press their children into an image predetermined by their own ego needs. Many are willing to take pot luck—to derive pride from what their children turn out to be. Michael's and Samantha's parents did it the other way around: they tried to make their children be what they derived pride from.

"About all some men accomplish in life is to send a son to Harvard," wrote author-editor Edgar Watson Howe in his typical manner, not mincing words. His thought could be broadened to include other men and women whose chief aim and accomplishment appears to be raising not only Ivy League offspring, but pretty ones and popular ones, athletic and good. In a word, to make them follow the rules of success so that they, the parents, may approve.

The rules of the success game are set down for children from birth. While still in maternity hospitals, except for those humanistic ones where babies and mothers share a room, infants learn there is a right time and a wrong time to want to eat and sleep. The baby who grows hungry too soon or sleeps too late learns the first rule of the game: nonconformity means hunger, or some kind of bad feeling. He is already under stress.

As a new family settles down at home, the game intensifies. Mothers and fathers, somewhat nervous in their new roles, decide to judge their success by comparing their babies to the babies of others. "Does yours sleep all night?" "How often do you feed yours?" I knew a mother who was ashamed to admit she had not toilet-trained her toddler.

"It seems so mean to make her sit on that potty when she'd rather play," she said to me—but not to her friends. "They'd say I was being soft."

The self-image of parents may easily rise and fall as their infant wins or loses the neighborhood competition. "No teeth yet? My Jimmy had two teeth when he was that age."

"Still not crawling? I wonder why?"

"My nine-month-old points to everything. Yours doesn't seem interested."

Each word is a knife wound carving out failure; their child is less good than someone else's.

There is, however, approval to be won in other rounds. Their baby smiles first—"No, it isn't a gas pain."

Their baby gurgles, "Mama," and echoes resound through the social circle.

Their baby drinks from a cup, eats solid food, rolls a ball, stands up and gets toilet trained, each act of growth a milestone on the road to success. Deep in the heart of parents is the warming belief, "When my child is best, I am best."

Although the stages in an infant's growth occur in sequence and can only with difficulty be forced by even the most competitive parents, parents continue to try . . . and continue, often, to deprive babies of the satisfactions of the growth process itself. Freud introduced us to a series of adult hangups attributable to too early weaning and toilet training; still parents persist in pushing babies toward growth attained faster and accomplishments achieved earlier than those of their friends' babies.

While infants are ignorant of the words of pressure put upon them, they are fully aware of the stress. More seriously, they begin to receive glimmers of a way to relieve that stress: make Mommy smile. When Mommy smiles, baby feels secure; so the trick becomes how to make Mommy smile. In groping for an answer, the baby finds himself playing the game.

By the time infants become children, they are playing the game in earnest. Rare are the parents whose ego does not drive them to the game board. Let me replay some of the scenes I myself have recently witnessed.

SCENE I

The parents and three small girls are playing with dolls in the living room. Suddenly the mother puts a record on the stereo, turns to the girls and says, "Show us how you do the hula." The two older ones, four and seven, begin gyrating and waving their arms; the two-year-old bounces up and down. Mother and Father applaud. The girls dance until the music ends, then return to their dolls.

SCENE II

It is a cocktail party with twenty or so men and women milling around a large dining room and living room. The children of the host pass trays of hors d'oeuvres. A big-busted woman swoops down on one of the children, a six-year-old boy who in self-defense wards her off with a tray of canapes. With a yell, she scrapes salmon and cream cheese from her bosom, drawing the horrified hostess to her aid.

"She made me choke," the little boy pouts.

"Look what you have done," his mother gasps. "Say you are sorry."

He remains silent, glaring.

"You tell Mrs. Adams you are sorry this minute," his mother orders.

Through clenched teeth the little boy spits, "I'm sorry." His mother does not notice: she has whisked Mrs. Adams into the bathroom.

SCENE III

In her bedroom in a small apartment, four-year-old Harriet is building a tower of blocks. She bites her lower lip and holds her breath as her fingers struggle to stack block on block. Her baby brother crawls through the door, inching his way toward the unsteady tower. In seconds, with a chubby arm he has demolished the tower, sweeping blocks across the room. From the kitchen Mother comes running at the noise—just in time to see Harriet raise her hand to strike back, glowering at the baby.

"Harriet loves her little brother." The mother's words drip from her mouth, cloying. The little girl forces a smile as she looks up at her mother in the doorway. She puts her arms around her brother in a loveless hug, still holding in one hand the block she never stacked atop her tower.

SCENE IV

We are watching a Little League baseball game. Chuckie comes to bat, his uniform loose over his small body; his stride important. He glances over his shoulder, both proud and nervous as he spies his parents watching from behind the catcher. They are as tense as he. Strike one! Chuckie shifts his position. His parents remain motionless. Strike two! Chuckie rubs his hands together, clutches the bat. Chuckie's father grips his hand into a fist. Strike three!

As the boy walks away dragging his bat, his father leans forward and grabs his arm. "Why didn't you take your time like I told you?" he asks angrily. Two tears spill over from his son's eyes and trail down his cheek. "For God's sake don't cry. You don't want the kids to think you're a sissy, do you?" The boy still looks down. "Oh come on," his father urges, "act like a man. Get in there and kill the pitcher next time."

Chuckie nods an O.K. and takes his place on the bench, suppressing his tears.

In each of these scenes, the star performers are children playing a role for the approval of their parents. In the first, the girls know that Mommy and Daddy love them when they do the hula because they show them off to friends and applaud. In the second, the little boy avoids his and his mother's embarrassment by going through motions that make everything all right. He used to consider it strange that you could say, "I'm sorry," and not feel it at all, and nobody would know the difference. Now he merely accepts it. In the third, Harriet understands that she is expected to love her little brother even at those times when she does not, and that Mommy would not love her at all if she suspected she hated him sometimes. It is easy to hug him so Mommy will smile, and to give him a pinch when she is not looking. In the fourth, Chuckie has learned a lesson for life: that to be a man, you cannot cry, and you have to win.

In relating the scenes above, I am not attempting to disparage parents, but rather to point out to them the deceptions they unconsciously wish on their children. Not "bad" parents—*most* parents. I did it myself several weeks ago when I took Darcy, now three and a half, to the ballet, which she adores. I am spellbound by the ballet, and I am proud that she, so young, is too.

We were drinking a ginger ale at intermission when a man approached. "Did you like the dancing?" he leaned over to ask Darcy. She remained silent, preferring not to answer what to her was a self-evident question.

I, however, could not let Darcy be Darcy. "Tell the man that you saw *The Nutcracker* last month," I prodded. Darcy still did not answer. The man left; we returned to our seats, and I spent the next hour hating myself instead of enjoying *Coppélia*. How much easier it would have been for both of us if I had merely smiled to acknowledge the man instead of using Darcy to give my ego a boost!

We are all susceptible to our ego needs. We must watch ourselves.

When children enter school, game playing is laid out in a different arena and rules are set down by new players, their teachers. The goal, however, remains the same—success—and the stress of needing to win intensifies. Since movement toward or away from the goal is reported regularly to parents, home and school join forces to close in on children. They feel compelled to get good marks, to make the team, to win office. How else can they win the acceptance of their teachers and a place in their parents' affection? How else, when from infancy they have been practicing to please their elders.

"I wanted to yell, 'Shit,' or make an obscene gesture," a student-body president admitted after commencement; he had played the game long enough.

For most young people, the game continues right from high school into college and beyond. A recent study revealed that students who do well in high school tend to do well in college—a not surprising fact when we realize that the rules of the game remain the same. The winners in high school make it into top universities like Harvard; the B and C students, into state universities; and the borderline cases into junior colleges or shaky private colleges that no one has ever heard of. As for the losers, they get hidden away in menial jobs, unemployment or early marriages.

Even marriages are made on the game board, for there are the right ones and the wrong ones, on which families and society pass judgment. The couple will settle in houses and communities approved or frowned upon, buy cars, grow lawns and raise children. Like their parents before them, they will do their level best to make those children good—and nimble and quick at jumping over the candlestick.

When Marilyn Horne sang with the Hamburg Opera last year, she received over forty curtain calls in one of the greatest accolades of all time. Her smile, however, was for a far greater accomplishment. "Never mind the curtain calls," she said afterward. "I just found out that my daughter got a ninety-three on her scholastic aptitude test for boarding school!"

WHICH WAY TO GO?

One wonders about the world's perspective. Let us look, for instance, at the contradictory foci toward which we train our children's eyes. *In the first place, we send children to school for the purpose of growth and learning.* Yet we do not evaluate growth or learning; we evaluate achievement. We measure French conjugations, English vocabulary and math equations; we measure scientific terminology and physical education feats—all from A to F or with percentage points.

Instinctively children know that marks have little relationship to learning, no matter how much significance we place on them. The truth is that tests test only what someone else considers important, and marks mark no more than a measurement in someone else's mind. Learning and growth take place elsewhere. Educators have not yet devised a system of marking them.

How, then, do we assess the real growth and learning that happens inside young people? Do we measure their self-awareness? Do we rate their creativity? Do we grade their decision-making, their follow-through, their accountability? Do we evaluate their empathy? Their kindness? Their sense of humanity? Do we hand out gold stars for their environmental concern?

Alas, no. On the contrary, not only do we fail to evaluate honest growth and learning in the life areas that will be a part of children forever, we call them frills and shy away from teaching them entirely. In such a topsy-turvy Alice in Wonderland situation, children have two ways to go, each painful. They can rebel and face the consequences, or they can play the game and cope with the stress.

Those who select the former option become non-homework-doing children whose parents nag; they become truants, dropouts and those who find ways to run away. The world is loath to forgive them. The latter group, while winning the world's favor, are apt to inflict unforgiveness upon themselves. While often not apparent for years, even until adulthood, in many children signs of stress appear immediately. A study by researchers Koszarny and Zbigiew revealed that children of perfectionist parents who place excessive expectations of success upon them frequently stutter. Other studies have related school pressures to stress symptoms as diverse as extreme sweating to bed-wetting.

Yet teachers, who are in the business of learning, and parents, who are in the business of growth, continue to be diverted from their objectives in their push for marks of achievement. The promise of good marks sells. It sells a school to parents, who determine its value on reading scores and Scholastic Achievement Test scores. It sells lesson plans and course outlines to teachers, who will themselves be graded by the ratings of their pupils. It sells toys—flash cards and workbooks that line toy counters from dime stores to fancy Fifth Avenue toy stores—proclaiming new possibilities for pushing a child to the top of the class. It even sells magazines, as a recent advertisement indicated. A smiling boy announced, "I'm the smartest in my class." The explanation underneath stated, "He reads *Newsweek*."

A second contradictory set of lessons we teach children develops around the theme of competition. As a nation and as individual Americans, we advocate a spirit of cooperation as a solution to many of our personal, national and world problems. For instance, we preach communication and compromise for healing the generation gap and holding marriages together. We set up programs of neighbors working hand in hand to minimize crime. We urge labor and management toward joint planning in order to reinvigorate the U.S. economy. And we urge the world's nations to face their common problems of poverty, terrorism and war together.

Yet, while we are talking cooperation, we are teaching competitiveness. Despite the words we speak, children receive through our actions the old lesson of Vince Lombardi: "Winning isn't everything; it's the only thing." Few corners of their lives remain as sanctuaries from the stress of being best.

"What did you get?" sweeps through the classroom as tests are returned, and at home after three o'clock.

"How much did your dress cost?" Money wins competitions.

"Which country club do you belong to?" Social status wins too.

"How many books did you read over the summer?" Sheer numbers gain top listing on the class reading chart.

"How many pounds did you gain over Christmas vacation?" Sometimes numbers win in reverse order.

"Are you on the first team?" Athletic prowess stacks up points.

"Did you get invited to the party?" Popularity has a head count.

"See who can be the first to clean up and get in line." Even speed wins.

Wherever children turn, they seem to be running for their lives in races lined up for them by adults. Chilling evidence of this attitude appeared in the newspapers when former President Nixon was interviewed upon the birth of Tricia's son, a few months following the birth of Julie's daughter. He said, "We look forward to their growing up and competing with each other, for nowadays boys and girls compete equally in everything."

Alas, they could also cooperate in everything, if we only showed them how.

A *third set of contradictions with which we confound our young people concerns the word—and the hope for—happiness.* Over the years, I have asked thousands of parents throughout the country what they want most for their children. "I want them to be happy," they reply almost unanimously. They are sincere, but what they really want is for them to be what they themselves think will make their children happy, not what their children determine. In other words, they define the happiness they wish *for*—and *on*—their children in their own terms.

Ann wanted to be a carpenter, but she followed in Daddy's footsteps and became a lawyer.

Buck wanted to stay home and read poetry, but he knew he had to play football to make his Dad happy.

Donny felt secondhand, but he acted happy for the sake of his adoptive parents.

Allison wanted to cry when her mother and father got a divorce, but she knew "that big girls act brave."

On a career guidance questionnaire Eunice wrote, "I want to be a mother when I grow up, but I know my parents will be embarrassed if I don't have a career, so I guess I'll be a nurse."

The obvious tragedy is that these young people and millions like them feel forced to achieve happiness as their parents see it. The more subtle and far more destructive tragedy is that they are not allowed to be honest about their feelings. They play the happiness game as though they wanted to. Rarely is a Eunice given the opportunity to voice her true feelings, and rarely is she even attuned to them.

For instance, Ann works a six-day week in a law firm at a profession she dislikes. She is tense and tired but too "successful" to quit —successful in the terms laid down by her father: lots of money and an upcoming partnership. She makes speeches to women's groups about law as a great future for women and publishes articles in law journals. But only on Sundays does her face relax as she traces a design to carve on a new cabinet or as her hand runs down the grain of a seasoned board.

Buck made the third-string football team and kept assuring his dad, "I'll be put up to second string soon." He never was, but he played hard when he got a chance. He stopped reading poetry and memorized football statistics instead, challenging his father with esoteric bits of information. A junior in high school now, he is a poor student and a poor athlete as well. Nothing interests him.

Donny used to tell his friends, "Boy, do my mom and dad love me. They love me more than your mom and dad do." Inside he never forgot that his "real" mom and dad did not love him at all.

Allison told the class in Show and Tell one day that her parents were divorced. "It is very important to be divorced," she said, "because you sign papers. And children are most important of all because they don't live with their mommy and daddy but can live in two places." She pleased her mother that day when she reported what she had said. And she cried herself to sleep almost every night.

Adlai Stevenson felt that at some point in life, everyone has to confront the problem of "making his public face the same as his private face." He hoped that each of us would eventually allow our true selves to shine forth, obliterating hypocrisy and deceit. Children caught in the pretend game react in quite the opposite way from the way that gentle statesman suggested. When pretending becomes overly stressful for them, they evade it, not by giving up their public face, but by giving up their private face. Pretend becomes what is real.

WHY PLAY THE GAME?

Why does Jack jump over the candlestick?

"Nature has her laws, and this is one—a fair day's wage for a fair day's work."

Benjamin Disraeli

"The only thing I ever got for nothing is measles."

My father

Why does Jack jump? Because Jack, like almost everyone—professor, plasterer or prostitute—works for a living. He gives what he can. The professor gives her mind; the plasterer his skill; the prostitute, her body. Each in turn receives the wherewithal necessary to keep on living. That, as Disraeli said, is the law of nature.

Jack follows that law too: he gives his heart so that he may receive materials for survival. Money for food and shelter are inconsequential to him for, like the lilies of the field, he knows his physical needs will be cared for. He works for far more essential currency: approval, with which to assure his self-respect.

When Jack feels rejected for whatever reason, real or imaginary, he struggles to earn love through the only skill he is aware of—his ability to please. He has been honing this skill, we must remember, since infancy.

He receives payment in what looks to him like love: his parents' praise, his teacher's good marks, acceptance from the world around him. He earns survival. However, let me state clearly that not every child who performs in a way that pleases his parents and teachers falls into the same category as Jack. While all are playing the approval game, not all are doing it for the same reason.

Some conform to the adult image of what they *should* be simply because it is what they *are*. Thousands of teachers are fortunate enough to have students who study because they are interested and excited and because they want to learn. I had little trouble identifying these students in my classroom, and I am sure this is true of other teachers as well: true learners are concerned with their discoveries; game players, with their marks.

I have had in the latter group students who haggle consistently over a plus or a minus and count point values on test questions in order to challenge my grading. Achieving was the name of their game, not learning. They were the students who invariably broke into a class discussion, no matter how stimulating, to ask, "Do we have to know this for the test?"

On the other hand, I have had in the former group students whom I could not get out of the room: they stayed to pursue their comments; they came in during free periods to question; they sought extra work in order to probe further. I even had one who, after turning back a corrected essay, asked me what mark he had received. "I forgot to look," he laughed.

Similarly, thousands of parents have children whose accomplishments and behavior delight and reward them, children who do what they do not to receive approval, but to feel good. There is a difference. For instance, four-year-old Harriet, whom we met earlier, pretends to love her little brother "as a big sister should"—she hugs him and pats his head and mouths love words when her mother is looking. With her mother out of sight, however, she pinches him, knocks him about and once even pushed him down the stairs. For fear of losing her mother's love, she hides the jealousy and resentment that she, like any normal four-year-old, feels. Since her mother expects a big sister to match the model in her mind, Harriet feigns the appearance. If she could help Harriet admit and share her moments of hatred for her brother, moments of love would come more freely more often.

Darcy, on the other hand, really loves her little brother. The difference shows. Her hugs and pats and gurgles are not staged for mother's approving eye. On the contrary, I constantly see Darcy, unaware, lean over and kiss Noah or tickle his neck till he giggles. I see her gently remove his hands from one of her toys and even guide his fingers on the typewriter keys when he gropes while she is "writing a letter." Sometimes I see her at the point of frustration we all reach from time to time, when she shouts, "No," at him, pushing his hands aside. As his curled underlip unfurls to cry, she turns to him wagging a finger and explains, "Sister is playing a game, and you can't spoil it. Now go away." Only as a last resort does she enlist aid with a plea of, "Mommy."

Parents and teachers can tell the difference between the two kinds of "being good" if they make an effort to observe. A tattletale plays the game to curry favor; a child who reports an incident is acting, often courageously, from his sense of values. It is not easy for a nine-year-old to tell a teacher, "I think you had better see what Jimmy is doing," when Jimmy is throwing stones at a window. It was not easy for a sixth-grader I know to face ostracism by alerting his teacher to the fact that a classmate had stolen the midyear exam from her desk drawer and was copying it for the class.

A show-off clowns in order to get attention; an ebullient child cuts up from her own sense of fun. A girl I know, for instance, does cartwheels while walking down the street because they make her "feel like a windmill."

One child picks his mother a handful of wild flowers on the way home from school to pave the way for a phone call from his teacher. Another hands her a bouquet of black-eyed Susans and dandelions because "I know yellow is your best favorite color."

Playing the game, then, is not all bad. For some children the rules of the game are the rules of their life, and they have no need for pretense. For others, however, the game is a self-effacing means to an end. They conform to what is expected of them not because they want to, but because doing so will please the people who matter to them.

For these children, life becomes a lie. Actors in a role, they never reach the end of the play; for if the curtain falls on their act, they feel that they will be left offstage alone, deserted. Like the dancer in the red shoes, they have to keep on performing.

We have already discussed instances of deliberate game playing, such as Harriet's attention to her baby brother and the little boy's burning, "I'm sorry." There are others that seem almost bizarre. Molly's mother never wanted her daughter to confront the ugliness of death. Once when a friend related having seen a large dog tear a smaller one apart, Molly's mother whisked her from the room. When, while driving in the car, they saw a dead animal on the road, she diverted the little girl's attention. "Look at that beautiful mountain . . . or tree . . . or horse," she would say so Molly would look aside. Once, upon seeing a squashed frog on the path where they were walking, Molly asked what it was and started to pick it up. "It's an old piece of shoe leather," her mother explained, and quickly pulled her along.

At first the little girl accepted and believed and thought nothing of it; but as she grew older, she became curious. Peering from the corner of her eye, she knew there was a dead woodchuck on the road; listening to stories, she heard about death; stepping over a dead frog, she saw decay. She learned about death, and she learned something else too: that her mother expected her to remain in the innocence of unawareness.

So Molly, quite consciously, decided to play the game. She closed her ears, averted her eyes and asked no further questions about dead frogs. So adept did she become that often she would spy a dead animal on the road before her mother saw it and herself point out an attraction on the side. "Look, isn't that lovely," she would exclaim to her mother's relief. And so she retained outwardly the innocence her mother required of her—like Rapunzel secure in her tower—and retained, therefore, her mother's love. What neither gave herself a chance to know was that sharing the hurt of facing death could have created a strong bond of love. Molly's mother, instead of diverting her daughter from upset and sorrow, could have acknowledged their mutual feelings and both given and gained support.

Len's game playing took a different turn. As a small child he relished the joy his parents and older sister took in Christmas—decorations, trips to see Santa Claus, anticipation of presents he would bring, cookies baked to leave at the fireplace, sleepless nights awaiting his arrival. Then dawned the day, early, with squeals and kisses to see what he had brought, and gifts opened one by one to prolong the wonder.

Christmas brought the family close in love and shared joy around the great red and white figure of Santa Claus. Len's sister discovered the truth of the myth, but, sworn to secrecy by her parents, held her silence around Len. The little boy, who became a somewhat bigger boy, continued to believe, and Christmas still held magic.

Then somewhere along the line Len stopped believing: he realized who left the gifts and ate the cookies and dressed in red and white. Instead of taking pride in his discovery, however, he found himself facing a dilemma. Since his parents expected him still to believe, what would happen to Christmas if he revealed the truth? More important, what would happen to him? He would no longer be special. Therefore, Len kept on believing . . . and kept believing . . . and kept believing. Christmas and his parents' joy in him continued as ever.

One day his sister faced him with, "You know there's no Santa Claus, stupid. Why pretend?"

Len went to his parents, shock disfiguring his face. "Is it true what she said?" he asked. "There is no Santa Claus?" The great game was over—except for tallying the score. Len was held and comforted and talked to in the serious voice his parents used for important occasions. His sister was spanked and sent to her room.

Parents of both children went to extremes to create happiness; yet were so blocked by their own interpretation of it that they eliminated it altogether. All they created was stress. Happiness is not a series of paintings hanging on a gallery wall, from which parents select one for their children. On the contrary, if happiness is to be seen as a painting at all, then it is each individual child who must be the artist.

We have seen children play the game when the game is theirs; we have seen others play the game in painful pretense. There is a third group of children who play the game without even knowing it: they delude themselves. Deep inside and long ago they have snuffed out the ulterior motives from which the second group operates, and in fooling themselves, they fool others. Eric Hoffer believes, "We lie loudest when we lie to ourselves." These children are the true tragedies for they cannot even say to themselves, "I know who I am.

I am a hypocrite." They have lost themselves and no longer know who they are.

Throughout this book we have met such children. There is Michael, the top student, the pride of his parents and teachers, the envy of his classmates, a satisfaction to himself . . . until after college he asked himself, "Why?" and answered by running away.

There is Lianna, the good little girl who became the best her mother could afford, who avoided the teenage rebellion her friends went through . . . until she attempted suicide.

There is Gregg, who according to the New York *Times* report was seen "as a humorous boy who joked and teased good-naturedly and who enjoyed sports . . . and earned good grades. His teachers liked him too and his neighbors thought him thoughtful and courteous." Then one day he chopped up his parents with an ax and jumped off a water tower.

There are children in your school and in your neighborhood who restrain their feelings and rechannel their behavior—and do so with such expertise that they delude not only the outside world, but themselves as well. Look around you. Is that goody-goody in fifth grade one of those children? Is that big wheel in the sophomore class? How about that child of yours who "never gives anyone trouble?"

Perhaps you fail to recognize children who fool themselves into playing the game. Perhaps you do not want to recognize them, for they make life so pleasant and problem-free. Are they not, after all, acting as you will them to act? Self-delusion festers, however, and at some point the putrefaction must seep out, like pus from a boil.

While the rewards of game playing—love and approval—bring survival, the cost is high. Many children cannot handle it and break down. Within a matter of months, two highly pressured suburban communities whose high schools boast an average acceptance of eighty-five percent of their graduates to top colleges, faced teenage suicide. In another city a mother found her sixteen-year-old daughter suddenly unable to speak a word. A twelve-year-old boy refused to leave his bed. A teenage girl lost thirty pounds in as many days. A boy overdosed on heroin. Teachers report children bursting into tears for no apparent reason. Psychiatrists cannot meet the burgeoning need for help among the country's children and adolescents who,

in their attempts to live up to adult expectations, come to the point
of collapse.

HOW TO PLAY THE GAME

Those who are able to handle the cost of their game playing fall
into two categories. *One group uses rationalization in order to live
with their pretense.* They may cheat in school, exonerating themselves in a myriad of ways. Sam, for instance, stole an exam ahead of
time. "I learned more by getting hold of it than if I hadn't done it,"
he explained. "It was like having a take-home exam where I could
look up all the answers." Hope plagiarized her English term paper,
shrugging off accusations by rationalizing, "Everyone else does it."
Both convinced themselves that their acts of dishonesty were not
only forgivable, but justifiable.

Rationalizers apply similar skills to varied situations. They may
shoplift (they do in such increasing numbers that many stores forbid children under sixteen without parents), tossing away their guilt
with, "The store won't miss one little item. They have lots of
money." They may lie to their parents, divesting themselves of guilt
by telling themselves, "My parents will be happier if they don't
know."

They may be adolescent girls who burn in shame and a sense of
failure for being unpopular with boys. "I don't know why anyone
wastes time with the dumb boys in our class," they rationalize to
their parents, their classmates and themselves. They may be nonath-
letic boys who ward off their parents' disappointment with, "Sports
are for the bird brains." Whoever they are, they are young people
who, yearning for acceptance, weave themselves a web of lies and,
struggling in the web, find a way to extricate themselves—by rationalization.

"No man for any considerable period," wrote Nathaniel Haw-
thorne, "can wear one face to himself and another to the multitude
without finally getting bewildered as to which may be true." These
children end their bewilderment through the process of rationalization, which enables them to wear only one face.

*A second group of children handles the cost of game playing
differently: they have no need to rationalize away guilt or self-*

dislike; they disallow feelings altogether. They go through the motions of compliance with indifference, having snuffed out excitement and anger and love, pity, joy, hatred and whatever else might have welled in their hearts.

They become, in a phrase coined by Dr. Burton White of Harvard, one-dimensional students—empty academics. Grace, for instance, is the super student her parents want, but nothing excites her; she pursues no interests. "Even a computer is more fun," a classmate admits.

The Malloy sisters are like the Stepford wives: attractive, obedient, pleasant—but they just go through the motions of life. Good students at school, good children at home, they cause no trouble. Neither do they make a commitment or stick their necks out for anything. They fit the description of Emory University professor Martin Kaplan as he writes about today's youth: "They seem to want nothing more than to be told what to do, think, believe and cherish by their teachers and parents so that they may dutifully regurgitate those approved facts and values so that in turn the society in which they want so desperately to succeed will duly reward them."

Les is another example. Although only in the eighth grade, he knows he wants to be a stockbroker like his father.

"Why, Les?" I hoped to hear a note of passion in his reason—*any* reason: Hungry greed for the money it would bring, swelling pride at controlling the world's economics, ego smugness at the status it entails.

But no. "Why, Les?"

"I don't know. There's nothing else to do, and Dad could get me a job in his firm."

So Les apes his father, much to the latter's gratification, by sporting Brooks Brothers suits, carrying his books in a leather attaché case and pretending to read the business section of the New York *Times.*

Here then are young people crying out in their stress by *not* crying out. They are nodding in agreement and smiling and following silent commands. They are jumping for their lives, back and forth over candles. As long as parents confuse children with angels, and teachers confuse them with robots, our children will suffer the stress of game playing. They will struggle for survival's sake to become those angels and those robots their world demands.

Matthew's gospel poses a searing question to the adults in the world of those children: "What is a man profited if he shall gain the whole world and lose his own soul?"

Dare we answer? Only when parents and teachers listen for the cries of their children, echoing unheard through the games they play for their sake, only when they hear those cries will the souls of children be saved.

PART THREE

◆

Adults to the Rescue

There was an old woman
Who lived in a shoe,
She had so many children
She didn't know what to do.
She gave them some broth without any bread,
She whipped them all soundly and put them to bed.

CHAPTER IX

◆

Answering the SOS

Humpty Dumpty sat on a wall,
Humpty Dumpty had a great fall.
All the king's horses and all the king's men
Couldn't put Humpty together again.

Behavior is caused. Almost a hundred years ago Ivan Pavlov jolted the world with that fact as, by ringing a bell, he conditioned dogs to salivate in anticipation of food. Since that time social scientists have taken hold of the idea and with it pursued the actions and reactions of human beings.

Pavlov's following arose not merely from the realization that behavior is brought about by outside forces, but from the infinite implications lurking in the thought that if behavior is caused, then it can be changed. What began simply as canine salivation has since led to the ultrasophisticated techniques we know today, such as brainwashing.

Some psychologists use conditioning to readjust our neuroses. Criminologists develop rehabilitative programs based on it. Urban planners take into account Pavlovian principles when they design housing complexes. Followers of John Dewey's "progressive" movement in education base teaching methods on the effects of positive reinforcement. Politicians condition voters in their maneuvers to be elected. Husbands and wives after long years together react with conditioned reflexes. Behavioral change in Pavlovian terms has become a part of our lives without our knowing it any more than Pavlov's dogs knew it.

Behaviorists tell us that while almost all behavior can be changed by conditioning, recently formed behavior changes more readily than long-standing behavior. Children, whose behavior is less ingrained than that of adults, are therefore particularly malleable in the hands of behaviorists . . . and of parents who borrow their techniques. What is adaptation but a kind of conditioning that makes difficult situations bearable?

We met in Chapter VIII children conditioned to play adult games for the sake of survival. In Chapters IV, V, VI and VII, we met those who rebel when adult conditioning efforts overburden them with stress. All cry out for help, their behavior sending an SOS. Parents, teachers and often society at large, reeling from the shock of the stress signals, seek to alter the behavior they see; and, usually unknowingly, use techniques straight from behaviorist pages. Some techniques work, reversing behavior patterns constructively; others fail, further aggravating them.

HOW BEHAVIOR CHANGES

Anthony M. Graziano, editor of a masterful collection entitled *Behavior Therapy with Children,* suggests the following six major ways in which behavioral change can be effected. It is worthwhile, I think, for parents and teachers to review them in order to understand how they are approaching their children and how they might more effectively approach them.

1. COUNTERCONDITIONING

Counterconditioning entails evoking positive feelings from a child in a stressful situation that has previously evoked negative feelings. For instance, a child who fears tigers in the dark as he lies alone in bed at night may be counterconditioned by having pleasant sensations created for him in the dark. Someone may sit by his side and stroke him. He may cuddle a woolly toy. He may hear his mother's voice singing a lullaby. He may play a music box. He may hear his father speaking in the next room. After a period of time, the fearful connotations of darkness may be converted to connotations of comfort and security.

I have seen teachers use counterconditioning to alleviate the stress of examinations. Some give children a piece of candy to suck. Others play soft music. Many walk among the students, patting a shoulder, whispering a friendly word, patting a head. Even a simple smile helps when you recall the usual stern expression of the typical exam proctor.

2. EXTINCTION

Extinction is a relearning process by which negative responses to stress are eliminated by removal of the reward the child has heretofore gained through his behavior. For instance, if a child throws temper tantrums when not getting her way in a matter, it is probable that parents have been reinforcing her behavior through heaping attention on her—trying to calm her, cajoling her into appeasement, at the very least getting upset and screaming themselves. The object of extinction conditioning, therefore, is to turn off the attention and to walk away from the tantrum in calm oblivion.

It has always seemed to me that schools should try the technique of extinction when faced with behavioral problems. What do they do? They suspend or expel students who act disruptively, relieving them of homework chores and the boredom of classes. What have these students wanted? Just that—to avoid homework and classes. The school's action, therefore, merely reinforces the behavior; it certainly does not alter it. It would appear wiser to me to keep the student in school, devising new kinds of work that might involve him, at worst require him to behave.

3. DISCRIMINATION LEARNING

When a child reacts with the same signs of stress to different kinds of situations, behaviorists say she is generalizing from a single experience. For instance, a little girl developed an intense dislike of men during a lengthy period of harassment by her father, recently divorced by her mother. Unable to cope, the child began lashing out —kicking the doorman, spitting at her grandfather, running away when her uncle came near, refusing to let the male nursery school teacher approach her. In short, she generalized a negative response to one man—her father—to include all men.

With time and patience her mother and the other men in her life were able to help her focus her feelings on the specific stimulus that had evoked them—her father, who frightened her. With love and affection, they were able to re-create her trust in other men.

Many teenagers generalize their hostility to an overly authoritative parent by rebelling against all authority figures, from their teachers to the President in Washington. If even one adult stops judging and damning them long enough to build a bridge of trust, their behavior may begin to show discrimination. Although acting no better to the domineering parent, they may develop less hostile relationships to other adults.

4. REWARD

Whenever we applaud seals going through their paces at the circus, we are recognizing the principle of changing behavior through bestowing rewards. Each time they balance the ball, their trainer tosses them a fish which says, "You've done a good job," and with such a reward, the seals continue to learn new tricks.

The A a teacher gives a student serves as a similar reward: success breeds success. Mother smiles and hugs when the toddler climbs onto the toilet for the right reason—he has his reward. Dad tosses his daughter the car keys when she drives carefully—she too has her reward. As a result, the former continues to use the toilet and the latter to drive with care, for rewards reinforce behavior.

They do more than that: they also *change* behavior. Let us say the girl above is not in general a careful driver. However, when her father *does* see her stop fully at a stop sign or pull slowly into the driveway and commends her, rather than criticizing when she *does not*, he is using reward to change her driving habits. Chances are that he will be successful, too.

Emma Stevens is a great kindergarten teacher in Valdosta, Geor-

gia. I never saw her punish a misbehaving child. I have seen her, instead, reward children with praise when they are not misbehaving.
One little boy in particular kept disrupting the class by alternately
jumping from his seat and kicking his feet back and forth. As the
children sat in a circle one morning, the little boy was momentarily
still.

"I want you all to notice how beautifully Willy is sitting," Emma
pointed out to the class. Then, turning, she added, "Willy, I am really proud of you." The children did what Emma had taught them
to do when they wanted to express support for a classmate: they
applauded. The little boy pulled himself to his full height of two
feet sitting down, smiled broadly, and remained still for the rest of
the morning.

5. PUNISHMENT

Punishment is probably the most common method used to effect
changes in behavior. It is also the least successful, as is indicated by
the high recidivism rate in prisons, especially in juvenile correction
facilities. Where it does alter behavior, it usually creates such pent-
up resentment that the behavior finds a different or a postponed
outlet. For instance, when a mother denied her daughter television
as punishment for a poor report card, the girl did not study more
and improve her grades: she spent her evenings on the phone talking with friends. When her mother then forbade telephone calls, the
girl withdrew sullenly to her room nightly, cutting off all communication with her parents.

Spankings have been the last resort of parents and—legally in
many states—of teachers as well. Yet we have been told repeatedly
that we do not convert a man simply by silencing him. A child who
is caught stealing pennies from his mother's purse may not be
caught again after a thrashing; he will be more careful. A belt
applied to a fourteen-year-old who staggers home drunk from a
party may prevent his returning home next time, but will probably
not prevent his drinking. Noah at ten months receives the equivalent of a spanking when his mother gently slaps his hand as he
reaches for ashtrays and hot coffee. He has not learned to stop

reaching, but he has learned to shake his head and gurgle, "No, no."
How effective is punishment?

6. SOCIAL IMITATION

Role models serve as a powerful force in conditioning a child's behavior. We know the child raised in love learns to love and, con-
versely, the child abused and beaten learns violence. The child who
observes his parents enjoying the satisfaction of hard work and a job
well done stands a far better chance of learning industry than the
child with parents on welfare, which perpetuates itself.

Television having the impact it has upon young people, it is safe
to assume that as many or more role models come from the tube.
Many psychologists and judges hold television responsible for the violence young people emulate. When a nine-year-old held up a New
York City bank with a toy gun, extracting one hundred dollars, he
said it was because "I saw guys do it on TV." A few years ago,
murders were committed with coat hangers in various parts of the
country after a coat hanger murder appeared on a television series.

Similarly, television role models have positive effects. A teenage
boy I know settled what might have turned into a free-for-all with
his sister because "that's how they did it in 'Little House on the
Prairie.'" Darcy plays school with her dolls in exact imitation of the
teacher on "Romper Room," and I think all of us speak a little more
gently after watching Mr. Rogers.

When parents are concerned over the behavior of their children,
let them look to themselves. Their honesty, their anger control, their
enthusiasm, their ability to deal with reality, their self-acceptance
can go a long way toward creating similar qualities in their children.

ANSWERING THE CRY OF STRESS

Surely, changing destructive behavior is important. To focus attention solely on changing it, however, without attempting to understand what the behavior communicates is defeating for both parents
and children. While the outward appearance may change, inwardly
the stress and frustrations of non-coping remain. Determining how
children *feel* is a good starting point for change.

A blunt, "How do you feel?" usually elicits a response no more revealing than a mumbled, "O.K." Nagging accomplishes little beyond irritation, a slammed door and a shouted, "Leave me alone!" Another way to the answer must be found. I suggest the three directions of a railroad crossing: stop, look and listen.

STOP

Stop nagging and prying. There are ways to draw out answers more efficiently than by questions such as "How?" and "Why?" Let me outline other suggested lines of questioning for each of the five stress-reactive behaviors discussed earlier in the book.

Aggression: "Something awful must have happened to make you so angry."

Beginning with this question in the face of a child's temper outburst over an incident that happened in school, a mother poses no threat. Her voice is warm. She is not disapproving, but empathetic; not against him, but on his side. He wants an interested ear in which to release his anger; she provides it. Trusting her, he can talk.

Self-destruction: When their little girl banged her head against the wall in frustration, her parents found a way to reach her. "Why are you doing that?" only made her bang harder. Her mother stroked her hair instead, speaking in a gentle voice. "You feel bad because the puzzle is so hard to put together, don't you?" Her daughter kept banging. "I know that hurting yourself sometimes makes the bad feelings go away." She rubbed her forehead. "But oh, that sweet head! Let's see if we can't find a different way to make the bad feeling leave." Soon the little girl was able to pour out her self-disparagement over the fact that her brother could put the puzzle together and she could not. From that admission, mother and daughter could discuss her feelings.

Escape: "When you are reading in your room, you feel nice and secure, don't you?" a father says, distressed over his son's fear of social competition.

"Yes."

"It's a lot different when you're with your classmates at a party, isn't it?"

"You bet it is," the boy begins. "There everyone is trying to be funny and grown-up, and I just stand around like a dummy."

"It sounds to me as if they're the ones acting like dummies, not you."

The boy, assured that his father is not going to criticize him, is willing to open up.

Apathy: "If you could do anything you want in the whole wide world, what would it be?" a father asks his apathetic, all but lifeless thirteen-year-old.

"Nothing."

"I remember feeling like that at your age." The boy shrugs. "It was easier to do nothing than something," the father continues.

"Yeah."

"I guess it's just a stage men go through, growing up."

"I suppose." The boy pauses. "What did you do about it? You're not like that now."

A conversation begins.

Playing the Game: Even with a game-playing child, one sentence may break down a wall of resistance, giving a glimpse of the interior.

"I'll bet you get tired of being so darned good all the time," might do it.

Or, "What do you suppose would happen if you didn't study for tomorrow's test and failed it?"

Any answer at all would serve to open a dialogue.

These, of course, are merely suggested openers, guidelines to follow. The actual words of questions asked young people in the hope of eliciting their feelings are less important than sensitivity and sincere concern. Children, like clams, close up tight when they fear being pried open, safe within their sea shells of defense.

LOOK

Look at your children. Looking is far easier than asking questions, for it involves less vulnerability: only *you* know what you see. A child's physical posture speaks loudly of his feelings—shoulders drooping, head hanging down, or neck tense and stiff. Eyes actually

say more than lips: they speak of hurt, anger, self-hatred, disappointment—or of hope, curiosity and joy. Clenched fists, furrowed brows,
yawns convey a message. No one need translate the signs for you:
you know if you look.

A child's appearance speaks in loud voices too—clothing, hair,
cleanliness. In the middle school years, many girls hide behind long
hair falling across their face, shrink into oversized shirts and jackets.
In high school, many boys strut their sexuality, wearing shirts open
to the navel and denims tight at the crotch. What is your child's appearance telling you?

Look, too, at your children's friends, at their habits and their
haunts. Notice whether they bring friends home after school or
whether they prefer going to someone else's home. See what they do
for recreation—the games they play, how they win, how they lose.
Tune your eyes in as receivers for your children.

LISTEN

Finally, listen to the voices of your children, those articulated and
those communicated through silence. It is easy for sound to rush
upon us, linger a moment and then pass away like a train, leaving
only the impression of noise. Children's voices come and go similarly, leaving us perhaps a little shaken by the decibel level, but too
often unmoved by what the voice says—or does not say. Listen. Be
moved. Hear the anger; hear the wishes; hear the fears in shouts and
songs and whispers. And in silence, hear how a child accepts what
he is.

Several years ago I visited Torrey Home for Girls, a small alternative correctional facility in the Bronx, New York, where each girl
had her own room to decorate and be responsible for. All but one of
the girls had fixed their rooms with posters, a bedspread, had per-
fumes lining the bureau and pictures on the walls. That one girl had
left her room as she found it—bare and untidy, reflecting total uncaring. The house mother explained that the girl had been shifted
from foster home to foster home all her life and was actually afraid
to fix her room up, afraid to become attached to it for fear of having
to move on once again.

Yet, when I visited, her self-pride could not be restrained: she cleaned her room, made the bed neatly and laid a bandana across the bureau for color. "I hope you don't look in my room," she tossed at me as I wandered through the building.

What she was really saying was, "Please, oh please look in my room because it is mine, and it is me, and I want you to like it."

Your children also may not say what they feel.

IDENTIFYING SOURCES OF STRESS

A second important step to take before attempting to change the behavior of children is to identify the sources of stress from which their behavior stems. It would be pointless to try to get rid of a headache with aspirin if someone were persistently hitting you on the head! It is equally pointless to ignore pressure points in a child under stress.

PHYSICAL SOURCES OF STRESS

The first checkpoint might well be health. While we have seen how stress manifests itself bodily in an array of psychosomatic illnesses, we can also see it the other way around: while stress creates ill health, ill health also creates stress. Poor vision causes strain, as any eyeglass-wearing individual knows when she has to get through the day and the glasses have been left behind. Children with faulty vision are under stress every day of their lives—as preschoolers, reaching, touching and trying to grasp; as students, unable to see the board clearly or to read the words, labeled as slow.

Children with impaired hearing suffer a similar fate. Ricky struggled along until fifth grade before an eighty percent hearing impairment was identified. By then he was already burdened under the stress of being labeled "a dummy."

There is no need to elaborate on the myriad of emotional problems stemming from neurological weaknesses: dyslexia has become a household word. Yet, hundreds of thousands of children whose aberrant behavior sends shock waves from their home or school into the larger community are found to have learning disabilities caused by long overlooked minimal brain damage.

It would be time-wasting to list here all the physical problems that serve as possible stressors to children, for they are legion. Parents should be on the alert for them, however, from tip to toe—falling hair to flat feet, both of which I have seen.

STRESS FROM EXPERIENCE

An equally important area to search for sources of stress lies within children's own experiences. What has happened recently in their lives? In an earlier chapter we reproduced the Holmes and Rahe chart of stress-rated experiences and translated them into the world of children. Many of these experiences take place at home—death or illness of a parent or grandparent, divorce, remarriage, moving, parental arguments, physical abuse, a new sibling, loss of a pet. Some arise at school—entering a new school, change of teacher, difficult work, tests, loss of a best friend, competitive events. Others arise in the outside community—stay in a hospital, witnessing an accident, a vacation trip, overnight at a friend's. And some arise in secret places where no one sees—where there are fears and sadism and sexual abuse.

At four, Dodie began throwing temper tantrums. Her parents ruled out sibling rivalry since the "new baby" was not new any longer.

"She is spoiled," a friend suggested.

"She is high-strung," they countered.

"Maybe she's just going through a stage," hoped the grandparents.

As the stage persisted, however, and Dodie's misery became more and more evident, her parents sought professional help. The explanation seemed to be that Dodie was afraid her mother was going to die. Why? Because she went to the hospital to have a baby, and somehow hospitals and dying had for her become synonymous—even with a delayed reaction.

UNREAL EXPECTATIONS AS A SOURCE OF STRESS

A third source of stress motivating destructive behavior in children is that of expectations. I mention it here only in passing since it has been dealt with in many examples throughout the book. However, so strong a stressor is the pressure to meet unrealistic expecta-

tions that parents and teachers need continual reminding. Not every
child can go to Vassar. Not every child can be beautiful. Not every
child can be a football hero. Not every child can have charisma to
win friends and influence people. They cannot, though the world
urges them down those pathways to success and acceptance. Parents
must counteract what the world holds out: they must set their sights
by what their children *are*, not by what they *wish* they were.

Impossible expectations on the part of parents, teachers and peers
probably provoke more stress-related problems among the young
than any other source. They begin early: Lonnie still wet her pants
when she was five because her mother had determined that she
would be toilet-trained at two. They become magnified in school:
Alfred developed into a masterful liar because, as teacher's pet, he
dared admit no wrong. They reach a climax at adolescence: Jill
smoked pot because her friends considered her one of the crowd,
and she could not let them down.

Some wit added a verse to the Beatitudes that went, "Blessed are
those that expect nothing, for they shall not be disappointed." In
seriousness, I want to emphasize the fact that parents and teachers
should have expectations for children. Without them, adults are de-
linquent in their responsibility; without them, children lack the self-
confidence that comes when adults believe in them. However, let
those expectations be founded on the reality of children themselves,
not on unfulfilled wishes and ego trips for grown-ups. With sound
expectations, parents and teachers can swell with pride and children
find fulfillment in knowing, "I can."

An old proverb says, "Small children disturb your sleep, big children, your life," from which parents may find comfort in knowing
they are not alone—not in the problems they encounter and not in
their anguish over them. Had Humpty Dumpty been a little boy instead of an egg, I feel sure his parents could have put him together
again where all the king's horses and men failed. Parents have more
at stake. And children, unlike eggs, are mendable. Humpty Dumpty
sounds self-destructive to me; perhaps he did not consider himself an
acceptable egg, a belief his parents could have reconditioned.

When faced with behavior contrary to their conception of "normal" or "right," parents tend to panic. Yet, troublesome behavior is

frequently normal. Teenagers drive their parents half crazy, yet as Anna Freud points out, "Adolescence is by its nature an interruption of peaceful growth, and the upholding of a steady equilibrium during the adolescent process is in itself abnormal." That should enable many a graying parent to heave sighs of relief!

Mental health experts estimate that about seventy percent of college freshmen suffer from varying degrees of depression, manifested in heavy drug involvement, drinking, promiscuity, exhaustion—or in rebellion against authority. As the heroine of a *Current Lifestudies* story expressed her blues, "It's like I live inside one of those little glass balls where it snows all the time."

Drs. Spock and Gesell have calmed the nerves of millions of parents by presenting stages of growth through which children pass. If I remember rightly from my own early motherhood, I survived the terrible twos, the agreeable threes, the assertive fours, the formidable fives and so on. Thank heaven my children are well into the tolerable twenties! Certain behavior, therefore, however bothersome, is normal and to be expected: parents, like the legendary Eastern potentate seeking a sentence applicable to all occasions, may safely say, "This, too, shall pass away."

However, much of the behavior parents question and dread will not go away by itself, any more than a blister on the heel will go away as long as the ill-fitting shoe continues to rub. The solution is to remove the shoe. Behavior, like blisters, is caused. When the causal factor is identified and removed, a change can begin to take place. What might require years of analysis in adults can often be effected in children by altering the circumstances of their environment. Where does one go to start?

WHO ELIMINATES STRESSORS?

I. CHILDREN HELP THEMSELVES

In the final analysis, all change comes from within. Even though a rubbing shoe brings on a blister and removal of the shoe makes it disappear, the shoe is only the stressor. The body itself in response to the shoe causes the blister and gets rid of it. So it is with behavior: stressors bring it on, but it is children themselves who make their behavior happen. It is, therefore, children who will ultimately make their behavior change.

Hans Selye writes in *The Stress of Life*, "The mere fact of knowing what hurts you has an inherent curative value." Thus, it is important for young people to probe inside themselves in search of their stressors. If a boy cheats in school, it is not enough for him to write off his desire to achieve an A as the stressor; he has to look further. He can be guided in the following train of thought:

I cheat in order to get an A.
My parents are pleased when I get an A.
When they are pleased with me, they love me.
When I do not please them, they do not love me.
They would not love me if I did not get an A.
What I really mean is that they love the A I get, not me.
Therefore, I have to get A's all the time.
But sometimes I don't know the material well enough to get an A.
Cheating is a sure way to get an A.
I cheat.
Cheating is a sure way to make my parents love me.

The stressor in this boy's life—and he is only one among millions —is that he believes his parents do not accept him as he is, but accept him only as an achiever.

Let us follow another line of self-probing as it applies to a five-year-old girl who has kindergarten in an uproar.

I cry when Mommy leaves me at school.
When I cry, Mommy stays.
If I didn't cry, Mommy would go home.
My new little sister is at home.
She and Mommy would be together all morning without me.
I don't want to share Mommy with the new baby.
I want to have Mommy all to myself the way I used to.
I knew then that Mommy loved me.
I felt good.
I'm not sure Mommy loves me when she is with my baby sister.

I hate my sister for making me share Mommy.
But I know I am supposed to love her.
That makes me feel even worse.

The stressor in this child's life is a combination of jealousy and guilt, a heavy burden for a five-year-old. Yet, just as the older boy can journey into himself to find the source of his stress, so the younger child can be guided by parents to do the same. *Identifying the cause of their upset is their primary assignment.*

Once children have been able to articulate what is bothering them, *they can go on to the second step: observing themselves with enough objectivity to identify their behavior.* The boy will know he has been cheating; the kindergartener will know she has been crying. Both had been sending out stress signals over a period of time which, unheeded by adults, intensified. When teachers suspended the boy for cheating, he did not stop cheating; he just became better at it. When Mommy called the little girl a baby for crying at school, she cried longer and louder. Only when they identified *what* they were doing and *why* they were doing it was their behavior susceptible of change.

Some children honestly do not recognize their behavior. When your child insists, "I wasn't screaming," he may really believe it. When a student accused by the school librarian of disturbing others defends herself with, "I wasn't talking," she may be unaware that she was. One little girl I saw, however, was fully aware of her behavior as she played in the front yard with a neighbor. Rubbing a handful of mud through her hair and down her dress, she gurgled in delight, "I make my mommy mad." She consciously had identified her behavior as disobeying Mommy and probably instinctively knew that the source of her stress was her mother's cleanliness fetish.

Eliminating the source of stress is the third step. Highly competitive twin high school boys were able to do this with some help. Courting situations in which they could compete, they chose the same elective courses and tried out for the same teams. Each had to win—get the better mark, score the most goals—to prove himself. As a result, each was reacting destructively to the stressful situation: one boy became sullen and withdrew; the other became aggressive and rebellious, both at home and in school.

A guidance counselor took them in hand, helping them through the process we have been discussing. With his help they were able to identify their stressor as the need to assert identity by rising above the other—not an uncommon need in twins. Their reactive behavior was easily identifiable: fighting from one, escape behind a closed door from the other.

The remaining problem was devising a way to eliminate the source of stress. The solution was to have them select different classes and different teams, but who would get the one they both wanted? The answer cost a penny—flipped to make the arbitrary decision for them. Although their solution did not eliminate competition between them completely, it minimized it to the point where each could drop his defensive behavior. The real stressor may have been parental pressure to succeed, but even with that remaining, they worked out a viable living arrangement.

Eliminating stressors is not always as simple as it was for the twins; often it is highly complex. The boy who cheated in order to secure his place with his parents would have a far more difficult task. How could he eliminate his insecurity? Maybe he could not, but he could try: by communicating his fears to his parents, who might respond . . . by finding areas other than academics in which to excel and gain parental approval . . . through greater diligence, achieving A's without cheating . . . best of all, by coming to the realization that above and beyond being an achiever, he is a person.

In the case of the kindergartener filled with jealousy and resultant guilt, her parents have to take a major role in helping her eliminate the source of stress. Since the baby cannot be parceled out for adoption, stress alleviation has to come from the child herself. Constant reassurances of love and a great deal of individual attention can rebuild the trust she had before the baby was born. Perhaps you recall my own experience with Eric, who showed his jealousy of Amy by chewing up all his reachable clothing. The hours I spent with him alone eventually reassured him of a firm place in my love, and the chewing stopped.

Sometimes a child must learn to live with stress because there is no possibility of eliminating it. Parents are divorced; a mother is an alcoholic; a grandfather dies; a child is deaf; a dog runs away; a brother is a math whiz—these are realities that no child can change. He can, however, learn to accept them instead of fighting them through reactive behavior.

When children are caught in stressful situations over which they have no control, the greatest help a parent or teacher can give is not pity and not an excuse for inadequacy, but a tight hold on reality. I remember a young girl in junior high school where I was a guidance counselor. Her mother was an alcoholic whom she found lying in a stupor almost every day upon her return from school. Hurt and resentful, the girl refused to study and showed interest in nothing but boys. She was failing her subjects, losing respect among her classmates and, worst of all, hating herself.

"What's the point?" was her response when teachers suggested she try. Looking around, she saw her classmates' mothers sharing their lives—giving parties for them, driving them to lessons, baking for PTA events. With her mother drunk every day, she could not even have a friend visit. "What's the point?" indeed. Yet her teachers and I were able to help her work through the reality of her problem. The thought process went something like this:

My mother is an alcoholic. [The source of stress]
I am angry because of that.
It's not fair because I didn't make her an alcoholic.
It's not fair because I can't stop her being an alcoholic.
So I have given up on everything. [Behavioral response]
Although I can't control *her* behavior, I can control *mine*. [Reality]
I gave up on life.
I am miserable.
I can make myself try to live again.
I can study and get good marks. I can go to college. I can have a career.
Then I will be my own person.
My only way out of this misery is to start trying. [Behavior change]

Enabling a young person to live with a bad situation is not a quick and easy job. It takes time, patience and endless repetition. The end result, however, is worth the effort—"Trouble creates a capacity to handle it," Oliver Wendell Holmes told us. The earlier a child is helped to handle it, the more self-confidence she will gain.

Children grow strong from adversity when the adults in their lives are themselves strong enough to confront it and cope. The parents of a little boy who was born with cerebral palsy were strong enough. By the time he was in nursery school, he could accept his classmates' stares and giggles with the explanation, "I have a sickness, but the name is too big for you to say." Then he would articulate "cerebral palsy" syllable by syllable.

Even children facing the ultimate stress of dying can be helped to accept it and make the most of the years or months that are left to them. "They handle it," says Dr. Paul Gabriel of New York University Medical Center, as he talks of terminal patients, "often far better than their parents."

While the stressors most children face are less dire than impending death, they are nonetheless heavy burdens, the shouldering of which may demand overlooked abilities. The following questions asked of themselves might reveal surprising strengths:

1. WHAT SKILLS HAVE I TO HANDLE THIS STRESSFUL SITUATION?

One young boy discovered that his years of piano practice paid off, for on the night before school exams, instead of pacing the floor sleeplessly, he began turning to Chopin to relax. "What better time to play a nocturne?" laughed his parents. A high school girl became a Candy Striper at a local hospital when going home after school to a nagging mother became too much for her. A fifth-grader struggling over long division eased her stress by helping her third-grade brother with subtraction.

Confidence is a reward in the adventure of self-discovery. It takes little imagination to know the pride in a young person who finds within herself not simply technical skills which enable her to cope, but qualities of character.

"I have the *patience* to wait this out," she may surprise herself to realize.

"I am too *honest* to cheat."

"My *compassion* will override my anger."

"I have too much *self-respect*."

"I still have my *sense of humor.*"

In the process of her search for skills, she may discover a more valuable treasure—herself.

2. "HOW CAN I KEEP BUSY?"

A twenty-four-hour day may seem endless to young people in the throes of stress. Sleeplessness adds uneasy hours to their nights; lack of involvement turns days into boring drudgery. The solution is to find ways of shortening the day and of becoming physically exhausted enough for sleep.

When children select preoccupations according to their own inclinations, parents may see them spending hours at activities a far cry from the schoolwork they had hoped for. I know parents who complained bitterly because their daughter, who loved horses, shoveled manure in a stable on weekends—"and she doesn't even get paid." They missed the point: for the first time in years, their daughter was excited about doing something.

Scott's parents were equally appalled when their son got permission from a local garage to watch the auto mechanics after school. They had fought his fascination and skill with cars, pressuring him into a college-preparatory academic program instead. The result had been that he not only continued with failing grades, but began getting into trouble as well. During a year at the garage he learned to fix cars. He also learned to work hard enough at school to pull his grades up—"so I can work here when I graduate." Help often comes in strange and wondrous guises.

When young people get turned on through any constructive involvement, more often than not their whole being turns on. As a teacher I have seen scores of students drag themselves through school year after year until something excites them—maybe photography or art, maybe being in a play or learning to handle lighting, maybe a science project, maybe even falling in love. But that one area of excitement, like an electric switch, lit up the whole person.

While keeping busy makes the hours rush by, it may require a partner—physical exercise. The recent *Perrier Study: Fitness in America* claims that eighty percent of all people who exercise feel less tension and find themselves better able to cope with stress than they did as non-exercisers.

Schools and communities abound in opportunities for young people, exercises to fit every taste. There are teams for the competitive, from the sometimes violent ice hockey to the more gentle badminton. Teams for even the very young are available in such sports as swimming, baseball or skating. There are solo sports like golf, tennis, gymnastics; and ballet is growing in popularity. There are recreational activities such as running, bicycling, body building and hiking. The young person who can urge himself into some physical undertaking will probably sleep better and will generally have a more positive outlook on himself and on life.

3. "WHO WILL LISTEN TO ME?"

Stress experts agree that all of us need a "significant other" in our lives, just as a pressure cooker needs a steam release valve. The tensions of almost any normal day can build up stress to the point of explosion: noise on the street, interruptions, arguments, inefficient services, our own inadequacies. It is not difficult, then, to recognize the intensification of stress in young people strung tight with the additional frustrations of academics, peer pressures, sibling rivalry, parental demands and their own growing up.

The irony is that at a time when children most need an understanding ear, their antisocial behavior deafens it. Parents "don't understand"; teachers "don't care"; and "Nobody likes me." What a feeling of isolation! Of course, stress intensifies and, of course, behavior reacts against it more dramatically!

Before abandoning themselves in their misery, young people can be helped to find at least one person to whom they feel free to talk. A parent? Perhaps not, since the relationship may suffer from mother or father's own stress-shaken emotions. A teacher or guidance counselor? Maybe. Jay Sommer, the 1981 national Teacher of the Year, considers sharing the problems of New Rochelle's high school students (many of whom are not even in his classes) one of his prime functions. An older brother or sister? Very often, yes. One girl I know makes lengthy weekly phone calls to her sister in college, but her parents do not complain of the cost: "It's cheaper than a shrink." A rabbi, minister, priest; an aunt or uncle; a family friend; parents of a classmate; a classmate; a neighbor; a nurse or doctor—

all of these have become significant others in the lives of young people.

II. PARENTS HELP CHILDREN RELIEVE STRESS

Young children, obviously, cannot undertake alone the program outlined in the preceding pages; they require parental guidance. Most older children as well cannot embark on a self-help program without suggested guidelines to follow and without continual encouragement. Therefore, it is to be assumed that parents be an intrinsic part of their children's self search for relief from stress—overtly or subtly as the child's age and needs demand.

Above and beyond that underlying help, there are specific steps parents may take to alleviate the pressure of stressors.

1. CHECK THE HEALTH OF THEIR CHILDREN.

In times of upset, the pediatrician or family physician is the best starting point. With a clean bill of health as reassurance, parents should reassess two other important factors—diet and sleep. Since this area has been covered in Chapters I and III, I shall not reiterate here.

2. EXAMINE THEIR OWN TENSIONS.

A few years ago two professors at the University of Wisconsin studied the effect of mothers' stress on the way they handled their children. Results were revealing: the more stress a mother felt, the more she punished her children. In addition, since stress in children created stress in mothers, they observed that the level of stress in children and the degree of maternal punishment were in direct ratio. We seem caught in a vicious cycle:

A child is stressed, displaying reactive behavior.

His mother becomes stressed in reaction.

She punishes him.

Punishment creates additional stress in the child, who then displays worse behavior.

In spiraling response the mother becomes even more stressed.

She punishes more severely.

As a result the child's stress mounts, and his behavior worsens. His mother . . . etc. etc. etc.

The only halt to this runaway pattern appears to lie in the mother's calling a truce to question herself: "How do I feel— honestly feel—about this child?" Anger over past hurts the child has inflicted on her communicates. Resentment over what she perceives as the child's ingratitude speaks loud and clear. Both build in the child stress to which the child responds with the behavior the mother finds intolerable.

"But I'm only human," parents say in exasperation. "I can't help feeling angry and resentful." They are not expected to deny their feelings; but if they sincerely want to relieve the stress symptoms their children evidence, they had better learn to cope with their stress in a more effective way. This entails assuming at least half the responsibility for the behavior-punishment-behavior syndrome that has evolved. When they can acknowledge themselves as part of the lockstep impeding change, instead of hurling full blame on their children, only then can change begin to happen.

Often, however, it is not the child-parent relationship that is causing stress, but the husband-wife tensions permeating the atmosphere in which a child lives. Physical fights and verbal altercations are not the only causes for trauma. Smoldering resentment that transmits itself even when masked by honied words unsettles children. Domination by either parent comes across as tyranny, which children assail. Children tremble most of all before silent anger, communicating itself through tight lips and glowering looks. A wife who feels unappreciated, a henpecked husband, a relationship grown stale—all play a part in the stress-reactive behavior of children.

Parents who resolve to stay together "for the children's sake" should be made aware that although divorce may temporarily shatter children, a hostile relationship may be far more corrosive. If they cannot put their relationship together for their own fulfillment, either by themselves or with the help of marriage or family counseling, then perhaps separation may save them all.

Parental tensions stem, of course, from sources other than their children or the marriage. Finances, social status, job satisfaction prey heavily on adults. Decisions of health, career, relocation and aging

parents weigh them down. While such stressors cannot be eliminated, they can be handled in nondestructive ways. For instance,
they can be shared with children, as they are between husband and
wife: as Hans Selye says, when the source of stress is understood, it
is more easily borne.

3. SPEND TIME WITH THEIR CHILDREN.

When children most need love, they are least lovable. Their antisocial behavior drives away parents who in turn drive them away—
sometimes consciously, to boarding schools and camp; other times
unconsciously, into the streets. Recent lawsuits have even succeeded
in securing legal divorces of children from parents and vice versa.

Dr. Theodore I. Rubin, psychiatrist and author of *Lisa and David*,
a sensitive account of adolescents, says, "Love is still my chief thera-
peutic tool." In the hands of parents even more than psychiatrists,
that tool can do an even better job of reshaping lives, for it is parental love above all else that children seek. Loving attention lavished
on children wraps them in the security of being accepted, approved
of, wanted (a state adopted children rarely if ever achieve), and in
that security they begin to cope. Since coping children find
fulfillment before their non-coping siblings, they have no further
need of the destructive behavior through which they have been crying for help. Life becomes easier for everyone.

Let parents and teachers, therefore, spend time with their children. It is easy to be with the "good" one and all but impossible to
be with the "bad" one; yet it is the latter who is crying out for
love. Time spent measures love in the language of children far more
accurately than the more common currency: money.

In the words of Dr. Leontine Young, onetime Executive Director
of the Newark Child Service Association and author of *The Frac-
tured Family*, "Relationships grow through shared experiences, and
sharing takes time together. Time is no guarantee of closeness, but it
is necessary for that intimate knowledge upon which all closeness
depends."

4. ORGANIZE A ROUTINE FOR THEIR CHILDREN.

Routines tend to settle children. When every day becomes a special occasion—a shopping trip or visit to grandmother's or overnight
at a friend's—chaos becomes the norm. At no time can the child

relax in the comfort of knowing, "It's time for this, and soon it will be time for that." Since even happy chaos creates stress, stress inevitably becomes the norm too.

Reassessment of children's daily and weekly life patterns quickly reveals whether routine exists for them or not. If not, it often can be established by eliminating the overplanning of activities parents fall victim to; a regular sequence of play after school, homework, dinner, a little television and a story or reading before bed can relieve stress far more than daily surprises.

I saw a mother settle a seriously distressed preschooler during a year of highly charged divorce proceedings by surrounding him with the comfort of a routine. Nursery school attendance took precedence over everything, the child missing it only when he was sick. His mother even limited her own life during that year in order to assure no absences from school. Naptime after lunch was adhered to regularly and playtime in the afternoon, in the park, at home or with a friend. Together they watched Mr. Rogers on television while dinner was cooking, and the evening hours they shared until bedtime. Special events took place on weekends—a visit with Daddy and an occasional trip to a show or the zoo, shopping or such. This mother turned what could have been traumatic into a time for mending.

5. REEVALUATE EXPECTATIONS FOR THEIR CHILD.

As discussed earlier in the chapter, parents' expectations for their children are frequently shaped by their own shortcomings and thwarted hopes. How many young Judy Garlands are there pushed into stardom and desperation by their mothers? Countless, and all in the guise of helping, yet causing lifelong pain.

Parents, therefore, must question whether their expectations distress their children when their children's behavior distresses them. Junior's anger in having to follow in dad's footsteps may be showing; sister may be getting even with mother for social pushing. "Peanuts" tells us that happiness is a warm blanket—yes, if a child happens to want that blanket. When parents give children the dignity of determining their own sources of happiness, they may also eliminate themselves as their children's chief source of stress.

Another kind of expectation calls for reevaluation as well. For instance, when a mother tells a child, "Clean your room," what does

she mean by "clean"? Does she mean sweep and dust? Does she
mean pick up toys? Does the bed have to be changed? Can books
and papers remain on the table? Must the windowsill be wiped?
Often because the mother's and child's interpretations differ, the
former winds up disappointed and the latter, angry over one more
failure. Specific directions offer favorable odds that the job will be
done with a minimum of stress.

One mother was taught this by her two-year-old, who balked every
night when told, "It's sleepy time."

"Not sleepy time," she finally managed to explain. "It's beddy
time." She was right, for sleep meant lights out, while bed meant a
story, a song, and kisses and pats. All that mother had to do was
clarify her language.

Similarly, it is important for young people to know the ground
rules by which they are operating and for parents to keep those rules
consistent. If children do not clean their room as expected, what will
happen? They have a right to know *beforehand*: will they have to
remain home over the weekend until the job is done? Will they
have to forfeit television for a week—or a month? Will Mother balance the score by refusing them a favor next time they ask? As long
as parents and children determine ahead of time whatever consequences will ensue, and adhere to that determination, stress for
both of them will be minimized.

III. SCHOOL HELPS

While children themselves and their parents remain the major
factors in eliminating sources of stress, school too serves as an important support. I say this with some trepidation since, over the years,
school has become the scapegoat of all children's ills, and parents in
their rush to attack often turn it into a battleground instead of a
place of learning.

School is the ally of parents in many ways. First, it provides professional opinions and facts on which to base expectations. Through
diagnostic testing, begun early and continued regularly, learning
levels can be determined and met, eliminating overburdensome
demands that lead to frustration. Shirley Gillis, Connecticut's 1981
Teacher of the Year, emphasizes the value of diagnostic test-

ing not only in her own kindergarten classes, but in preschool education in her entire community. "When we discover what children can do and cannot do as early as nursery school," she explains, "we have a head start on preventing disruptive behavior."

Although early diagnosing is best, belated diagnosing is better than none. When junior high schools realize that well over half of their "problem children" are poor readers or nonreaders, they will be in a position to tackle and solve the problem—of reading, that is; the problem of behavior may solve itself as a result.

If schools act as parental allies by identifying problem areas of learning, it follows that they offer further help in solving those problems. Children are not mass-produced like cars; their learning, therefore, cannot be put in place on an assembly line. Each must be handmade. Since handmade learning entails individually planned programs for children, many schools give up before they try. "We haven't the staff. We haven't the money," they cry, and parents are reluctant to insist.

Yet I have spoken with thousands of teachers in schools equally limited in staff and money who insist on teaching *children*, not *classes*. There are kindergartens from Connecticut to Georgia, New York to Utah, where teachers individualize learning. There are first-graders in Indiana and Colorado following their own work plans under the guidance of their teachers. Elementary schools in rural towns in New Hampshire and in urban New York boast elementary schools where children have tailor-made learning. In junior high and high schools in North Carolina and Missouri, California and Brooklyn, New York, a single teacher is meeting twenty-five or thirty individual needs in one classroom.

How individualized learning relates to improved behavior is no puzzle to teachers. "I have no behavior problems," Elaine Barbour told me at a time when her fifth grade was filled with "troublesome" children from other schools. It is no puzzle to parents either. "They have become different children," exclaimed surprised parents after Kate Dennis knocked down the walls and opened up teaching in her one-room schoolhouse.

If parents find their children stuck in schools and with teachers that are a far cry from the ones just described, there are three measures they might take:

1. They can try to change the school. This can be done and *has* been done by parents all over the country through nonhostile, persistent effort.
2. They can switch schools. This entails moving to a better school district or paying the price of private schooling.
3. They can compensate at home for the school's inadequacy. Diagnostic testing can be done outside, with parents themselves, student tutors or professionals filling in learning gaps that appear.

School can be parents' greatest ally in still a third way—dealing with children's emotional turmoil. Dr. June Christmas, retired Commissioner of New York City's Department of Mental Health, claims, "School for many children has always been a place where stress produced at home could be relieved in a variety of ways." The variety of ways has increased in recent years as the stresses have grown.

Some schools schedule weekly guidance sessions in which students and counselors discuss problems—even in elementary schools. Pat Oyeshiku, California's 1981 Teacher of the Year, turns every Friday of her Ethnic Literature and Reading classes into rap sessions over personal concerns. "I know the kids can't concentrate on work when they've got problems," she says, and so she takes it upon herself to help solve them. In many cases students turn informally to a single teacher or to the school nurse for guidance. I recall endless talks after school with students whose emotional burdens were so painfully heavy that I marveled at their ability to get up each morning and go through the motions of a day.

IV. THERAPY HELPS

It would be incomplete to consider bases covered in alleviating stress without mentioning the enormous field of therapy that has proven of great value. Outside help has lost the stigma once associated with it when parents considered it for "crazy" or "sick" children. Today most people accept it as an aid beyond home and school for young people whose behavior indicates overwhelming stress with which they are unable to cope.

The most common kinds of therapy involve regularly scheduled visits to the therapist while the child lives at home, attends school as usual and generally continues in his normal routine. What kind of help the child receives depends on his particular needs and on the therapist's preference. She may decide on family therapy, in which the whole family meets with a psychologist to work out the dynamics which may be causing behavior problems. Or she may feel group therapy is better for a particular child: here he joins a group of other people, either young or of varied ages, and together they share problems, learning from each other and contributing as well. Or she may rely on individual therapy with a psychologist or psychiatrist, meeting as infrequently as bimonthly or as much as five times a week.

On the other hand, problems may be of such a nature that the therapist recommends hospitalization, either in the wing of a regular hospital devoted to mental and emotional problems or in homes and hospitals specifically handling those kinds of patients. Where children have become heavily involved in drug or alcohol abuse, where they are suicidal, where the family dynamics are too destructive to offer help and where a child is schizophrenic, hospitalization may be advised. I have seen young people put back together after stress damage in as little as three months in hospitals like New York's Roosevelt or Payne Whitney. I have seen others make adjustments in psychiatric hospitals such as Long Island's Hillside over a period of a year, in which they attended school and took on regular jobs in addition to receiving therapy.

There are few jolts so traumatic to parents as learning that their children need hospitalization for emotional problems. Psychiatrists do not recommend it lightly, and second opinions may be warranted. However, should it become necessary, parents can learn to accept it, not as a sign of their failure, but as an answer to their child's cry for help.

When a child is churning in icy water over his head and screams, a parent has no hesitancy about plunging in, heedless of the cold cutting through him or of his own faulty swimming. Yet when children yell "Help!" in the desperation of their stress, parents are loath to take the plunge. If they don't recognize behavior as the cry for help it is, they can push their children further into the maelstrom. Yet parents are made to be rescuers.

Wednesday's child is drowning, and parents are closest to pull him to shore. There is always hope. No matter how destructive a child's behavior, there exists hope that underneath the stresses from which behavior stems awaits a person in anticipation of fulfillment.

The Indian poet Rabindranath Tagore reminds us, "Every child comes with the message that God is not yet discouraged of man." Let parents be no less hopeful than God.

CHAPTER X

❖

Raising Children Who Cope

If wishes were horses, then beggars would ride.
If turnips were watches, I'd wear one by my side.
If "ifs" and "ands"
Were pots and pans,
There'd be no work for tinkers!

The English language boasts no single word, I believe, with which we are more able to flagellate ourselves than the two-letter word "if." If wishes were horses or cars or first-class seats on a 747, then not only beggars, but all of us would ride. If wishes were brains and beauty, charm and good luck, the world would be as painless as Orwell's 1984—and as unlivable. Though our children would be born as images of perfection, it would be *our* images, not *theirs*, which designed them. Peopled thus with Barbie and Ken dolls, would our world not ache for the relief of a flaw?

Yet flaws, our own and our children's, drive us to most of the "ifs" we use for whips:

—"If you study, you will do well."
—"If you lose weight, you will look right."
—"If you obey, you will get ahead."

Each condition translates broadly into, "If you are smart and beautiful and good, we will love you." But for reasons lurking where no one dares look, children often can't study; they can't stop eating; they won't obey. Barbie and Ken will not be die-cast by their parents' wishes. Bewildered by flesh-and-blood children so different from their plastic images, parents and teachers respond in their own imperfect ways, compounding hurts and regrets until years later they feel the lash of "if."

—"If we had listened . . ."
—"If we had spent more time . . ."
—"If we had said, 'I love you' . . ."
—"If we had understood . . ."

"If" comes too late for listening and spending time and loving and understanding. Wishes are not horses, and our children rarely become what we anticipate. Therein lies the pain. The remedy is not to devise a scheme that will assemble children the way we will them, but to repattern our thinking so that children may assemble themselves the way their unique blueprints intend.

WE ARE WHAT WE ARE

Hans Selye's words echo through my mind: "Parents will greatly minimize stress when they realize that not all of their children are racehorses; some are turtles."

We are what we are, and not entirely self-made but affected by a mingling of our heritage and our surroundings. Our parents bequeathed us genes which predetermined our appearance, and they passed along weaknesses and strengths which predisposed us for life's assaults. In addition, they created for us an environment to which we responded by becoming the people we are. Genes and environment inextricably overlap so that, as with the chicken and the egg, we can no longer tell for sure which is cause and which effect.

Watching me cut out paper doll clothes the other day, Darcy, still not four, asked for the scissors to cut them herself. I let her try, bracing myself for screams of frustration, but none were forthcoming. Slowly, frowning in her intensity, she cut around the dress and the tabs, not evenly, but proudly. Now I am out of a job. Was Darcy born with adeptness at small motor skills which gave her confidence to tackle so complex a task? Or has her mother created in her so strong a self-image that she dares attempt the impossible? Which came first?

"I'm pretty," she said, looking at herself in the mirror. She is right. But does she feel pretty because her genes brought together hazel eyes, a pointed chin and translucent skin to form a cameo? Or because she mirrors love in the faces of people around her, which makes her feel pretty? I know equally good-looking children who will not even look in a mirror and who fling away compliments with, "I'm ugly!"

Where the difference lies we cannot hope to answer here or possibly anywhere, for opinions reinforce the argument on both sides. We know that no two children grow up in the same environment even within families, for an older or younger sibling rearranges circumstances to the point of total change. We know further that parental responses to their children, even to twins, differ, creating separate environments for each child. Therefore, studies that report varied personalities emerging from a single family in order to disclaim the effect of environment are as inconclusive as those that show identical twins with dissimilar traits in order to disclaim heredity. No one knows for sure.

We are certain, however, that what we are is in large measure attributable to our parents, be it the union of sperm and ovum that initiated us or the dynamics of their personalities that surrounded us from birth. Furthermore, we can be certain that our parents' genes and personalities evolved from their parents, which evolved from their parents, which evolved . . .

That being the case, we can be equally certain that we, parents of our children, bequeath the same to them. Generations are like an optical illusion which at one moment seems to be moving outward and at another, moving in.

Haven't we all looked at ourselves in a mirror with another mirror behind reflecting our image down an infinite line of images in mirrors as far as our eyes can discern? We might think of the face in the second mirror as that of our children, perhaps not with the contour or the expression we intended to put there, but with what we *did* put there nonetheless. The genes implanted in us and the surroundings in which we grew shaped that face, which in turn will shape the face in the third mirror and so on and on and on.

James Barrie's little minister says, "The life of every man is a diary in which he means to write one story and writes another." We could say the same about parents, for the biography of their children which they intend to write often runs far afield of their original prospectus. What were the chapters planned but never written for the tens of thousands of young people locked in detention homes? For the young prostitutes in bondage to pimps? For the teenage drug pushers and their little brothers and sisters shooting up in the school lavatory?

When parents hold newborn infants in their arms, what are their dreams as they look into the heavy-lidded eyes? Aren't they dreams of laughter and learning, happy marriages, children and grandchildren? Aren't they of joys ahead? At what point do those dreams fade, merging into statistics of violence, sickness, divorce and death?

"All I ever wanted for him was happiness," a mother wept over the body of her son, dead from an overdose of heroin. What story had she intended to write, and where had it run away from her? Social scientists at the University of Michigan have discovered that before boys are fifteen years old, the attitudes that lead to success or failure are already formed. One wonders whether parents are aware of the turn their story is taking as the plot begins to thicken.

The chapter parents write on home life may not read as they had outlined it: sibling rivalry creeps in; Dad weekends at work; Mother's temper is shorter than planned; the house is too small and crowded; and the hero of the story may be fat and graceless. That is not part of the original script.

School introduces subplots against parents' will: undone homework and a subject failed, fights with teachers and competitive pressure and kids who coax and tease. Sex enters the story when parents are unprepared, then there is the push to get into college, to stay in college and to graduate from college; job applications and rejections, marriage and divorce.

"All I ever wanted for him was happiness!" Parents do not lay out stressors like an obstacle course for their children to struggle through. They do not have to—life does it for them. From Go to Finish is no easy route, nor is there any reason for it to be. Survival depends, as Adam and Eve discovered, not on living in Paradise, but on coping with the real world outside. In the same way, each of us and each of our children, like each of our parents before, are thrust into reality despite hopes and plans for us to remain in Eden.

EQUIPPING CHILDREN TO HANDLE STRESS

The job of parents is not to remove stressors, for in removing, they create them. Like the Hydra's head, we cannot chop difficulties off our children's lives and be done with the monster stress.

Since the world is fraught with stressors, the job of parents is to equip children to handle them. Chapter II introduced us to Sabbath day children, not those with stress-free lives, but those who cope with stress and keep on growing. The remainder of the book led us through the tears and torments of Wednesday's children, the non-copers. Behind the scenes of both move the adults in the lives of children, primarily their parents. How do they differ, the parents of Wednesday and Sabbath day children? What do the former do "wrong"? What do the latter do "right"? The answer would be Open Sesame to the magic door of happiness.

Do they spank them?
Do they teach them letters early?
Do they let them go on dates at fifteen?
Do they live in the country?
Do they live in the city?
Do they help them with homework?
Do they toilet-train them with ease?
Do their mothers work?
Do they have brothers and sisters?
Do they watch television?

Yes.

And no. The parents of coping and non-coping children do all of those things and do some of them and do none, for it is not those things that make the difference. The day-to-day, moment-to-moment decisions of parents do not alter the course of their children's lives. The attitude and underlying philosophy from which their daily decisions stem do, for in that attitude and philosophy lie the common denominators which psychologists and educators find among parents whose children are able to meet stress, cope with it and emerge victorious. That attitude and philosophy surround a child from the moment of birth, and even earlier as he unfolds in the watery world of the womb. To them he responds as his genetic makeup demands; from them he is shaped into the person he will be.

Common denominators exist among successful parents. I have described below the three major ones isolated by a composite of educators, psychologists and psychiatrists.

I. SUCCESSFUL PARENTS ENABLE CHILDREN TO SEE STRESS AS A POSITIVE RATHER THAN A NEGATIVE FORCE.

"Fun is when you feel challenged to do your best," writes psychologist Eda LeShan; and what is challenge but stress? Danger lurks in challenge, however, for it tests our mettle in contest with ourselves and makes us face an inevitable victory or defeat. How parents define victory and defeat makes the difference in a child's attitude toward stress.

When Chuckie stood at bat in the Little League game (Chapter VIII), he struck out. To his parents and, as a result, to him, his strikeout spelled defeat, which he read clearly in his father's face and in his voice. For Chuckie, playing baseball was less a way of having fun than a means of proving his worth. Unable to rack up a hit or, better still, a home run, he accepted both his batting average and himself as failures. So did his father.

Unfortunately, Chuckie is not an isolated case, for many parents put their own self-esteem in the batter's box along with that of their children. For them a hit means meeting a challenge; a strikeout means failing to meet it, and fun plays little part. Sadly, they not only miss the point of Little League baseball, but deprive their children of the stimulation of real challenge. The point is for Chuckie to win over *himself*. The real challenge is for him to meet his strikeout with courage: "I'll hit it next time!"

Courage, however, requires hope, of which Chuckie has little. So tied up with hitting the ball is his self-image that by not hitting it, he becomes "a loser." "I'll never hit it," his inner voice whispers in loathing of himself and baseball equally.

Making stress positive for children begins with the focus of challenge. Another father could handle the strikeout in such a way as to switch the focus from how his son hits the ball to how he reacts.

He could reinforce the boy's self-confidence by accentuating the positive: "Your stance is beginning to look like Reggie Jackson's," or "I noticed you are holding the bat lower," or whatever he truly observes.

He could offer a tactful suggestion: "Do you think you stepped forward too soon?" or "I'm not sure, but maybe you looked away for a split second."

He could encourage: "It was so close. I think you'll hit it next time."

Above all, he could make his son feel like a winner in the contest that matters: "You really swung that bat. I'm proud of the way you tried. I'm proud of you."

That son will respond positively to stress, thanks to his father, and will discover fun in meeting challenge. Obviously, he will not learn in one Little League game, but in many games, and from his parents' attitude he will learn over the years. As a baby, he probably learned to play with toys: to struggle to put rings on a stand or make jack-in-the-box jump up. His parents helped, but refused to do the job *for* him. He learned to walk, and his parents did not laugh when he fell down. He handled his own spoon at mealtime, and neither parent complained of the mess.

As he grew, they supported his efforts, letting him walk alone to first grade, frightened but feeling grown-up. He fell off his first bicycle and cried, and his mother marveled at his bravery. He did his own homework with his parents expecting only his best. He was awkward at his first party, and they understood his embarrassment. He crammed for spelling bees and learned to play a hard game on the tennis court. As third-string, he sat on the bench through basketball games, but his parents attended and cheered his team. In his senior year, they admired him for applying to Yale, even when he did not make it.

The parents of this boy helped him reach an understanding of challenge as competition with himself. They helped him enter it in the sense of adventure and win, even when he lost. Skinned knees, school marks and score cards bore no stigma in their home, for they came and went as mere details on the periphery of life's contest. The core was more important—their son himself.

II. SUCCESSFUL PARENTS TEACH ACCOUNTABILITY RATHER THAN OVERPROTECT.

In December of 1976, a letter appeared in *Time* magazine written by Virgil Langtry, the presiding judge when Gary Gilmore, then about twelve, was first referred to juvenile court, having been caught in the act of vandalism during a robbery. "Gary, you didn't do it. Don't let them tell you you did. Don't say a word, Gary, you didn't do it," were the words the judge heard the boy's father say. They are the words that eliminated his need to be responsible for the consequences of his actions.

"The boy quickly learned," the judge wrote. Yes, the father quickly taught. In overprotecting his son, he removed any possibility of Gary's developing accountability for his behavior. "Dad will get me out," young Gary learned. He went home on probation, got into trouble again and spent the rest of his life in and out of prisons for crimes of violence. Only when it was too late for even a father to shield him from consequences was he held accountable before a firing squad.

We are surrounded by incipient Gary Gilmores, not destined for murder, perhaps, but for destruction of other kinds. The husband who cannot admit his own share of blame in a family argument and the wife who languishes in self-pity over her husband's shortcomings destroy a marriage. Mothers and fathers who in frustration cut off communications with their children destroy their relationship. Teachers too threatened to listen when students complain destroy the process of learning. Human lives lie in ruins on all sides of us, razed by someone's inability to say, "I am responsible for some part of this situation."

Parents make the difference. When they allow their children to be hurt, their children learn to cope with hurt. When they insulate them, they develop no coping skills. If sidestepping hurt were a life-long possibility, if as adults we had the choice to be hurt or not to be hurt, some value might be attributed to early lessons in evasion.

This, however, is not the case: difficulties and problems beset us throughout life, *and they hurt.*

"I wish I could always be there to protect him," sighs a mother in a toothpaste commercial on television as her son tumbles off his bicycle. Then, settling for mere dental protection, she adds, "But I know I can't." Some mothers can, and fathers too, to the detriment of their children. For instance, when Billy was not selected as a contestant in the Cub Scout pie eating contest, rather than let him suffer and survive disappointment, his father bought him his own pie, pushed him among the contestants and shouted, "Get in there and win!" Billy was not a very nice boy when he grew up.

The parent who hands her five-month-old every toy she points to, rather than letting her reach for it and crawl, overprotects. The parents who will not leave their wailing toddler with a baby sitter overprotect. The urban parent who walks her fifteen-year-old to school overprotects. Parents who do homework for children and who switch teachers when their children are unhappy and who blame the other child when theirs gets into trouble overprotect. I know them all. I know parents who in fury removed their eight-year-old from a private school when the teacher found her stealing, and a mother who sued when her high school son, caught with answers up his sleeve, was accused of cheating. They taught the lesson of Gary Gilmore's father.

Others teach different lessons, fortunately. Abby's mother watched her cry when a neighborhood child tossed away a treasured spool she offered him as a token of love. She did not scold or call the boy's mother; she watched Abby go to her room and cry because she knew she was watching her learn to survive. Falling down hurts, yet parents who let their children risk it teach a lesson far more valuable than walking, roller skating or skiing: they teach the lesson of "I can."

Sometimes it is "I can" because the alternative is worse: *not* walking or roller skating or skiing. When parents retreat from the homework war, letting their child fight her own nightly battles, she may quickly discover that the consequences of not doing homework are worse than the agony of doing it. Or when parents refuse to support a child's lie told to evade an invitation, the embarrassment of being caught lying may prove far worse than the embarrassment of declining an invitation with honesty.

I remember as a teenager wearing too much makeup, which drove my father to threats of punishment.

"Leave her alone," my mother said. "She'll tone it down when her friends laugh at her." She dared the censure of her friends so that I could learn from the mockery of mine.

At other times, however, the "I can" is learned in the face of no alternatives. Children *have* to visit the dentist, *have* to attend school, *have* to live with brothers and sisters who may draw more attention, *have* to live with themselves. Unavoidable events occur: dogs die and grandparents die and parents separate and brothers and sisters leave home. Children worry and weep and go on living because they have no alternative. No parent can insulate them against these hurts; when children know they can survive, no parent needs to.

A shampoo is torture to Darcy; yet the other day when she was visiting me, I suggested we wash her hair.

"Do I have to?" she asked.

"I think it would be a good idea," I answered tactfully.

"But do I have to?" she insisted.

I abandoned tact. "Yes."

With no alternative, we had no trouble shampooing.

I am reminded of Eric as a tiny boy needing a spoonful of medicine that tasted awful. He began to cry and squirm when my mother pulled him into her lap. As I bent over to pin down his arms and legs, my mother asked him, "Shall I force it, or will you take it nicely?"

Through tears Eric looked up. My mother had given him an alternative. "Force it," he said.

Coping is a gift of freedom, for adults as well as for young people. We live on the brink of sickness, accident, heartbreak and death every day of our lives, like helpless victims of fate. Yet, in learning to handle the stresses that emanate from our circumstances, we refuse to be victims; we take control. Death may still claim a child's beloved pet and divorce rend him from the security of his home; a friend may still turn on him, and he may still fail in his strongest efforts. However, given past experience in hurting and the confidence of having endured, he will not be at the mercy of fate: he will control his own person, if not the way of his world.

Graduates of EST spend four eighteen-hour days of humiliation and exhaustion in order to penetrate "the secret." Children can learn it early in their lives, for the secret is simply this: you are in control of your life. As we discussed earlier, you cannot do much to alter the way you are—heredity and environment have already done that. You can, however, do everything to decide the way you act. What people do to you is *their* problem. What you do in response is *your* problem. That is coping. Parents, like the rent-a-car company, can put children in the driver's seat if they start early enough. All they have to do is let them face their own difficulties. All they have to do is bear the pain of the pain their children bear.

III. SUCCESSFUL PARENTS KNOW HOW TO LOVE.

"I love my mommy," a tiny blond girl said one day as I interviewed her "mommy" for an article.

"How can you tell you love her?" I asked.

As though having pondered the question before, she replied, "Because I like to give her things."

Out of the mouth of that babe flowed a definition that wise men have been discovering every century or so for the past two thousand years: loving is giving. While it may seem more truism than truth, millions who nod their heads in agreement have little idea of what giving includes. Loving is giving: few may challenge the definition, but the lives of many fail to live up to the concept. Many of those "many" are parents, whose children wither in lovelessness.

"We loved him," exclaimed the dazed parents of a sixteen-year-old who shot himself in the basement. Maybe so, but the boy did not believe it, as repeated entries in his diary indicated: "I'll never be what Dad wants," he wrote one time, and another, "I don't blame them [his parents] for hating me." Whatever love his parents felt was not transmitted to their son, who in his difficult adolescent years needed it for a lifeline. They failed to save his life, not because they did not love him, but because they did not know how to reach him with love as he drowned in his anguish.

Had they known what the little daughter of my interviewee knew, their son might not have sought death as the only means of ending his desolation. Loving is giving— But giving *what?* Giving *how?* The boy's parents did not know.

In our acquisitive society, giving frequently limits itself to the materialistic; yet even the little girl knew better than that. When I asked what she liked to give her mother, she told me, "Kisses, and when her head hurts, I pat it wif a wafclof." St. Paul himself was hardly more eloquent when in First Corinthians he described love as "patient and kind."

Parents, like the human beings they are, often enter love relationships with their children while they themselves are hung up on ego needs developed in childhood and passed down through the years. Sometimes these ego needs block the communication of love, which they feel but do not express. For instance, children of strongly achieving parents may receive the message that if they do not reach the peaks of achievement, they will be rejected by their parents. Whether this is fact or a figment of their imagination is far less important than whether children *believe* it is fact. Truth as they, not their parents, perceive it is the only truth to which they respond. The trick then is for parents to reassess the means they are using to communicate love to their children. What are they giving?

There are, I think, three major areas in which parental giving translates into love.

1. GIVING GUIDELINES

A cartoon some years ago showed the parents of Dennis the Menace ringing a neighbor's doorbell, while the couple inside cringed behind a chair. "It's them," they whispered, "and they've got *him* with them." "Him" was a spoiled brat who would destroy everything in sight while his parents looked on with never a "No."

I have met Dennis's parents over and over again at school. They were the ones who, when called in to discuss a behavior problem, threw up their hands sighing, "I can't do a thing with him." If parents can't do anything with their children, they had better take a look at what they are *not* doing.

Children need guidelines. According to Dr. Lawrence Kohlberg of Harvard's Center for Moral Education, the first step in learning moral values lies in following rules. Until small children learn to do what is "right" because Mommy and Daddy say so, they cannot grow into a more complex understanding of values and, finally, into the assimilation of a personal code of morality. Since the learning process as Dr. Kohlberg outlines it must follow a logical progression of steps, children not given parental rules of "right" and "wrong" cannot graduate to higher moral levels. America's prisons are overcrowded with men and women who were not given the opportunity to pass Step One.

Children want guidelines. Not only does license place too great a burden of decision-making on them, but it transmits the feeling that no one cares. Actually, if they are allowed to do what they will, no one does care.

"Can I have a piece of candy?" a child asks.

"No, it's too close to dinner," Mother answers.

"Please. Just one."

"I said, 'No.'"

The child begins to whine and cry. Mother grows annoyed. If in desperation she relents, while the child gets the candy he fails to get the feeling that what he does matters to his mother. If she perseveres, there is no candy and temporarily no peace in the house, but the security of maternal love.

"I can't bear to hear her cry," a father explained one day. He was leaving for a shopping trip, having told his two-year-old daughter that he could not take her that day: he had promised their older child a time alone. When the little girl cried, he tried to remain resolute but, finally weakening, he picked her up and carried her to the car. "All right, you win!" he told her. It is difficult to say which child suffered more in the long run: the younger, who learned she could manipulate Daddy with tears, or the older, who learned that Daddy could not be trusted to keep his word. Both got the message that Daddy did not care enough to avoid the easy way out of a problem.

Children have ways of begging parents to follow through on rules they have laid down. Darcy used to climb on the couch to reach the one light switch that had no cover over the wires. "No," we would say. Staring us in the eye, she would inch her finger closer and closer until we emitted a "No!" angry enough to convince her we were standing our ground.

Noah, almost a year now, tests us by holding his hand above the telephone receiver, his eyes bright in anticipation of our removing either him or the telephone altogether. The other day as my husband joined us in our increasingly severe "No's," he made a suggestion for Noah's learning experience.

"Why don't you slap his hand?" he said.

I looked at the round little hand hovering over the telephone, dimpled at each knuckle, and at the eyes alight with joy in the game.

"Why don't you?" I asked.

My husband lifted Noah and carried him to other fertile fields—the pots and pans in the kitchen.

In both cases, Darcy and Noah, like all children, were groping for guidelines, testing to ascertain the firmness of them and of us.

Following through on rules is often equally as painful for parents as for their children. I remember telling Eric and his friend Vince years ago that if they did not stop throwing stones through the window at Amy, I would take Vince home and keep Eric in his room. They didn't, and I did—drove thirty miles round trip to follow through on my word. I hated it but thought it was important for Eric to know that I would inconvenience myself for the sake of his learning. Inconvenience translates into love.

It speaks the same language to older children too. When Chris as a teenager balked at helping his father with chores, he was denied the privilege of driving the car.

"What's mowing the lawn got to do with the car?" he grumbled.

"It's Dad's car, that's what. You help him; he helps you."

I felt mean sometimes, especially when other people's children were allowed license that ours were not. For instance, we would not serve liquor at parties when the children were underage, although parents of their friends did. Chris nagged, begged, cajoled, but the answer remained, "No. It's illegal."

Furious, he retorted on one occasion, "Then I won't have a party at all," hoping, perhaps, that with arrangements all set we would relent. We longed to, knowing how much Chris wanted the party, and my heart ached for him—and for us. But serving liquor would be like saying, "Go ahead and break the law." It's easier; however, "easier" is not what makes children the people they deserve to become. So we let Chris call off the party.

Years later all three of our children confessed at different times, "You know, Mom, I'm really glad you were strict with us when we were growing up." I have not asked them why. I look at them—loving, contributing adults—and know.

2. GIVING SUPPORT

When parents comfort the crying infant, kiss the toddler's scraped knee, hold a hand before a tonsillectomy, enfold the shoulder bowed under the burdens of school, they are using time-tested remedies for stress. In each case the crisis is obvious, and they know by instinct what to do. Yet, in times of less obvious crisis they are apt unknowingly to turn away.

"Mommy, look at the picture I drew."

"Not now, Bud. I'm cooking dinner."

To a five-year-old, his picture has top priority. Regardless of burning beans or a falling soufflé, if Mommy ignores his picture he comes up with only one explanation: she is not interested in him.

"Daddy, guess what my teacher said in class today."

Daddy, not looking up, grumbles, "Later," into the newspaper he is reading. The little girl walks off; he has rejected her.

"My class is doing assembly tomorrow. You'll see me read the Gettysburg Address."

Too bad: Dad has a meeting at the office, and Mom has to take little sister for a checkup. Suddenly the coveted part in assembly no longer matters.

When parents are too busy or too tired or too preoccupied to share the lives of their children, their actions speak as clearly as though they said in words, "I am more interested in me than in you." Even *bona fide* excuses do not lessen the hurt.

A mother in Little Rock, Arkansas, holding a full-time job, told me, "I *can't* be too busy for my children. What else is more important to be busy for?"

There are few years, only seventeen or eighteen, when parents have their children to become involved in; and then they are off, entwined in other involvements, looking elsewhere for support. The fun of those early years, however, comes back with dividends to parents who invest their time.

"I never knew what fun weekends could be," a mother said, "until Josh and I began spending them together." Recently divorced and working full time, she treasures her Saturdays and Sundays with her son since their evenings together are short. No longer does she shoo him to watch television on weekend mornings. "I don't want to waste our good times," she explains.

There are a myriad of ways in which parents can demonstrate support for their children above and beyond what many of them are currently doing. The secret lies in realizing that events in their life, trivial as they may seem to adults, are important to them. When the child of a friend of mine wet his pants in kindergarten, in an effort to console him she shrugged it off with, "Oh well, we all make mistakes." The little boy became hysterical. He needed support in his humiliation, not a throwaway, for his act had made him look like a baby in front of his classmates—what his mother might need if she spilled soup down her dress at a business dinner.

School, which is the business world of a child, in which he spends almost half his waking hours, deserves more time and attention than most parents give. One PTA meeting and a cursory look during Open House are mere tokens of interest. Indifference until the end of the semester when report cards appear merely reinforces the impression of more parental concern for achievement than concern over the child. Since for almost ten months a year school is a major focus of children, meaningful support should be expected from parents for the same period of time. Let them attend *all* PTA meetings, work on a committee, help with fund-raising events, supplement the teacher's efforts. Only one thing thrilled my children more than taking cookies to the class party; that was Amy's volunteering to have her mommy wash and iron the kindergarten dress-up clothes!

According to a National Education Association report, "The apathy of parents is the greatest problem affecting teachers' instruction." I knew as a teacher, and most teachers know that their job is only half done unless parents continually reinforce the learning experience at home—not necessarily by aiding children in schoolwork, but by showing interest. Listening to children's chatter about

"What I did in school today," and "My teacher says," and "See my picture"—that shows interest. Dropping by to see a teacher, not only when something goes wrong, but when something goes right— like, "That was an interesting assignment you gave last night"—that shows interest.

Sitting through ball games and chorus recitals, assemblies at early morning hours and plays at night, even when your child is not the star—that shows interest. I cannot count the number of times I have seen parents walk out in the middle of a school event simply because their child had finished performing. Not only is such behavior disruptive and rude, but it evidences the most perfunctory interest in a child's school world.

Parents can also support children by supporting their friendships. They might include a friend in a special family outing and make a point of talking with a visiting friend, sharing her interests as well as those of their own child. I know families who enjoy close relationships with friends of their children long after they have graduated from high school and even college, whose children grew up confident of their parents' interest in them. On the other hand, I know parents who have destroyed friendships by mocking "that pimply boy" or "the dumb-looking kid" that came to the house, undermining the parent-child relationship as well. In between are the majority of parents who just pay no attention at all.

Supporting children in time of trouble is often difficult because children themselves become trouble. What parent has not been barked at as a scapegoat when a teacher overdisciplined? Or has not had endurance strained to the limit when a teenager fell in love? Or has not had a new toy hurled across the room when it was too difficult to play with? Yet it is at those difficult times that parental support is most needed: concern enough to listen, restraint enough not to lecture.

"You give great advice, Mom," a preteen declared as she suffered through ostracism by a class clique. The only words her mother had spoken were, "Let's talk about it."

3. GIVING MOTIVATION

In *The Pursuit of Loneliness* Philip Slater remarks that whereas parents of times past were primarily concerned over their children's outward actions, present-day parents are more concerned over their children's inner state. Motivation for acquiring acceptable behavior differs in each case, he continues: the former from fear orientation and the latter from love orientation.

Dr. Frederick Herzberg at the University of Utah picks up on the theme of motivation, defining it in terms of satisfaction and dissatisfaction. He says that when children alter their behavior because of punishment, they do not achieve satisfaction, but merely relief from dissatisfaction: the punishment stops. On the other hand, when children alter their behavior because of new insights into values, they are rewarded with the personal satisfaction of having grown.

"Psychological growth," Dr. Herzberg says, "is nourished by intrinsic factors called motivators." Parents are in the number-one position to trigger these motivators for, unlike most schools, they deal with a child's total development. Therefore, using Philip Slater's love-oriented approach, parents can motivate children toward growth, which in the process produces what we call good behavior. With fear-oriented techniques, however, while children may achieve good behavior, they bypass psychological growth, which brings satisfaction.

Part Two of this book illustrated destructive behavior in response to stress, most of which developed as a result of neglect, punishment or autocratic rule. In punishment and autocratic rule, fear was the chief motivator used by parents, perhaps effecting behavioral changes for a time, but failing in the long run. Without love, there is little growth to sustain change.

Some years ago I did a survey of junior high and high school students in which I tried to ascertain their reasons for behaving in acceptable ways.

"When you want to do something and your mother or father wants you not to, what do you do?" I asked.

Answers ranged from, "I argue," to, "I do what I want," with the majority admitting they usually concede.

"When you obey," I then asked, "what factors are important in making your decision?"

Here the group split. About half responded to the effect, "They'll kill me if I don't." Their parents seem to motivate through fear.

Somewhat under half answered, "I might as well give in. They'll

win anyway." Their parents motivate, it appeared, by the power of
authority, which carries with it fear.

A small group spoke in these terms: "They do a lot for me. If it's
that important to them, I owe them one." This sounded to me like
love orientation.

Wise parents realize that internalized controls over behavior, once
developed, preclude the daily nagging and disciplining that both
weary and frustrate them, because a self-motivated child motivates
his total behavior. Parents who motivate through fear-oriented techniques find themselves forced to apply them repeatedly as their children face each new situation. Dr. Herzberg explains why: self-motivated children, in growing, have acquired mature values that regu-
late their behavior; others, like laboratory mice given electric shock
when they take a wrong turn, have merely learned to run through
the maze.

Although parents shoulder responsibility for their children's
growth and their decisions exert the greatest influence, we cannot
neglect to mention another contributing factor. School runs a close
second, and teachers have a long way to go toward creating environments conducive to the development of Sabbath day children. What
the late Prime Minister Nehru observed in Indian schools can be
seen in schools of all countries, not the least of which is America.
"At school children learn many things which are no doubt useful,
but they gradually forget that the essential thing is to be human and
kind and playful and to make life richer for ourselves and for
others."

Schools need to tone down competitiveness and motivate more
through group accomplishment, the value of which is illustrated by
endeavors such as Outward Bound. Teachers must begin to acknowledge and handle their own stress in order to prevent its blocking
their relationships with students. For instance, qualities identified in
a study by Turkish professor Dr. Necia P. Oner as personal warmth,
regard for students and flexibility help teachers establish the teach-
ing-learning process; authoritarianism, punitiveness and rigidity—
qualities that often emerge under stress—stand in the way.

Ewald Nyquist, New York's former Commissioner of Education,
worked toward creating a statewide school system that would de-

velop in students positive qualities for a future humanistic life. In a speech he told the state's district supervisors, "All teachers should emphasize human values by knowing how to establish a strong sense of personal identity in the student, a feeling of controlling his own environment through active participation in decision-making and a mission or purpose in his life." He saw a future peopled by such students as crime-lessened and joy-increased. Where there was failure, he attributed it not to the child, but to the teachers and the school.

While Dr. Nyquist's standards were high, perhaps too high for the State Board of Regents which, disagreeing, fired him, they can be attained. George A. Wingate High School, deep in the heart of Brooklyn's inner city, stands as proof. A blackboard jungle less than a decade ago, it has been turned into a model of urban education by Robert Schain, a principal whose priority is learning. Refusing to spend his time in punishing and policing, he spends it in loving both the person and the potential of his students. He has instituted a strong skills program to equip them, an array of school and community-based courses to stimulate them and a voice in decision-making to involve them. The result is what Diane Ravitch calls in *New York* magazine "a born-again school." It educates born-again students.

When parents and teachers can hear the cries of their children for the agonized signals of stress that they are, hope for a better world will arise, like crocus buds in spring. They can go a long way toward answering the SOS and toward raising children who, capable of coping, need emit no cries. Those children can go farther and faster, however, when other adults in the lifeworld of a child reach out to help:

— when manufacturers stop filling them with junk products to poison their bodies and their environments.
— when advertisers stop manipulating them into the buying syndrome.
— when television respects their minds.
— when their heroes and heroines assume the responsibility of role models.
— when the criminal justice system recognizes the rehabilitative power of human dignity.

— when legislators realize that good citizens grow in the soil of good food, good housing and good schools.

"All those who bear responsibility or wield authority in society have a solemn duty to work for the creation of a world worthy of human beings," writes Professor Langeveld in "The Favorable Assimilation of Profound Psychic Shock." All can help children grow in security, but overall others are parents—parents, who have a solemn duty to overcome society's pressures by holding up stress as a positive force . . . to teach accountability in a lax world . . . and to love when brutality surrounds. "The greatest of these is love"—St. Paul knew. The mirror of parental love creates the image of self-love, which like an amulet wards off the evils of *dis*tress throughout life. Children blessed with it face the Fifty-First Dragon with courage and face thousands of future dragons with the self-confidence of knowing they will overcome.

In a poem entitled "The Fortress," written "while taking a nap with Linda," Anne Sexton speaks for what all parents have the potential of communicating:

> *I cannot promise very much.*
> *I give you the images I know.*
> *Lie still with me and watch.*
> *A pheasant moves*
> *by like a seal, pulled through the mulch*
> *by his thick white collar. He's on show*
> *like a clown. He drags a beige feather that he removed,*
> *one time, from an old lady's hat.*
> *We laugh and we touch.*
> *I promise you love. Time will not take away that.*

Index

◆

146–48; and escape through illness, 150–51

Yale University study on violence, 90
Young, Dr. Leontine, 213
"Young Ones, Flip Side, The," 35

"Youth Terror: a View From Behind the Gun," 94

Zimmer, Andrew, 58–59
Zindel, Paul, 36